WASH...

# DMZ
## M.I.A.

**Will Dennis** Editor-original series
**Mark Doyle** Associate Editor-original series
**Robbin Brosterman** Design Director-Books

**Karen Berger** Senior VP — Executive Editor, Vertigo
**Bob Harras** VP — Editor-in-Chief

**Diane Nelson** President
**Dan DiDio** and **Jim Lee** Co-Publishers
**Geoff Johns** Chief Creative Officer
**John Rood** Executive VP — Sales, Marketing and Business Development
**Amy Genkins** Senior VP — Business and Legal Affairs
**Nairi Gardiner** Senior VP — Finance
**Jeff Boison** VP — Publishing Operations
**Mark Chiarello** VP — Art Direction and Design
**John Cunningham** VP — Marketing
**Terri Cunningham** VP — Talent Relations and Services
**Alison Gill** Senior VP — Manufacturing and Operations
**Hank Kanalz** Senior VP — Digital
**Jay Kogan** VP — Business and Legal Affairs, Publishing
**Jack Mahan** VP — Business Affairs, Talent
**Nick Napolitano** VP — Manufacturing Administration
**Sue Pohja** VP — Book Sales
**Courtney Simmons** Senior VP — Publicity
**Bob Wayne** Senior VP — Sales

Logo and front cover designed by Brian Wood

DMZ: M.I.A.

Published by DC Comics. Cover and compilation Copyright © 2011 DC Comics. All Rights
Reserved. Originally published in single magazine form as DMZ 50-54. Copyright © 2010
Brian Wood and Riccardo Burchielli. All Rights Reserved. VERTIGO and all characters,
their distinctive likenesses and related elements featured in this publication are trademarks of
DC Comics. The stories, characters and incidents featured in this publication are entirely
fictional. DC Comics does not read or accept unsolicited submissions of ideas, stories or artwork.

DC Comics, 1700 Broadway, New York, NY 10019
A Warner Bros. Entertainment Company.
Printed in the USA. Second Printing.
ISBN: 978-1-4012-2996-2

Library of Congress Cataloging-in-Publication Data

Wood, Brian, 1972-
  DMZ. M.I.A. / Brian Wood, Riccardo Burchielli.
    p. cm. - (DMZ ; v. 9)
  "Originally published in single magazine form as DMZ 50-54."
  ISBN 978-1-4012-2996-2 (alk. paper)
  1. Graphic novels. I. Burchielli, Riccardo. II. Title. III. Title: M.I.A.
  PN6727.W59D57 2012
  741.5'973—dc23
                                                    2012029978

# DMZ
## M.I.A.

**BRIAN WOOD**
WRITER

*NOTES FROM THE UNDERGROUND*
**LEE BERMEJO   PHILIP BOND
RICCARDO BURCHIELLI   FÁBIO MOON
DAVE GIBBONS   REBEKAH ISAACS   RYAN KELLY
JIM LEE   JOHN PAUL LEON   EDUARDO RISSO**
ARTISTS

*M.I.A.*
**RICCARDO BURCHIELLI**
ARTIST

**JEROMY COX**
COLORIST

**JARED K. FLETCHER**
LETTERER

COVER BY **BRIAN WOOD**
ORIGINAL SERIES COVERS BY **JOHN PAUL LEON**
DMZ CREATED BY **BRIAN WOOD** AND **RICCARDO BURCHIELLI**

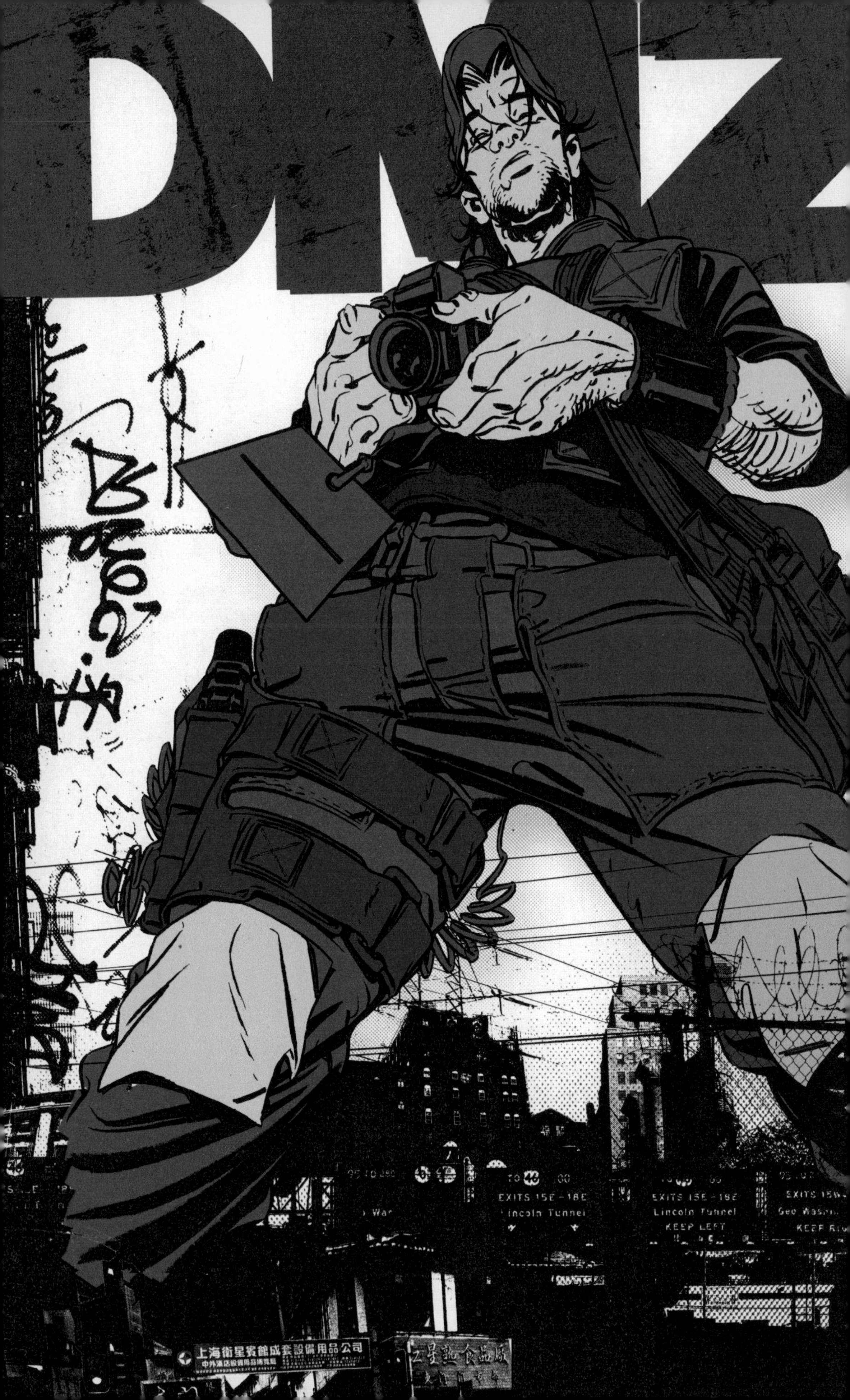
DMZ
EXITS 15E - 18E
Lincoln Tunnel
EXITS 15E - 18E
Lincoln Tunnel
KEEP LEFT
上海衛星賓館成套設備用品公司
中外酒店設備用品博覽組

Four years ago and totally against my will, I crash-landed in the middle of the DMZ.

Four years later I sit in a comfortable chair in a secure building with a killer view of the Lower East Side of Manhattan. I've negotiated hostage releases, exposed Trustwell's ties to domestic terrorism, broke the true story of Day 204, helped the city elect its first true government, and founded an independent news source.

I also lost Kelly Connolly, Zee, my father and mother, and probably my country too.

I bought and sold a nuclear weapon for Parco. I've worked both sides against each other numerous times. I still have blackmail material hidden all over the city, and I spend my time in the company of murderers. I don't like to think about people like Amina, and Jamal, Angel and Zee, who I've manipulated and used, all in the name of "getting the story."

"The Story" sits in front of me, in a thousand pieces all over this desk. If there's a big picture to be found here, I'm not seeing it yet.

Just a lot of smaller ones.

# Notes FROM THE Underground



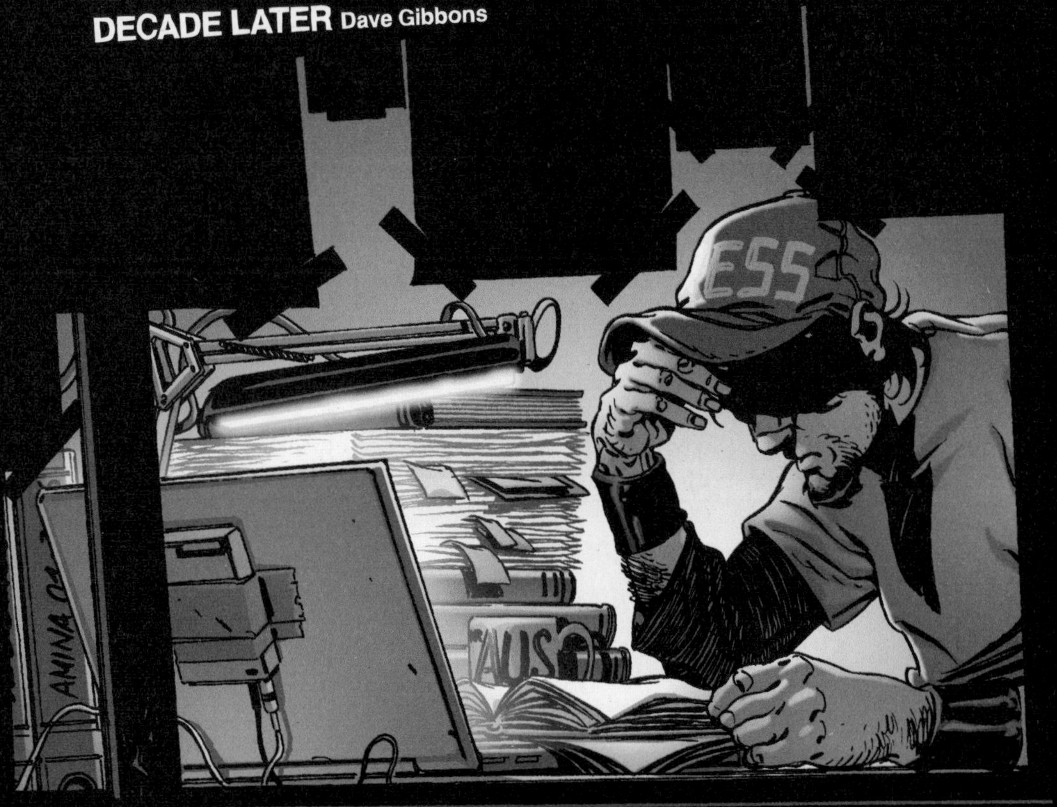

ESS
AMINA 04
AUS

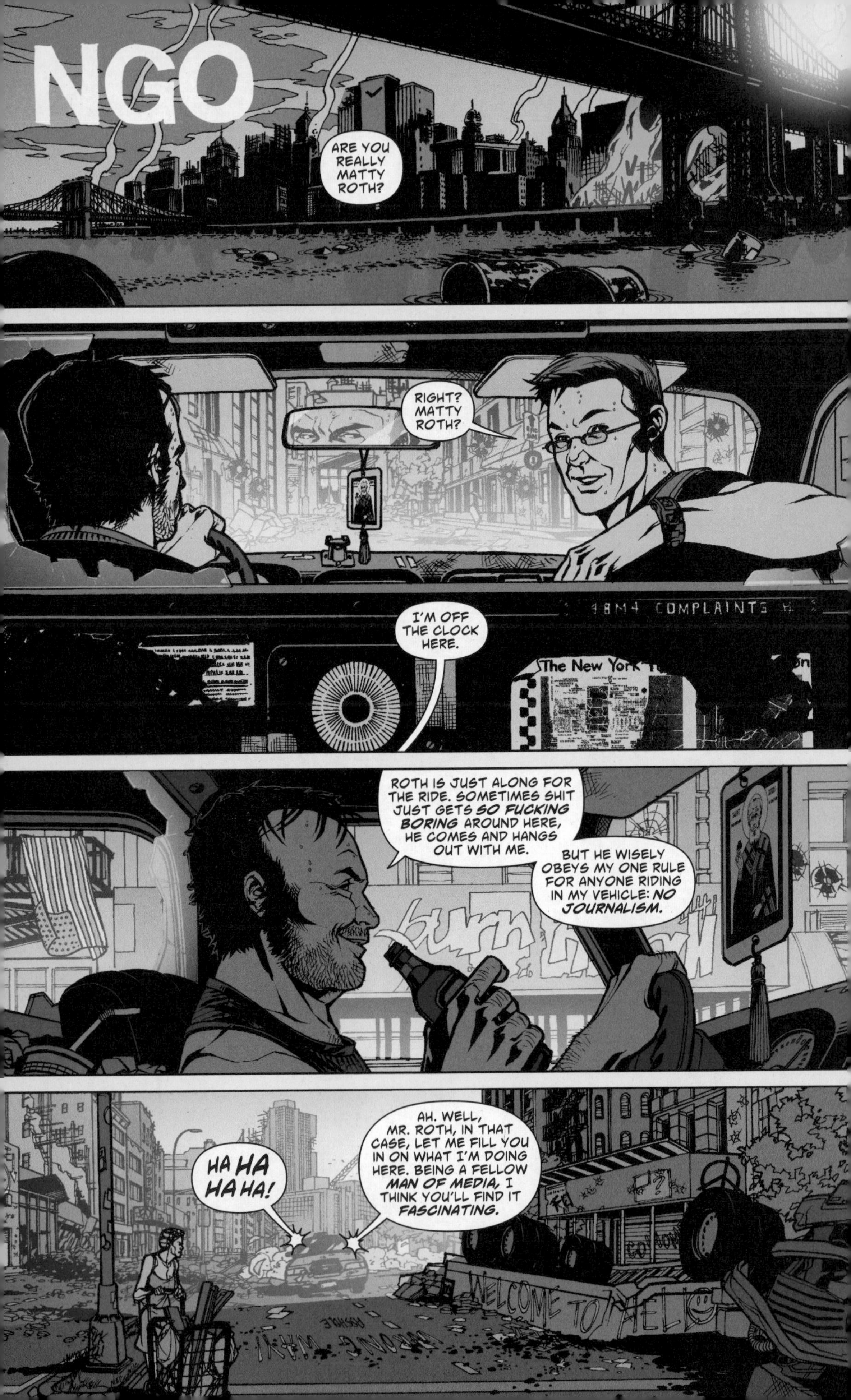
NGO
ARE YOU REALLY MATTY ROTH?
RIGHT? MATTY ROTH?
48M4 COMPLAINTS
I'M OFF THE CLOCK HERE.
The New York
ROTH IS JUST ALONG FOR THE RIDE. SOMETIMES SHIT JUST GETS SO FUCKING BORING AROUND HERE, HE COMES AND HANGS OUT WITH ME.
BUT HE WISELY OBEYS MY ONE RULE FOR ANYONE RIDING IN MY VEHICLE: NO JOURNALISM.
burn
HA HA HA HA!
AH. WELL, MR. ROTH, IN THAT CASE, LET ME FILL YOU IN ON WHAT I'M DOING HERE. BEING A FELLOW MAN OF MEDIA, I THINK YOU'LL FIND IT FASCINATING.
WELCOME TO HELL

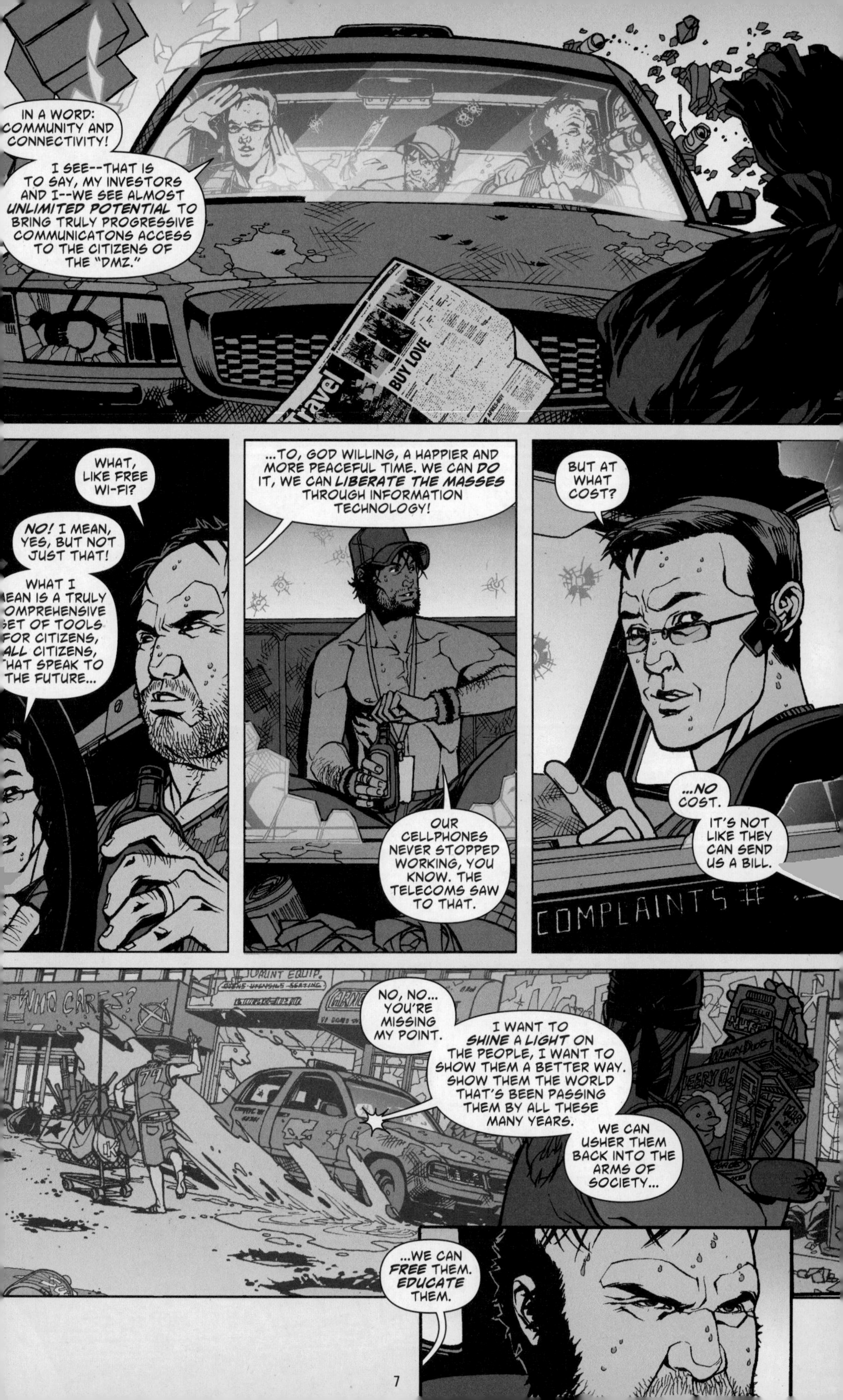

IN A WORD: COMMUNITY AND CONNECTIVITY!
I SEE--THAT IS TO SAY, MY INVESTORS AND I--WE SEE ALMOST UNLIMITED POTENTIAL TO BRING TRULY PROGRESSIVE COMMUNICATONS ACCESS TO THE CITIZENS OF THE "DMZ."
Travel
BUY LOVE
WHAT, LIKE FREE WI-FI?
NO! I MEAN, YES, BUT NOT JUST THAT!
WHAT I MEAN IS A TRULY COMPREHENSIVE SET OF TOOLS FOR CITIZENS, ALL CITIZENS, THAT SPEAK TO THE FUTURE...
...TO, GOD WILLING, A HAPPIER AND MORE PEACEFUL TIME. WE CAN DO IT, WE CAN LIBERATE THE MASSES THROUGH INFORMATION TECHNOLOGY!
OUR CELLPHONES NEVER STOPPED WORKING, YOU KNOW. THE TELECOMS SAW TO THAT.
BUT AT WHAT COST?
...NO COST.
IT'S NOT LIKE THEY CAN SEND US A BILL.
COMPLAINTS
WHO CARES?
NO, NO... YOU'RE MISSING MY POINT.
I WANT TO SHINE A LIGHT ON THE PEOPLE, I WANT TO SHOW THEM A BETTER WAY. SHOW THEM THE WORLD THAT'S BEEN PASSING THEM BY ALL THESE MANY YEARS.
WE CAN USHER THEM BACK INTO THE ARMS OF SOCIETY...
...WE CAN FREE THEM. EDUCATE THEM.

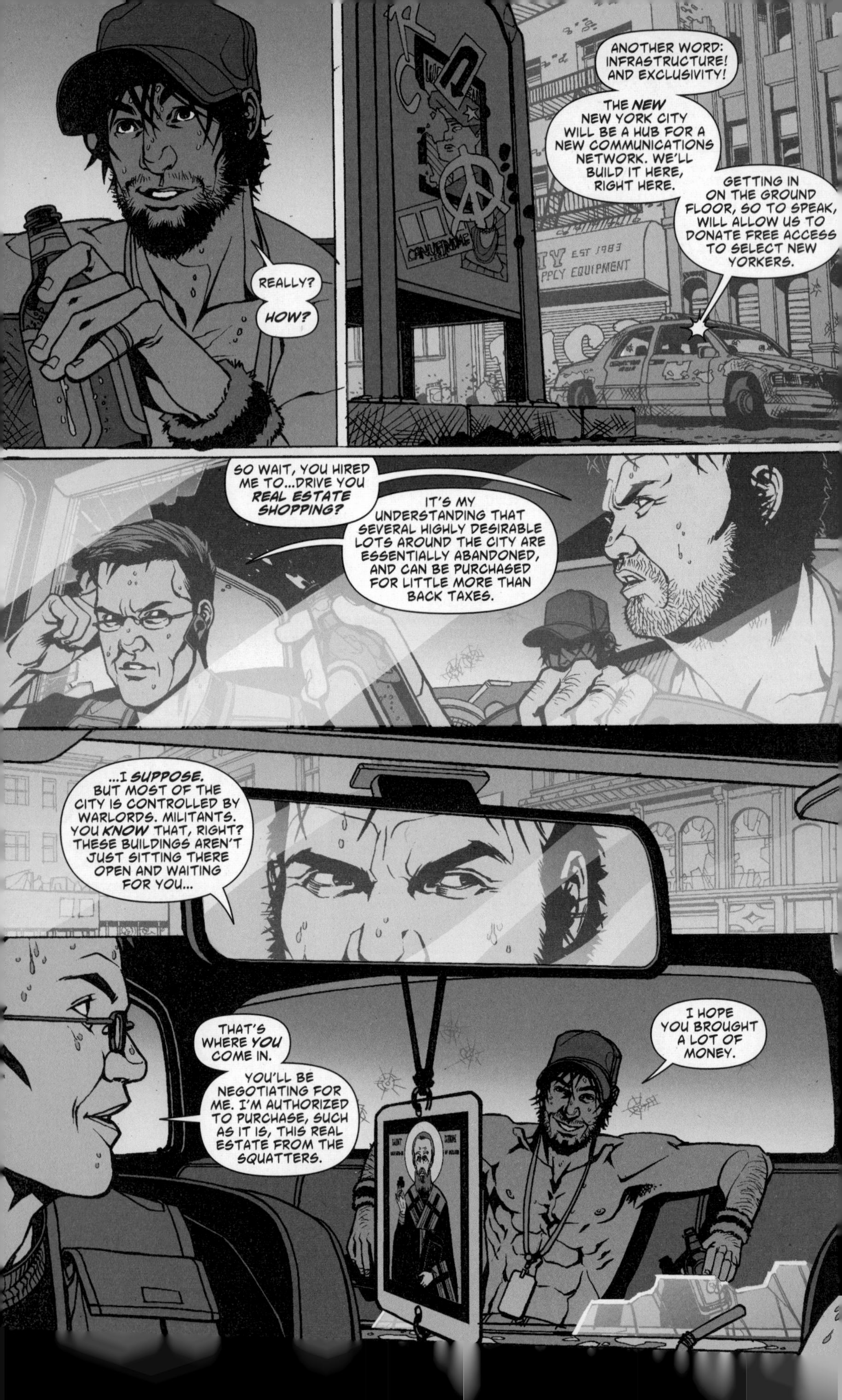
REALLY? HOW?
ANOTHER WORD: INFRASTRUCTURE! AND EXCLUSIVITY!
THE NEW NEW YORK CITY WILL BE A HUB FOR A NEW COMMUNICATIONS NETWORK. WE'LL BUILD IT HERE, RIGHT HERE.
GETTING IN ON THE GROUND FLOOR, SO TO SPEAK, WILL ALLOW US TO DONATE FREE ACCESS TO SELECT NEW YORKERS.
EST 1983
EQUIPMENT
SO WAIT, YOU HIRED ME TO...DRIVE YOU REAL ESTATE SHOPPING?
IT'S MY UNDERSTANDING THAT SEVERAL HIGHLY DESIRABLE LOTS AROUND THE CITY ARE ESSENTIALLY ABANDONED, AND CAN BE PURCHASED FOR LITTLE MORE THAN BACK TAXES.
...I SUPPOSE. BUT MOST OF THE CITY IS CONTROLLED BY WARLORDS. MILITANTS. YOU KNOW THAT, RIGHT? THESE BUILDINGS AREN'T JUST SITTING THERE OPEN AND WAITING FOR YOU...
THAT'S WHERE YOU COME IN.
YOU'LL BE NEGOTIATING FOR ME. I'M AUTHORIZED TO PURCHASE, SUCH AS IT IS, THIS REAL ESTATE FROM THE SQUATTERS.
I HOPE YOU BROUGHT A LOT OF MONEY.

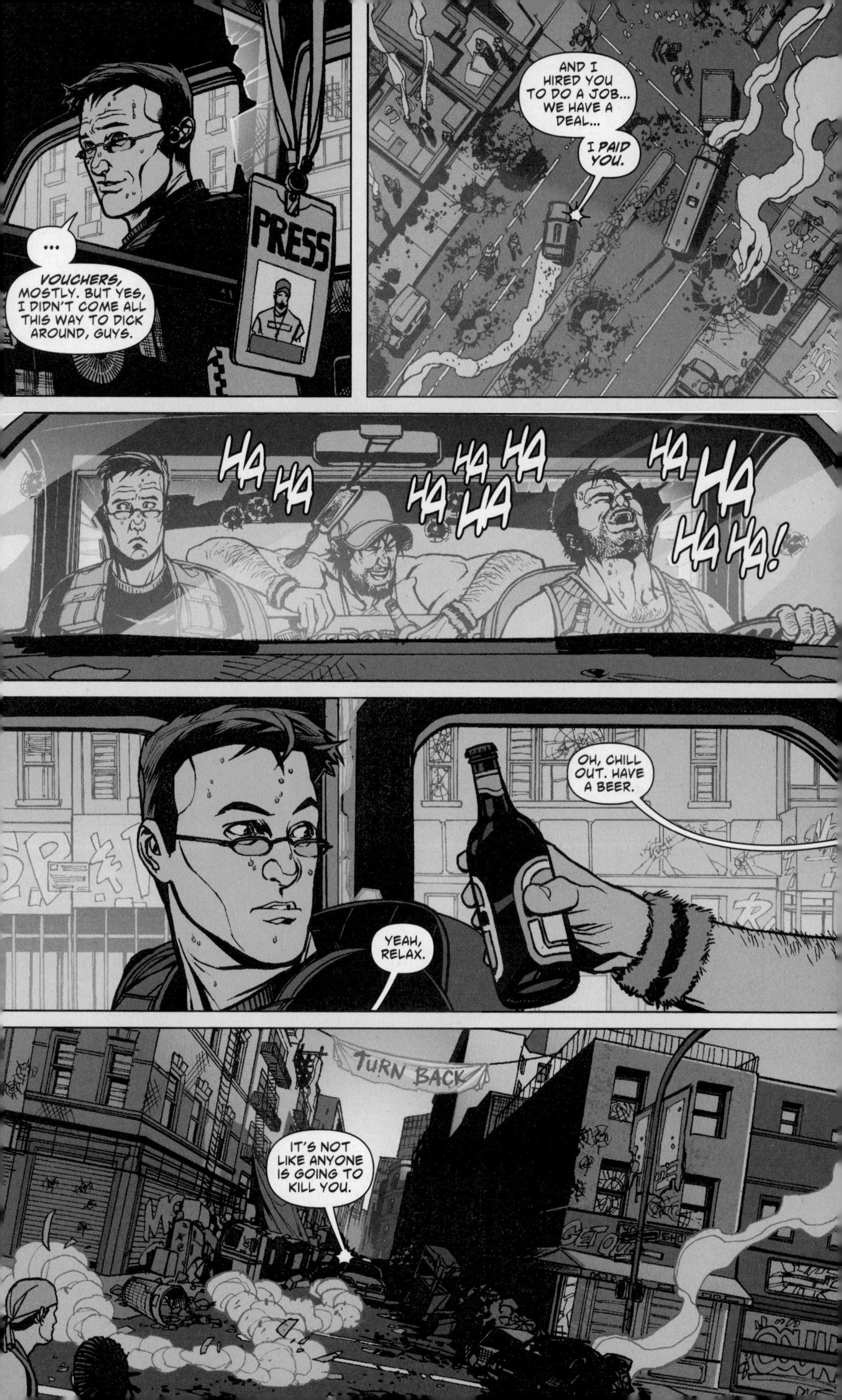
...
VOUCHERS, MOSTLY. BUT YES, I DIDN'T COME ALL THIS WAY TO DICK AROUND, GUYS.
PRESS
AND I HIRED YOU TO DO A JOB... WE HAVE A DEAL...
I PAID YOU.
HA HA
HA HA HA HA
HA HA HA HA!
OH, CHILL OUT. HAVE A BEER.
YEAH, RELAX.
TURN BACK
IT'S NOT LIKE ANYONE IS GOING TO KILL YOU.

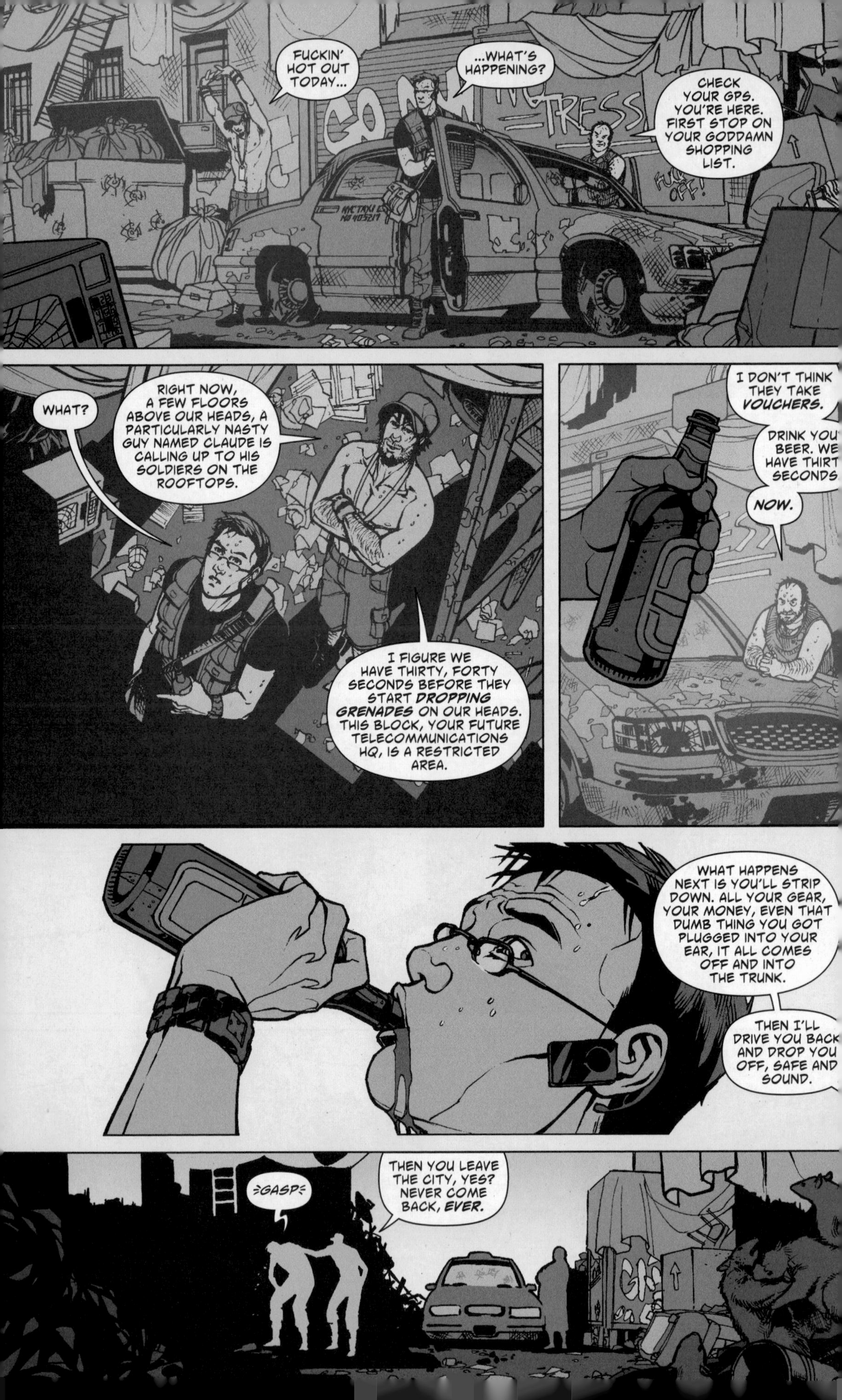
FUCKIN' HOT OUT TODAY...
...WHAT'S HAPPENING?
CHECK YOUR GPS. YOU'RE HERE. FIRST STOP ON YOUR GODDAMN SHOPPING LIST.
NYC TAXI
WHAT?
RIGHT NOW, A FEW FLOORS ABOVE OUR HEADS, A PARTICULARLY NASTY GUY NAMED CLAUDE IS CALLING UP TO HIS SOLDIERS ON THE ROOFTOPS.
I FIGURE WE HAVE THIRTY, FORTY SECONDS BEFORE THEY START *DROPPING GRENADES* ON OUR HEADS. THIS BLOCK, YOUR FUTURE TELECOMMUNICATIONS HQ, IS A RESTRICTED AREA.
I DON'T THINK THEY TAKE *VOUCHERS.*
DRINK YOU BEER. WE HAVE THIRT SECONDS
*NOW.*
WHAT HAPPENS NEXT IS YOU'LL STRIP DOWN. ALL YOUR GEAR, YOUR MONEY, EVEN THAT DUMB THING YOU GOT PLUGGED INTO YOUR EAR, IT ALL COMES OFF AND INTO THE TRUNK.
THEN I'LL DRIVE YOU BACK AND DROP YOU OFF, SAFE AND SOUND.
GASP
THEN YOU LEAVE THE CITY, YES? NEVER COME BACK, *EVER.*

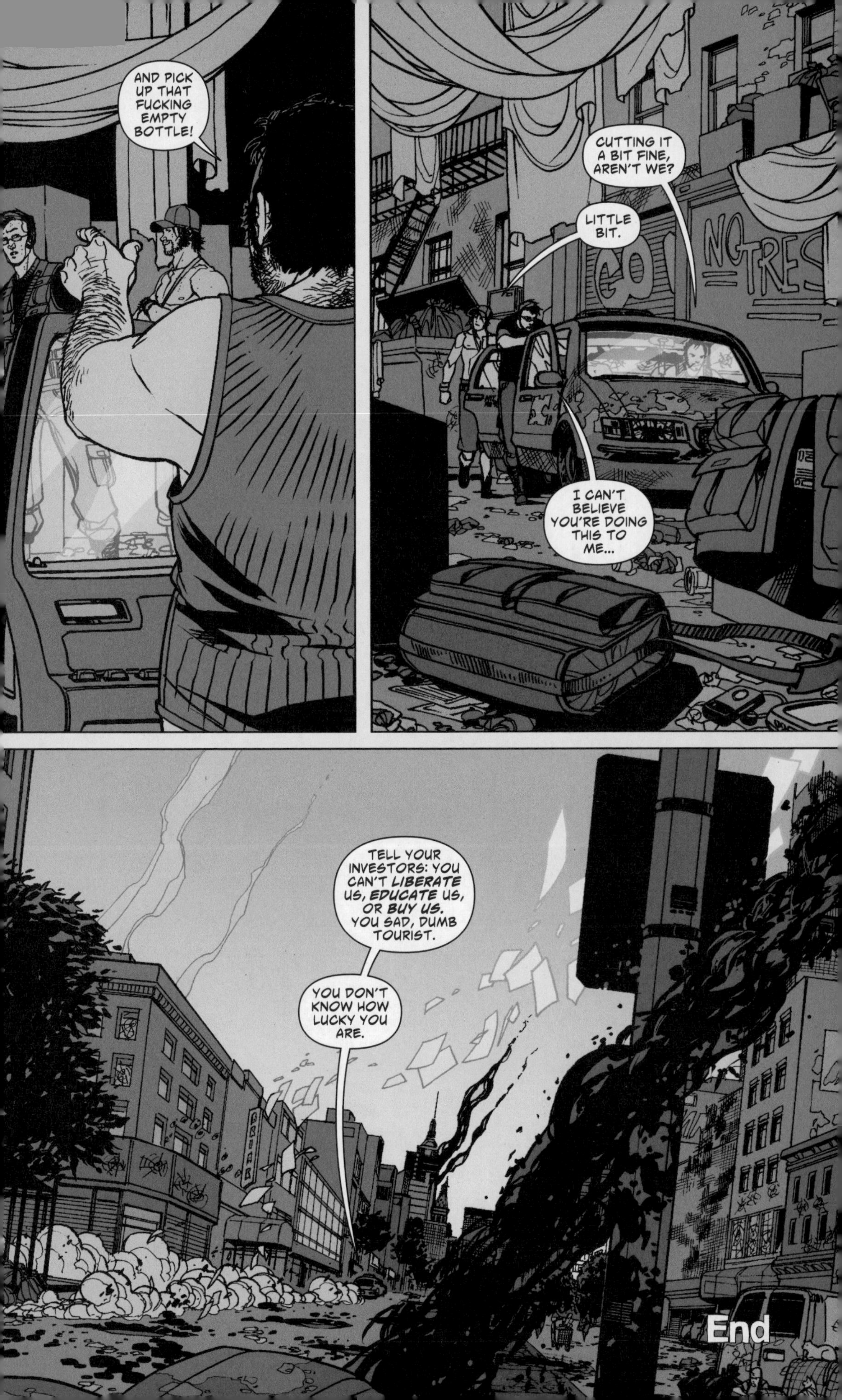
AND PICK UP THAT FUCKING EMPTY BOTTLE!
CUTTING IT A BIT FINE, AREN'T WE?
LITTLE BIT.
I CAN'T BELIEVE YOU'RE DOING THIS TO ME...
NO TRES
TELL YOUR INVESTORS: YOU CAN'T *LIBERATE* US, *EDUCATE* US, OR *BUY US*. YOU SAD, DUMB TOURIST.
YOU DON'T KNOW HOW LUCKY YOU ARE.
End

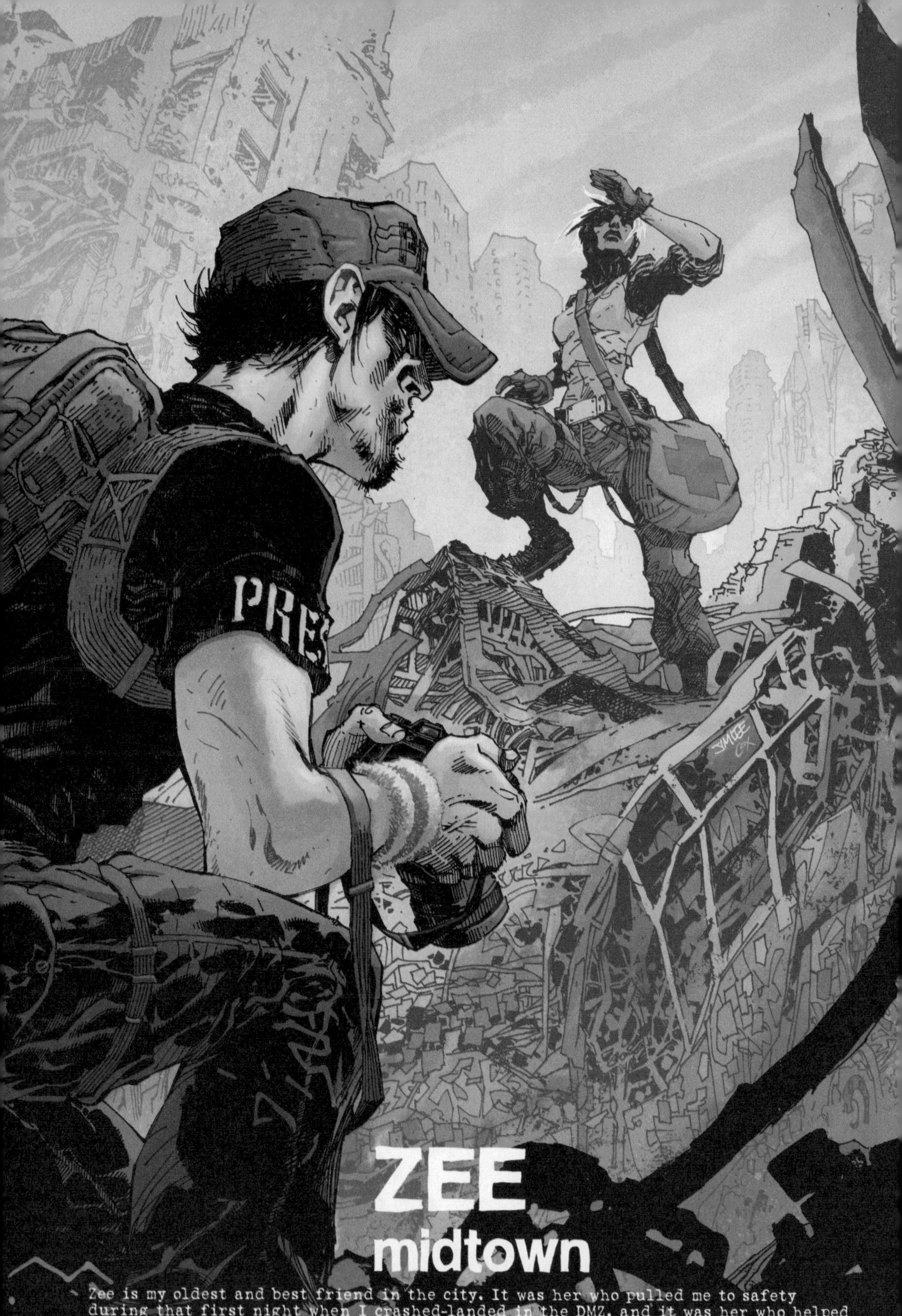

# ZEE
## midtown

Zee is my oldest and best friend in the city. It was her who pulled me to safety during that first night when I crashed-landed in the DMZ, and it was her who helped me establish the cred I needed to even function in the city. And, whether she knows it or not, it's her that has me constantly second-guessing my motivations and actions, and keeps the idea of impartiality and objectivity in the front of my head.

She demands such a high level of perfection from the people around her, though, that it's impossible to maintain in her eyes, and I'm constantly dealing with the fallout from her disappointment and anger. Sometimes I feel it'd be easier to just make my way in the DMZ without her around... but I find myself wondering if Zee and the DMZ are not one and the same, linked on some spiritual level, because I cannot imagine living in this city without her. I cannot imagine this city existing without her.

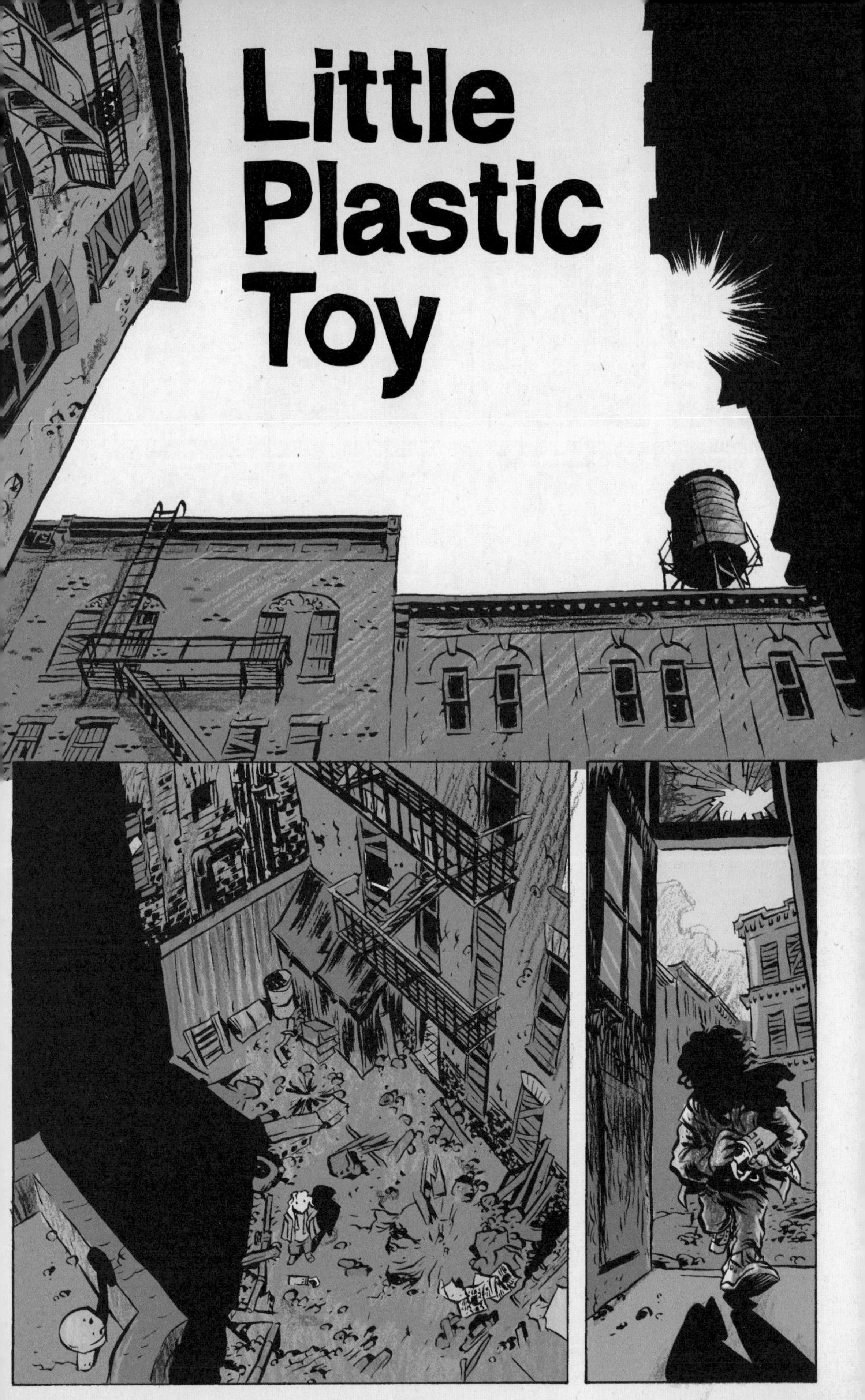
Little Plastic Toy

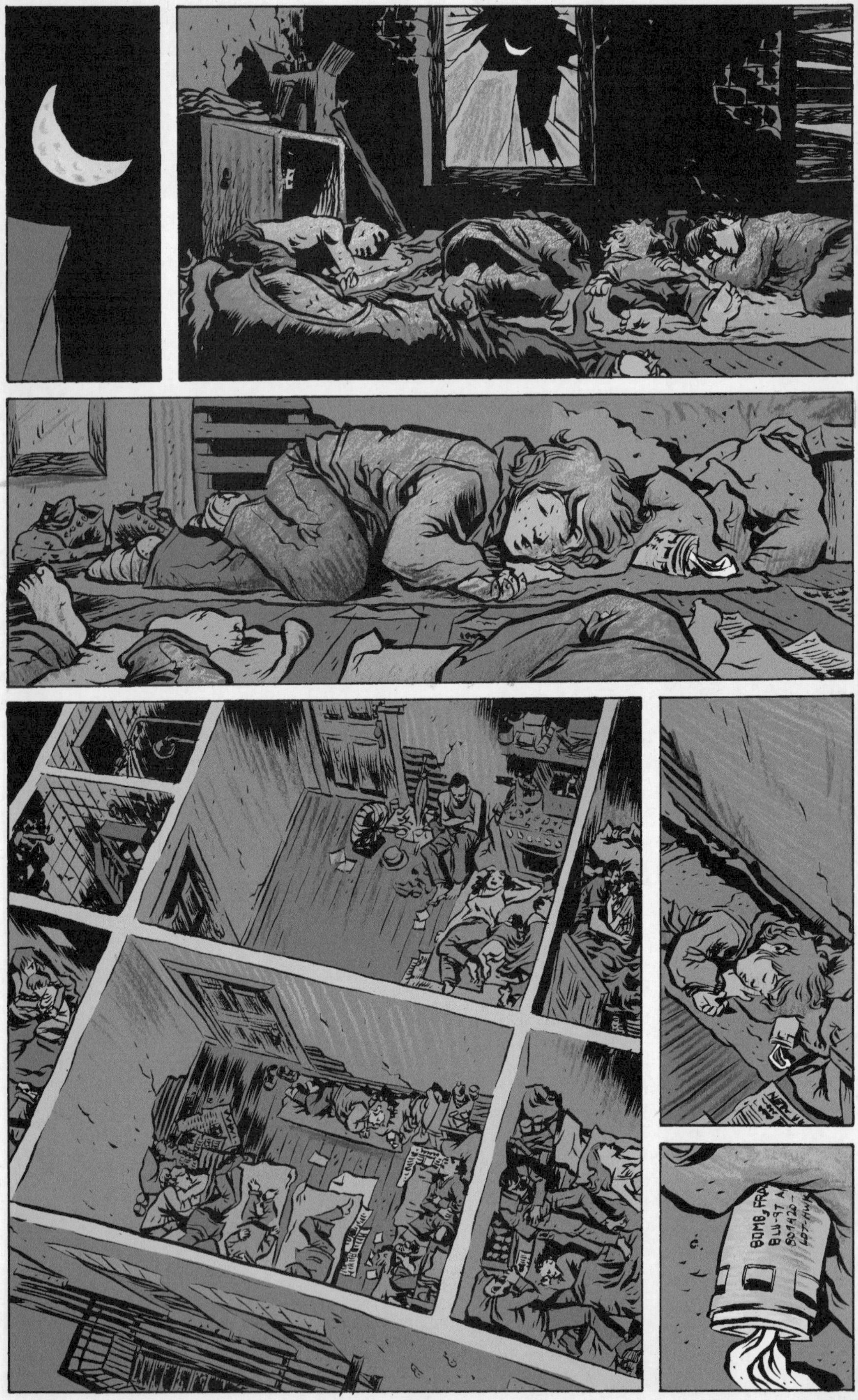
BOMB, FRA
BLU-97 A
801422-

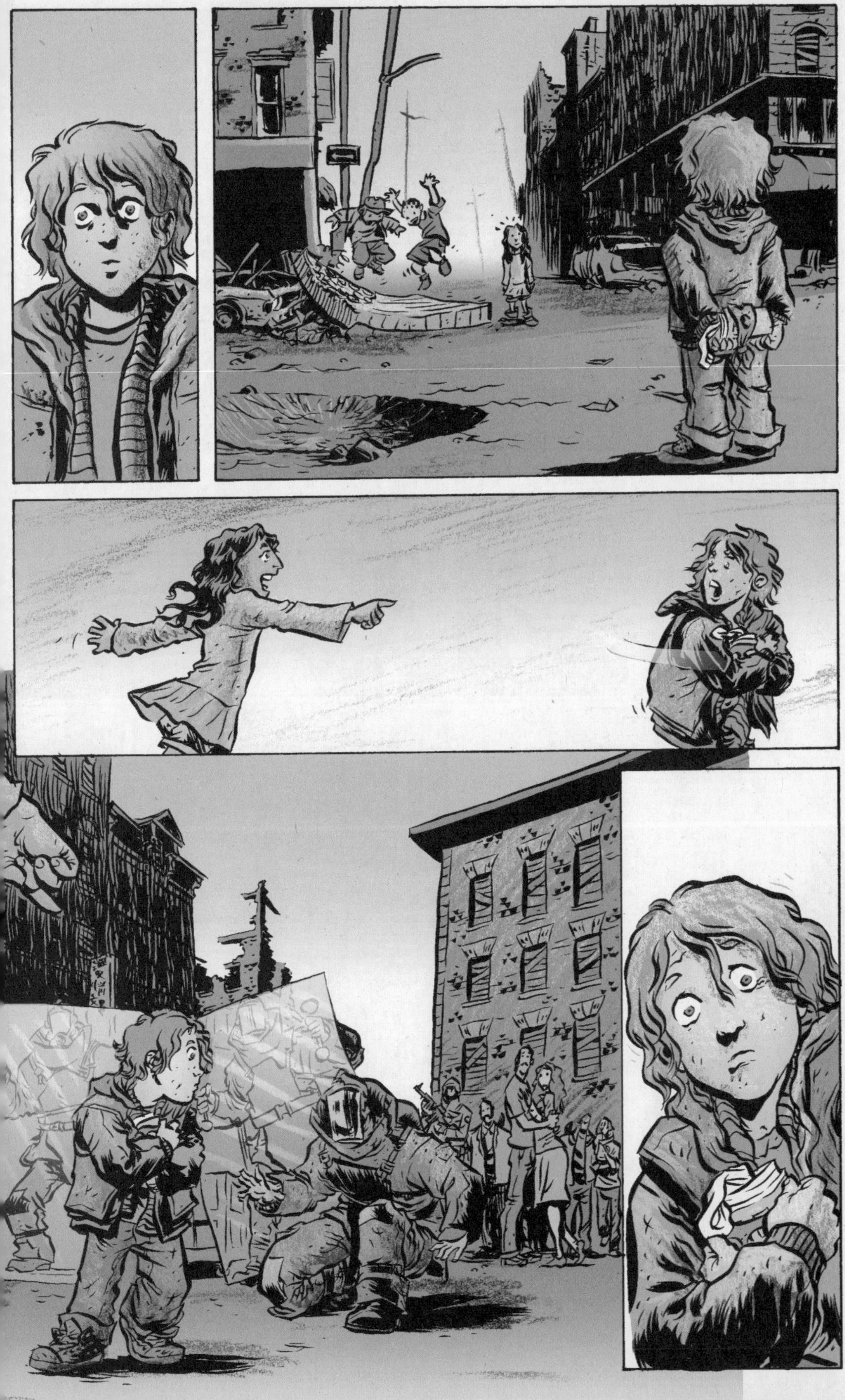

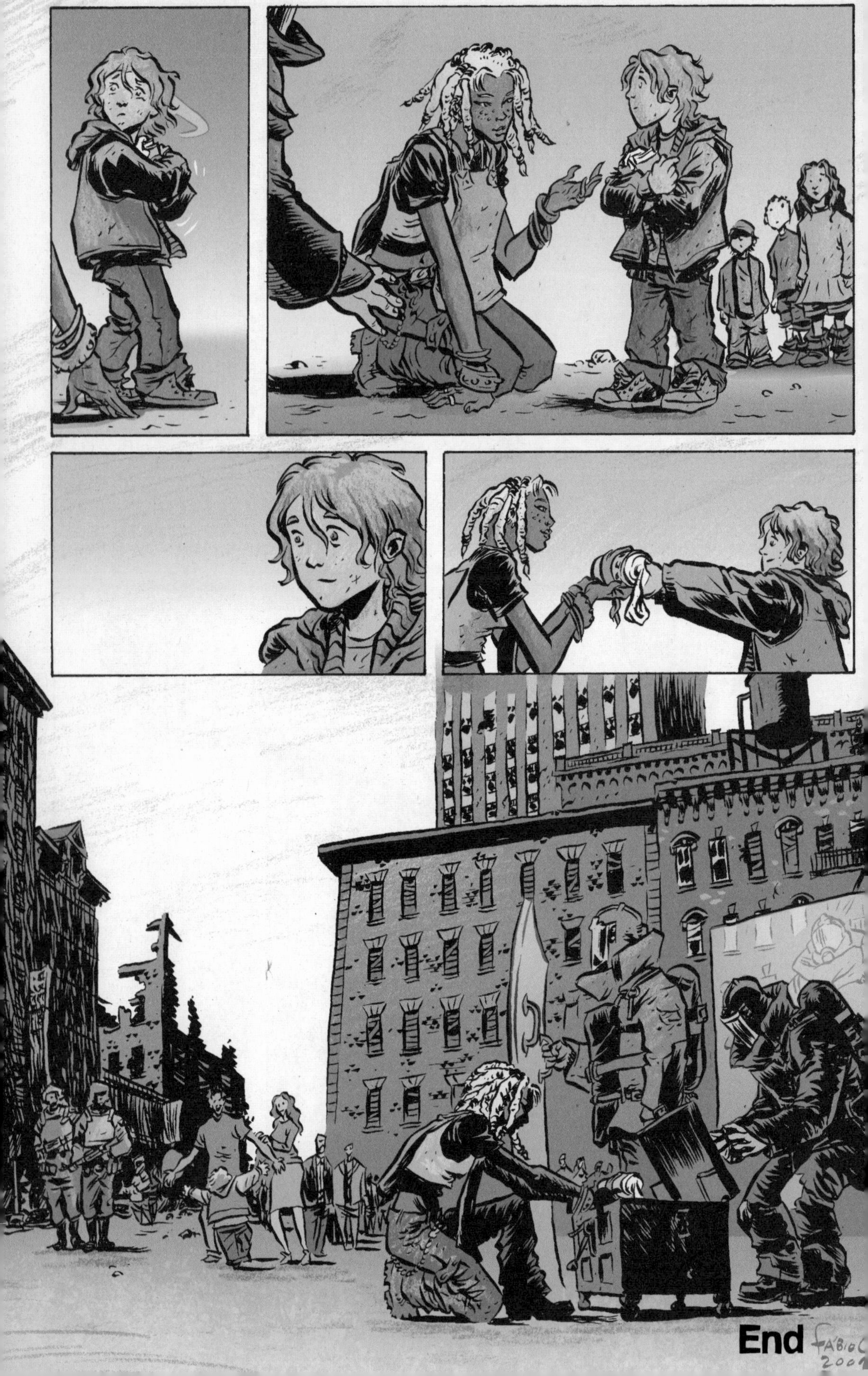
End

# Looted

**FIFTH AVENUE AKA MUSEUM MILE.**
**THE DMZ.**

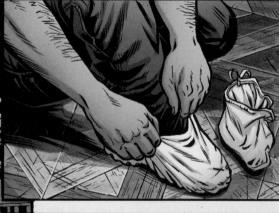

READY?

I THINK SO.

I got this call--routed to me via word of mouth and through trusted sources-- a story that was too good to pass up and worth the risk. I was given an address, an Upper East Side townhouse.

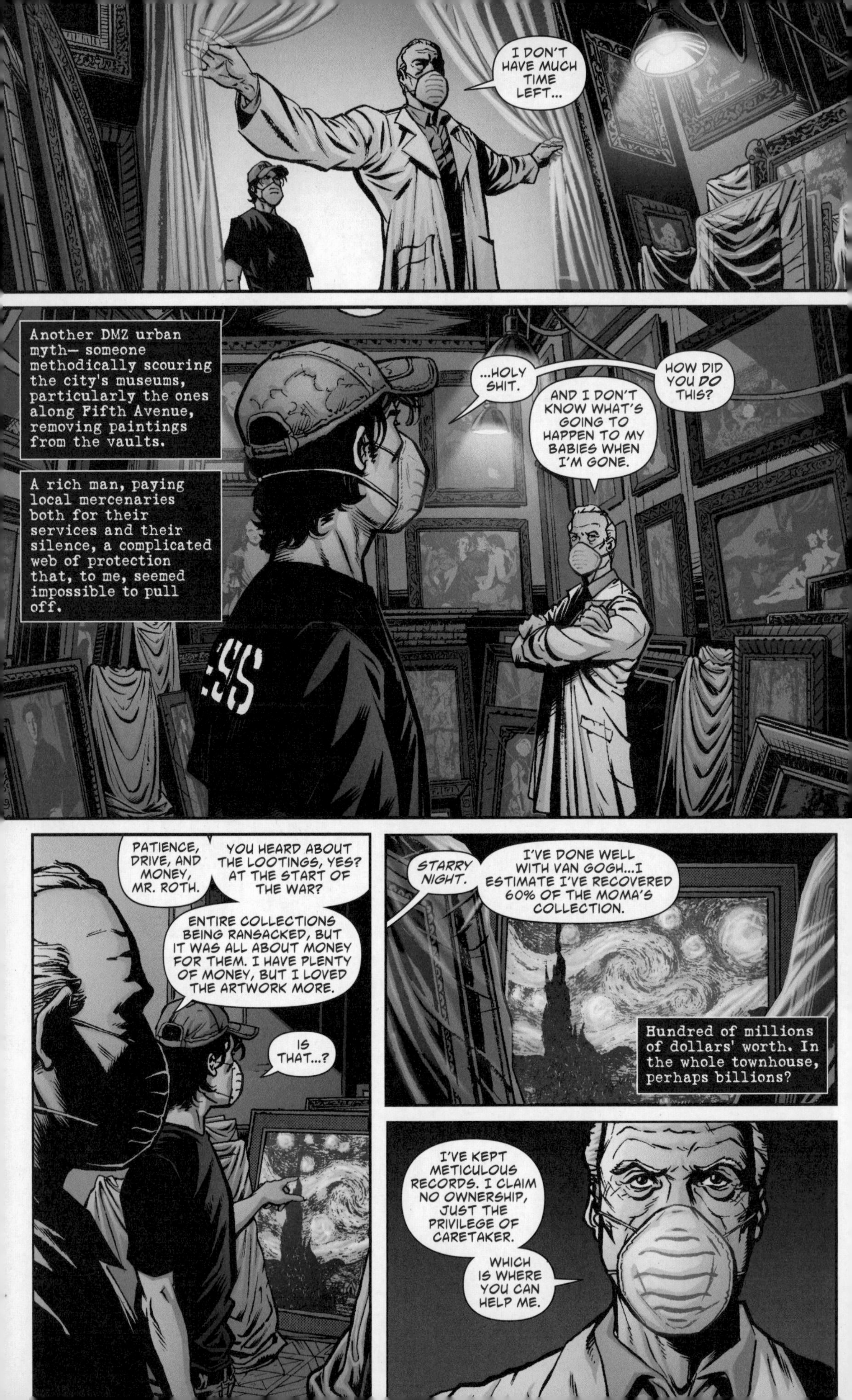
I DON'T HAVE MUCH TIME LEFT...
Another DMZ urban myth— someone methodically scouring the city's museums, particularly the ones along Fifth Avenue, removing paintings from the vaults.
A rich man, paying local mercenaries both for their services and their silence, a complicated web of protection that, to me, seemed impossible to pull off.
...HOLY SHIT.
HOW DID YOU DO THIS?
AND I DON'T KNOW WHAT'S GOING TO HAPPEN TO MY BABIES WHEN I'M GONE.
PATIENCE, DRIVE, AND MONEY, MR. ROTH.
YOU HEARD ABOUT THE LOOTINGS, YES? AT THE START OF THE WAR?
ENTIRE COLLECTIONS BEING RANSACKED, BUT IT WAS ALL ABOUT MONEY FOR THEM. I HAVE PLENTY OF MONEY, BUT I LOVED THE ARTWORK MORE.
IS THAT...?
STARRY NIGHT.
I'VE DONE WELL WITH VAN GOGH...I ESTIMATE I'VE RECOVERED 60% OF THE MOMA'S COLLECTION.
Hundred of millions of dollars' worth. In the whole townhouse, perhaps billions?
I'VE KEPT METICULOUS RECORDS. I CLAIM NO OWNERSHIP, JUST THE PRIVILEGE OF CARETAKER.
WHICH IS WHERE YOU CAN HELP ME.

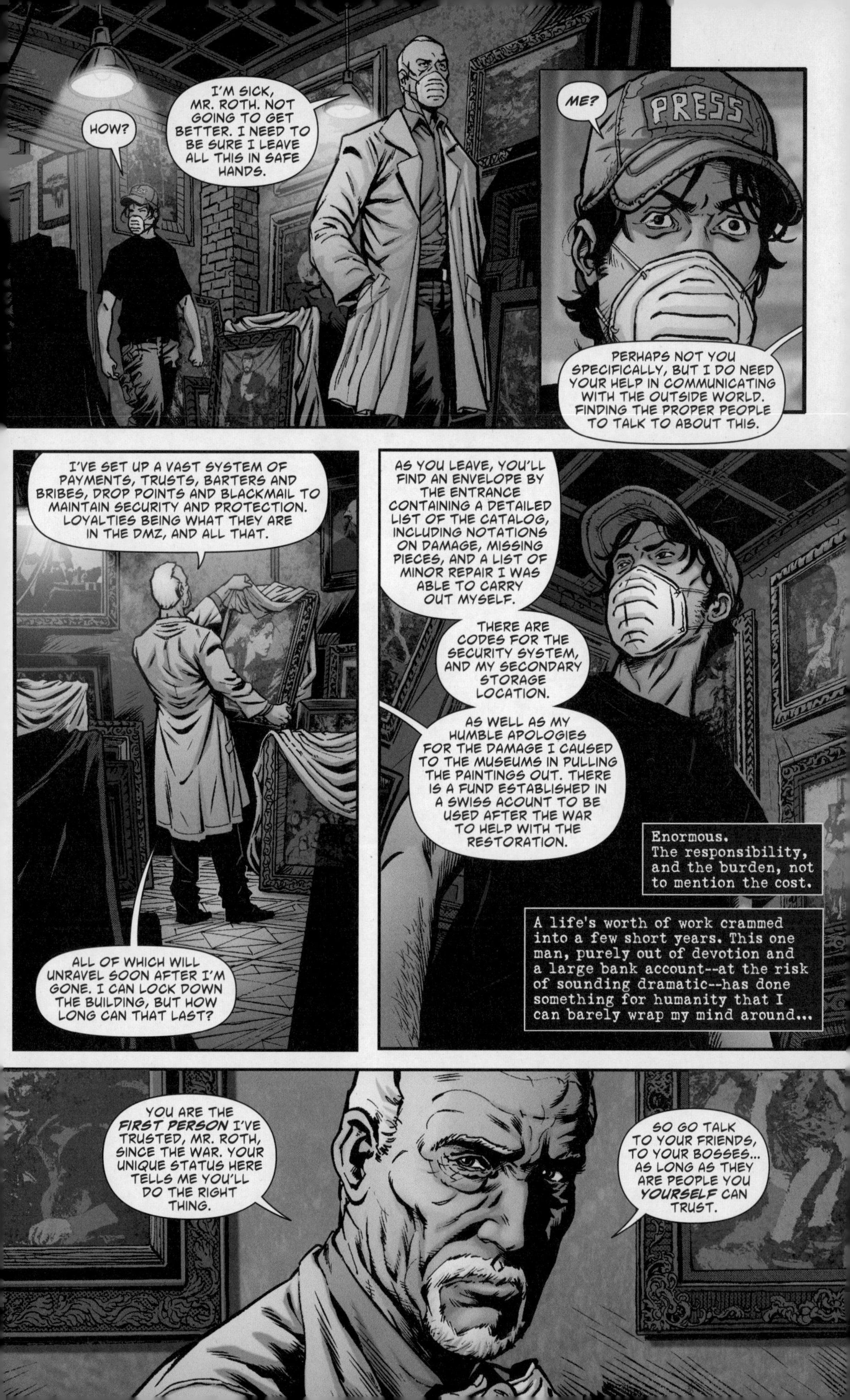
HOW?
I'M SICK, MR. ROTH. NOT GOING TO GET BETTER. I NEED TO BE SURE I LEAVE ALL THIS IN SAFE HANDS.
ME?
PERHAPS NOT YOU SPECIFICALLY, BUT I DO NEED YOUR HELP IN COMMUNICATING WITH THE OUTSIDE WORLD. FINDING THE PROPER PEOPLE TO TALK TO ABOUT THIS.
I'VE SET UP A VAST SYSTEM OF PAYMENTS, TRUSTS, BARTERS AND BRIBES, DROP POINTS AND BLACKMAIL TO MAINTAIN SECURITY AND PROTECTION. LOYALTIES BEING WHAT THEY ARE IN THE DMZ, AND ALL THAT.
ALL OF WHICH WILL UNRAVEL SOON AFTER I'M GONE. I CAN LOCK DOWN THE BUILDING, BUT HOW LONG CAN THAT LAST?
AS YOU LEAVE, YOU'LL FIND AN ENVELOPE BY THE ENTRANCE CONTAINING A DETAILED LIST OF THE CATALOG, INCLUDING NOTATIONS ON DAMAGE, MISSING PIECES, AND A LIST OF MINOR REPAIR I WAS ABLE TO CARRY OUT MYSELF.
THERE ARE CODES FOR THE SECURITY SYSTEM, AND MY SECONDARY STORAGE LOCATION.
AS WELL AS MY HUMBLE APOLOGIES FOR THE DAMAGE I CAUSED TO THE MUSEUMS IN PULLING THE PAINTINGS OUT. THERE IS A FUND ESTABLISHED IN A SWISS ACOUNT TO BE USED AFTER THE WAR TO HELP WITH THE RESTORATION.
Enormous. The responsibility, and the burden, not to mention the cost.
A life's worth of work crammed into a few short years. This one man, purely out of devotion and a large bank account--at the risk of sounding dramatic--has done something for humanity that I can barely wrap my mind around...
YOU ARE THE FIRST PERSON I'VE TRUSTED, MR. ROTH, SINCE THE WAR. YOUR UNIQUE STATUS HERE TELLS ME YOU'LL DO THE RIGHT THING.
SO GO TALK TO YOUR FRIENDS, TO YOUR BOSSES... AS LONG AS THEY ARE PEOPLE YOU YOURSELF CAN TRUST.

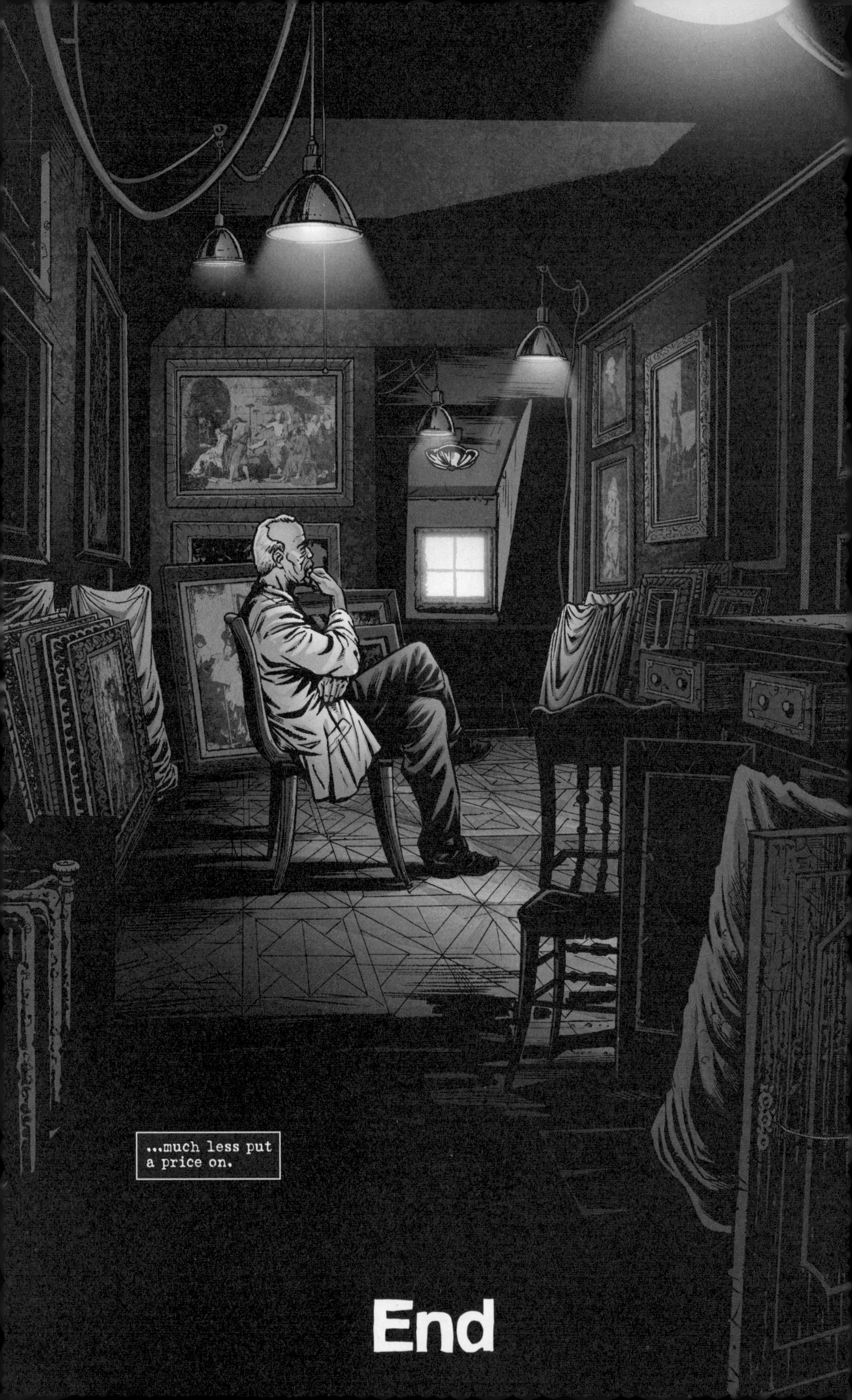
...much less put
a price on.
End

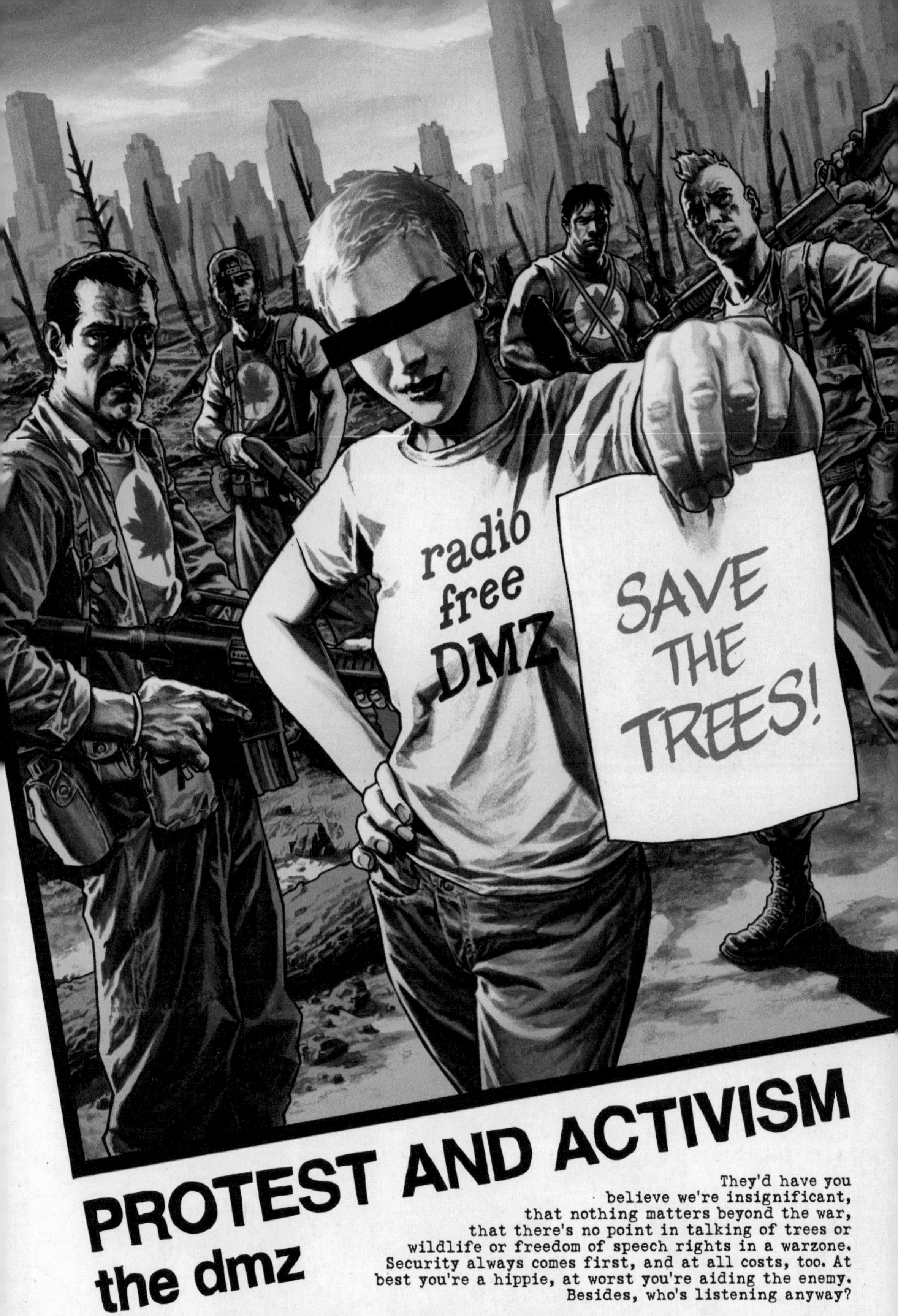
radio free DMZ
SAVE THE TREES!

# PROTEST AND ACTIVISM
## the dmz

They'd have you believe we're insignificant, that nothing matters beyond the war, that there's no point in talking of trees or wildlife or freedom of speech rights in a warzone. Security always comes first, and at all costs, too. At best you're a hippie, at worst you're aiding the enemy. Besides, who's listening anyway?

Soames, the leader of The Ghosts, summed it up: "At some point this war is going to end. And on that day, when the dust settles and we begin to take stock of the damage this stupid war caused, we will mourn the decimation of our parks and open spaces, the tainting of the water supply, the poisoning of the air and the destruction of historical areas. And, I firmly believe, the first question we'll ask is, "Why didn't we do something when we had the chance?"

"Our excuses will ring hollow."

# Heart of North Jersey

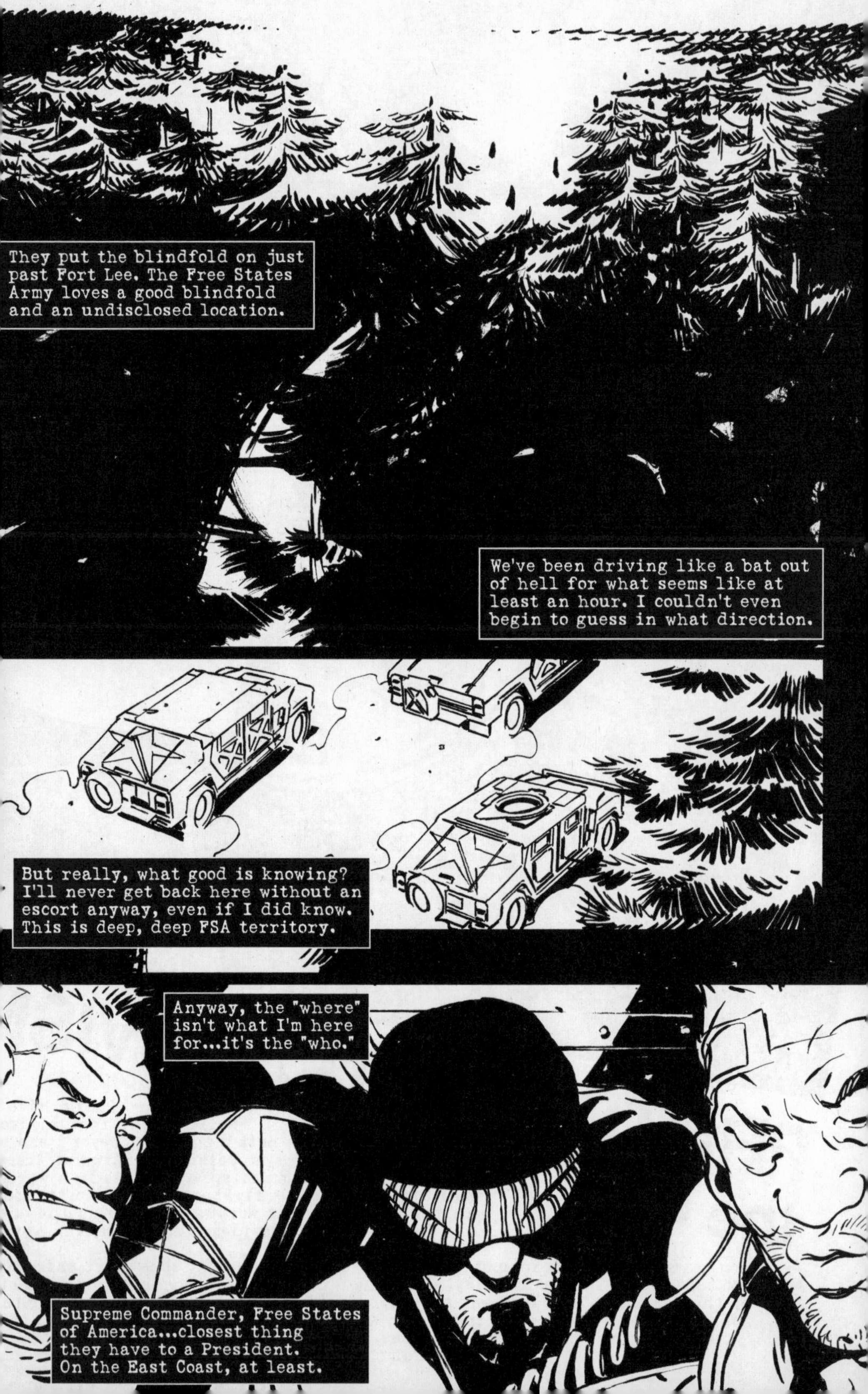
They put the blindfold on just past Fort Lee. The Free States Army loves a good blindfold and an undisclosed location.
We've been driving like a bat out of hell for what seems like at least an hour. I couldn't even begin to guess in what direction.
But really, what good is knowing? I'll never get back here without an escort anyway, even if I did know. This is deep, deep FSA territory.
Anyway, the "where" isn't what I'm here for...it's the "who."
Supreme Commander, Free States of America...closest thing they have to a President. On the East Coast, at least.

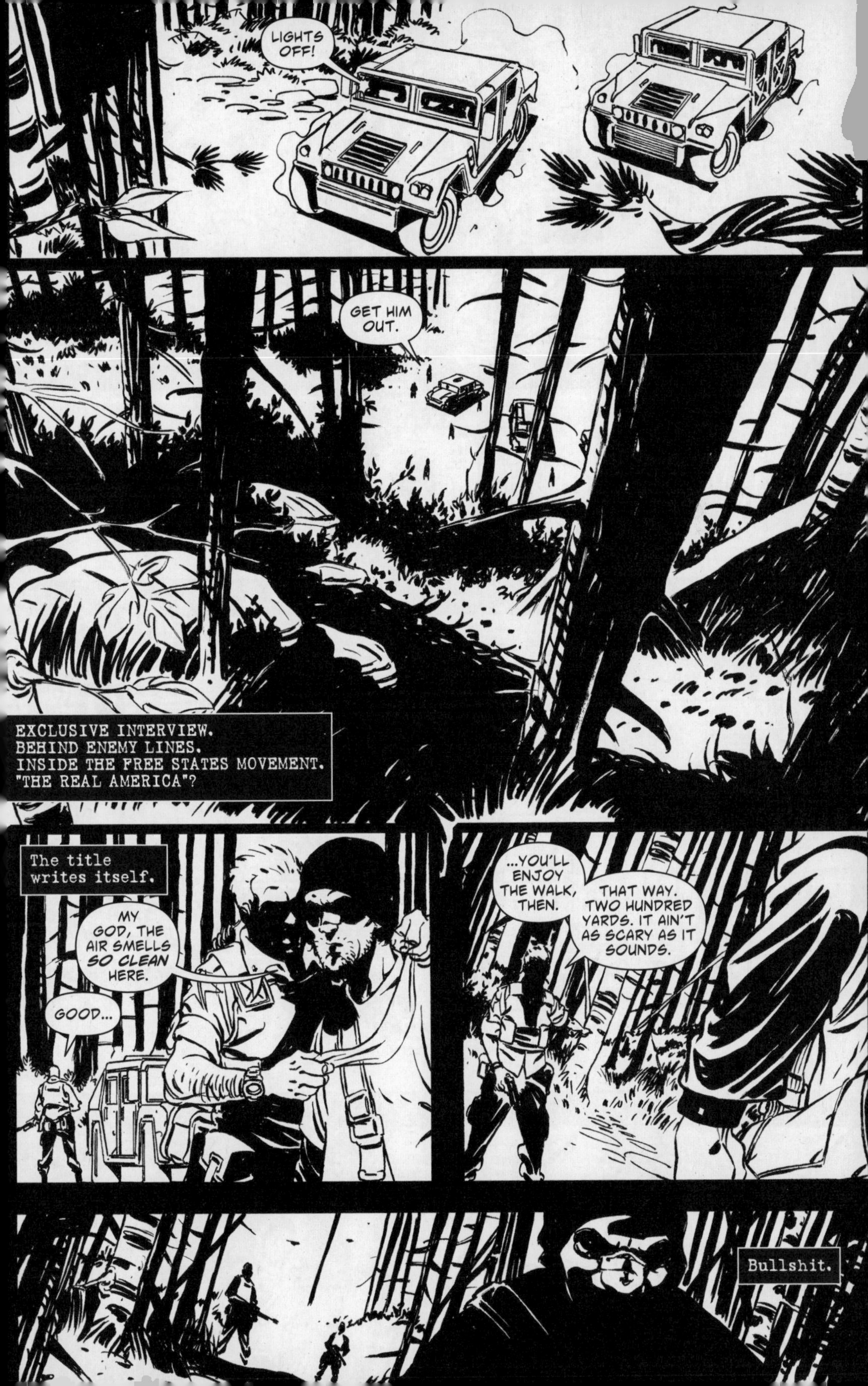
LIGHTS OFF!
GET HIM OUT.
EXCLUSIVE INTERVIEW.
BEHIND ENEMY LINES.
INSIDE THE FREE STATES MOVEMENT.
"THE REAL AMERICA"?
The title writes itself.
MY GOD, THE AIR SMELLS SO CLEAN HERE.
GOOD...
...YOU'LL ENJOY THE WALK, THEN.
THAT WAY. TWO HUNDRED YARDS. IT AIN'T AS SCARY AS IT SOUNDS.
Bullshit.

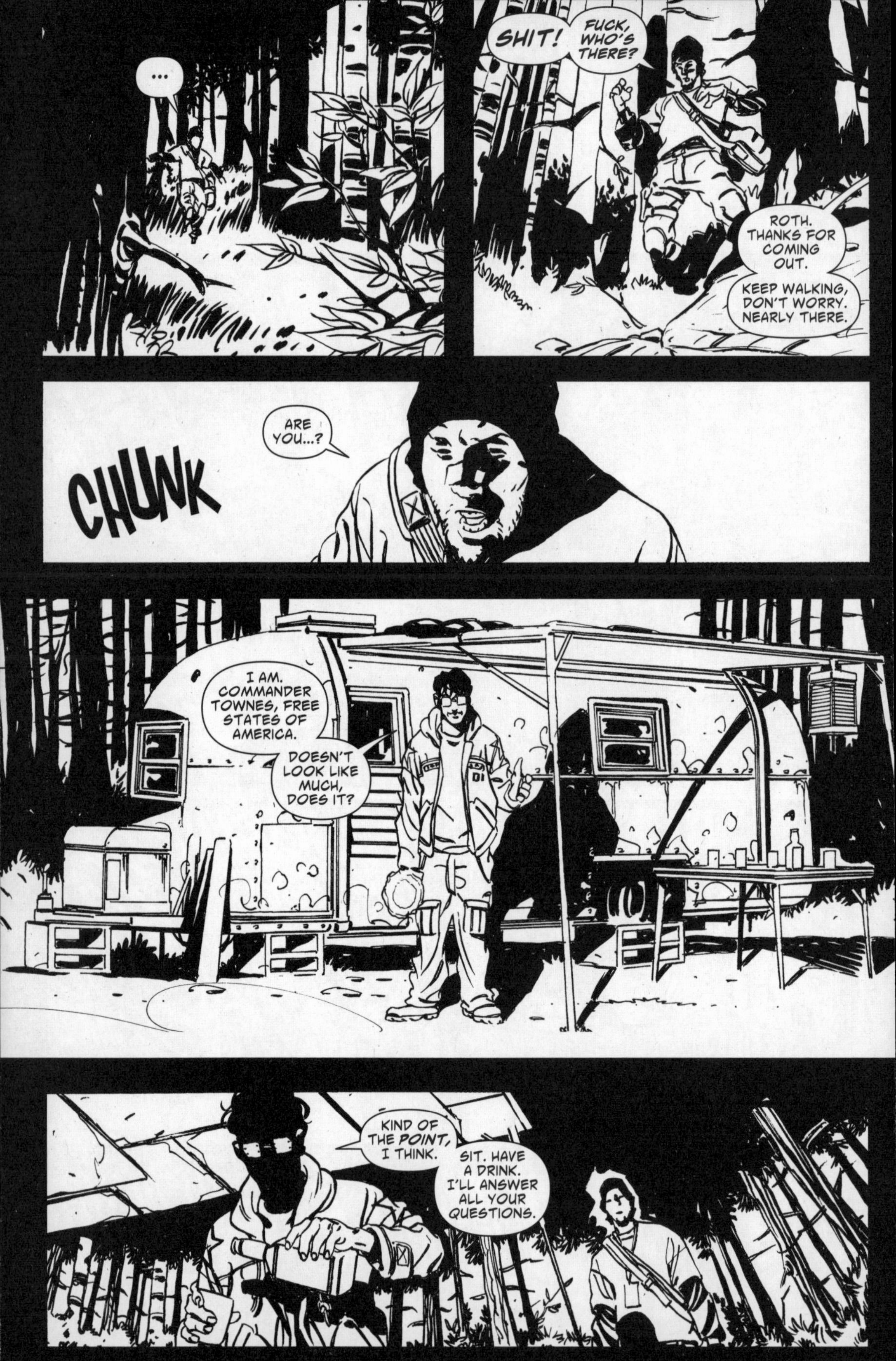
...
SHIT!
FUCK, WHO'S THERE?
ROTH. THANKS FOR COMING OUT.
KEEP WALKING, DON'T WORRY. NEARLY THERE.
ARE YOU...?
CHUNK
I AM. COMMANDER TOWNES, FREE STATES OF AMERICA.
DOESN'T LOOK LIKE MUCH, DOES IT?
KIND OF THE POINT, I THINK.
SIT. HAVE A DRINK. I'LL ANSWER ALL YOUR QUESTIONS.

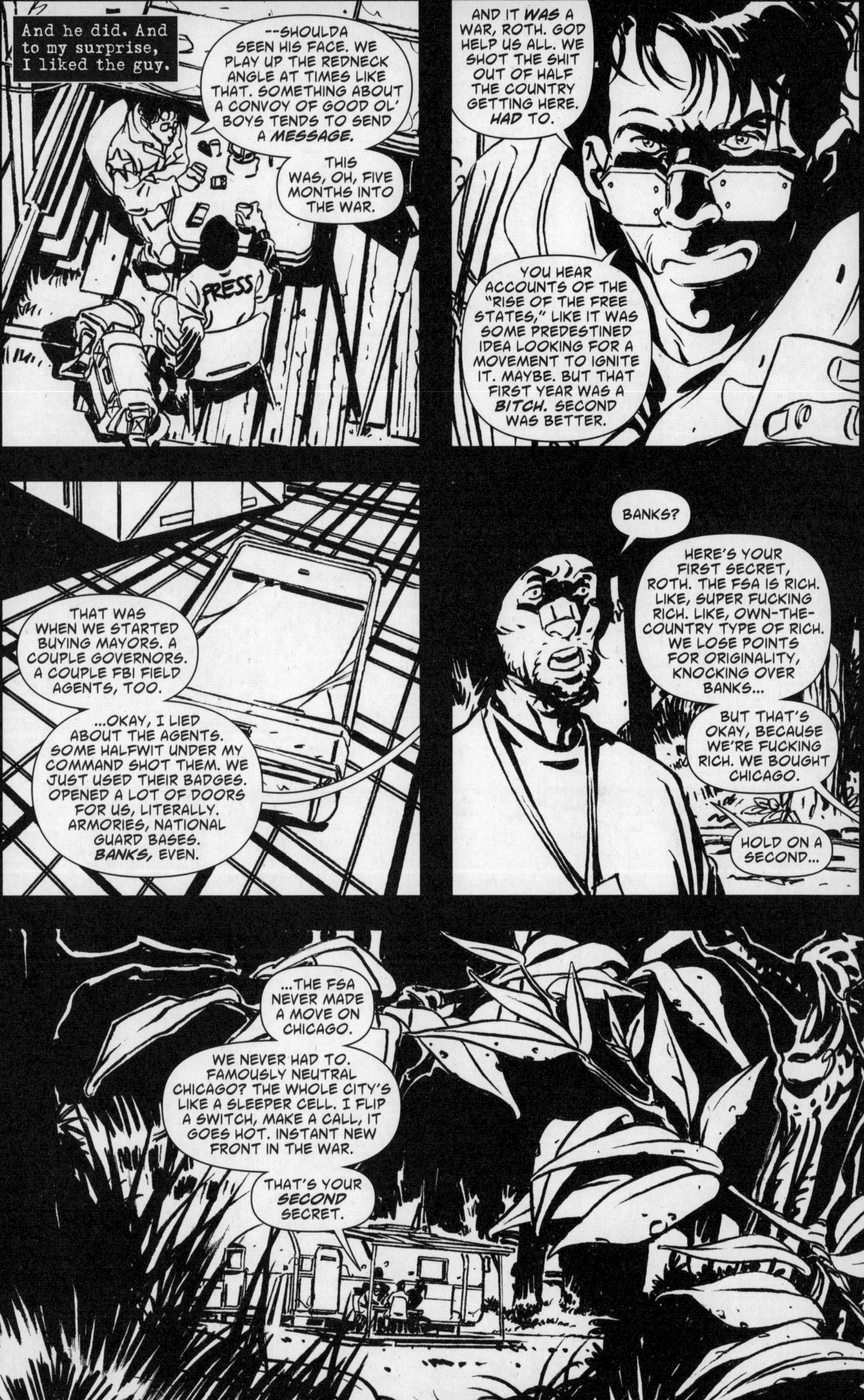
And he did. And to my surprise, I liked the guy.
--SHOULDA SEEN HIS FACE. WE PLAY UP THE REDNECK ANGLE AT TIMES LIKE THAT. SOMETHING ABOUT A CONVOY OF GOOD OL' BOYS TENDS TO SEND A MESSAGE.
THIS WAS, OH, FIVE MONTHS INTO THE WAR.
PRESS
AND IT WAS A WAR, ROTH. GOD HELP US ALL. WE SHOT THE SHIT OUT OF HALF THE COUNTRY GETTING HERE. HAD TO.
YOU HEAR ACCOUNTS OF THE "RISE OF THE FREE STATES," LIKE IT WAS SOME PREDESTINED IDEA LOOKING FOR A MOVEMENT TO IGNITE IT. MAYBE. BUT THAT FIRST YEAR WAS A BITCH. SECOND WAS BETTER.
THAT WAS WHEN WE STARTED BUYING MAYORS. A COUPLE GOVERNORS. A COUPLE FBI FIELD AGENTS, TOO.
...OKAY, I LIED ABOUT THE AGENTS. SOME HALFWIT UNDER MY COMMAND SHOT THEM. WE JUST USED THEIR BADGES. OPENED A LOT OF DOORS FOR US, LITERALLY. ARMORIES, NATIONAL GUARD BASES. BANKS, EVEN.
BANKS?
HERE'S YOUR FIRST SECRET, ROTH. THE FSA IS RICH. LIKE, SUPER FUCKING RICH. LIKE, OWN-THE-COUNTRY TYPE OF RICH. WE LOSE POINTS FOR ORIGINALITY, KNOCKING OVER BANKS...
BUT THAT'S OKAY, BECAUSE WE'RE FUCKING RICH. WE BOUGHT CHICAGO.
HOLD ON A SECOND...
...THE FSA NEVER MADE A MOVE ON CHICAGO.
WE NEVER HAD TO. FAMOUSLY NEUTRAL CHICAGO? THE WHOLE CITY'S LIKE A SLEEPER CELL. I FLIP A SWITCH, MAKE A CALL, IT GOES HOT. INSTANT NEW FRONT IN THE WAR.
THAT'S YOUR SECOND SECRET.

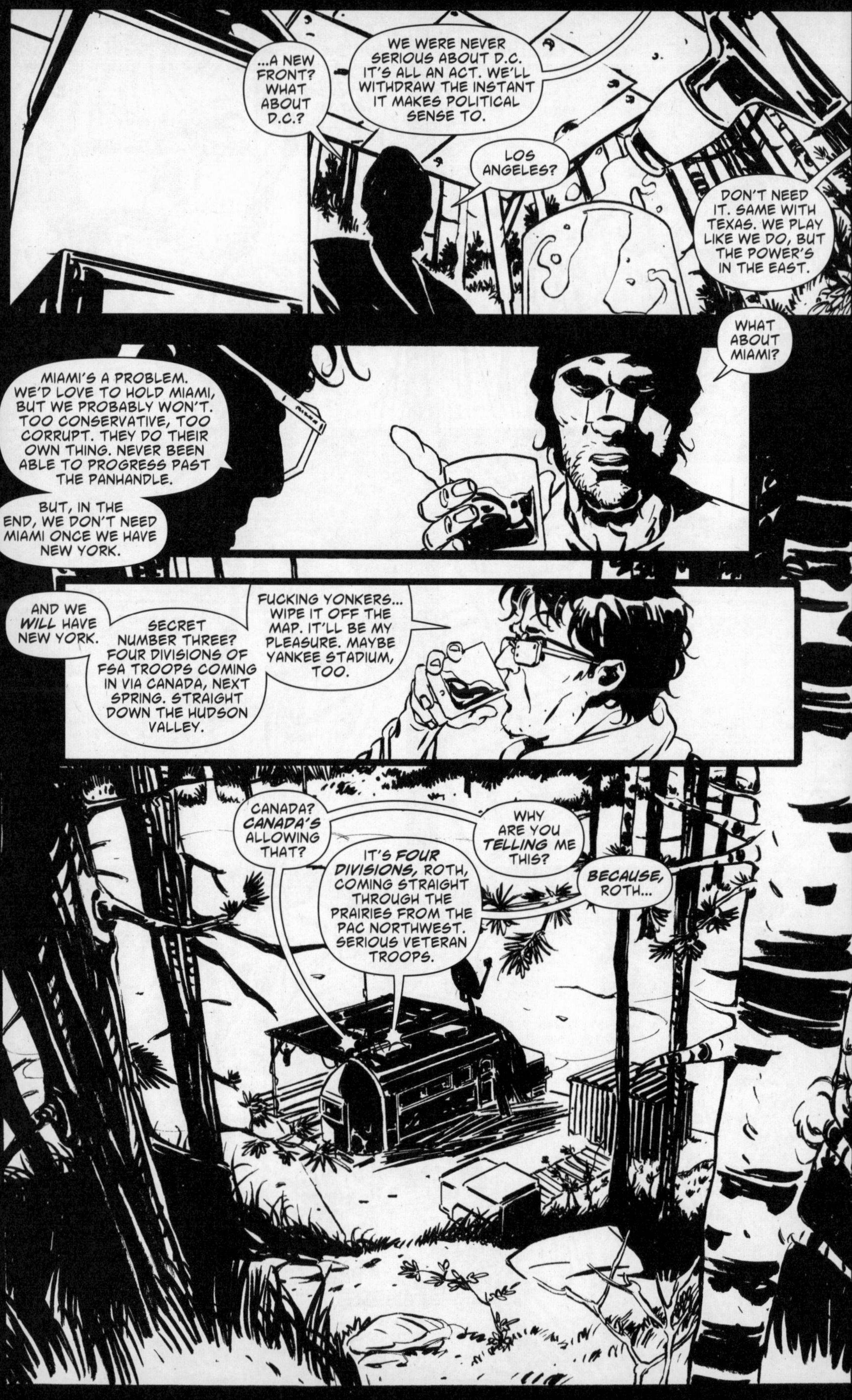
...A NEW FRONT? WHAT ABOUT D.C.?
WE WERE NEVER SERIOUS ABOUT D.C. IT'S ALL AN ACT. WE'LL WITHDRAW THE INSTANT IT MAKES POLITICAL SENSE TO.
LOS ANGELES?
DON'T NEED IT. SAME WITH TEXAS. WE PLAY LIKE WE DO, BUT THE POWER'S IN THE EAST.
WHAT ABOUT MIAMI?
MIAMI'S A PROBLEM. WE'D LOVE TO HOLD MIAMI, BUT WE PROBABLY WON'T. TOO CONSERVATIVE, TOO CORRUPT. THEY DO THEIR OWN THING. NEVER BEEN ABLE TO PROGRESS PAST THE PANHANDLE.
BUT, IN THE END, WE DON'T NEED MIAMI ONCE WE HAVE NEW YORK.
AND WE *WILL* HAVE NEW YORK.
SECRET NUMBER THREE? FOUR DIVISIONS OF FSA TROOPS COMING IN VIA CANADA, NEXT SPRING. STRAIGHT DOWN THE HUDSON VALLEY.
FUCKING YONKERS... WIPE IT OFF THE MAP. IT'LL BE MY PLEASURE. MAYBE YANKEE STADIUM, TOO.
CANADA? *CANADA'S* ALLOWING THAT?
IT'S *FOUR DIVISIONS,* ROTH, COMING STRAIGHT THROUGH THE PRAIRIES FROM THE PAC NORTHWEST. SERIOUS VETERAN TROOPS.
WHY ARE YOU *TELLING* ME THIS?
*BECAUSE,* ROTH...

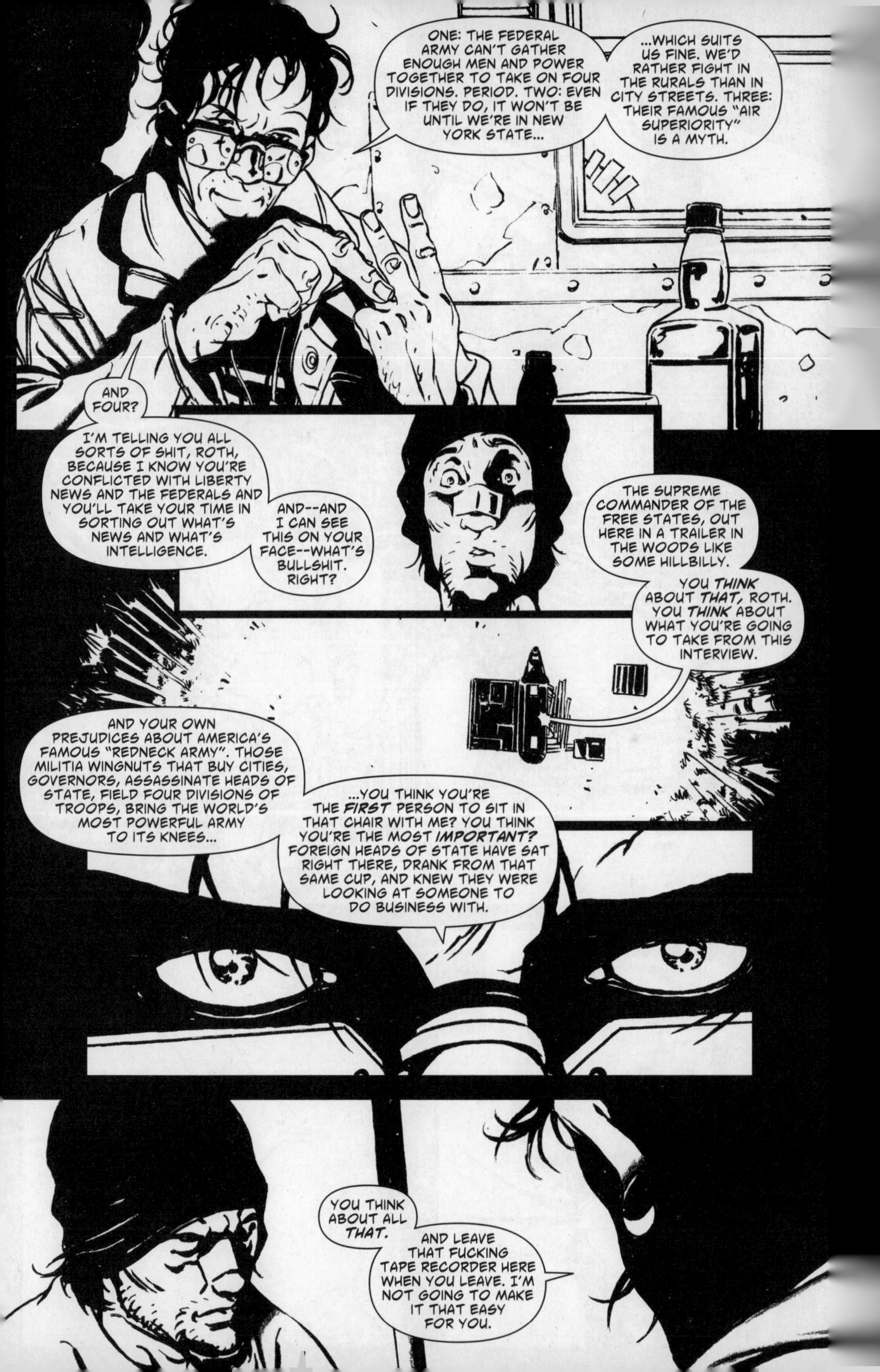
ONE: THE FEDERAL ARMY CAN'T GATHER ENOUGH MEN AND POWER TOGETHER TO TAKE ON FOUR DIVISIONS. PERIOD. TWO: EVEN IF THEY DO, IT WON'T BE UNTIL WE'RE IN NEW YORK STATE...
...WHICH SUITS US FINE. WE'D RATHER FIGHT IN THE RURALS THAN IN CITY STREETS. THREE: THEIR FAMOUS "AIR SUPERIORITY" IS A MYTH.
AND FOUR?
I'M TELLING YOU ALL SORTS OF SHIT, ROTH, BECAUSE I KNOW YOU'RE CONFLICTED WITH LIBERTY NEWS AND THE FEDERALS AND YOU'LL TAKE YOUR TIME IN SORTING OUT WHAT'S NEWS AND WHAT'S INTELLIGENCE.
AND--AND I CAN SEE THIS ON YOUR FACE--WHAT'S BULLSHIT. RIGHT?
THE SUPREME COMMANDER OF THE FREE STATES, OUT HERE IN A TRAILER IN THE WOODS LIKE SOME HILLBILLY.
YOU THINK ABOUT THAT, ROTH. YOU THINK ABOUT WHAT YOU'RE GOING TO TAKE FROM THIS INTERVIEW.
AND YOUR OWN PREJUDICES ABOUT AMERICA'S FAMOUS "REDNECK ARMY". THOSE MILITIA WINGNUTS THAT BUY CITIES, GOVERNORS, ASSASSINATE HEADS OF STATE, FIELD FOUR DIVISIONS OF TROOPS, BRING THE WORLD'S MOST POWERFUL ARMY TO ITS KNEES...
...YOU THINK YOU'RE THE FIRST PERSON TO SIT IN THAT CHAIR WITH ME? YOU THINK YOU'RE THE MOST IMPORTANT? FOREIGN HEADS OF STATE HAVE SAT RIGHT THERE, DRANK FROM THAT SAME CUP, AND KNEW THEY WERE LOOKING AT SOMEONE TO DO BUSINESS WITH.
YOU THINK ABOUT ALL THAT.
AND LEAVE THAT FUCKING TAPE RECORDER HERE WHEN YOU LEAVE. I'M NOT GOING TO MAKE IT THAT EASY FOR YOU.

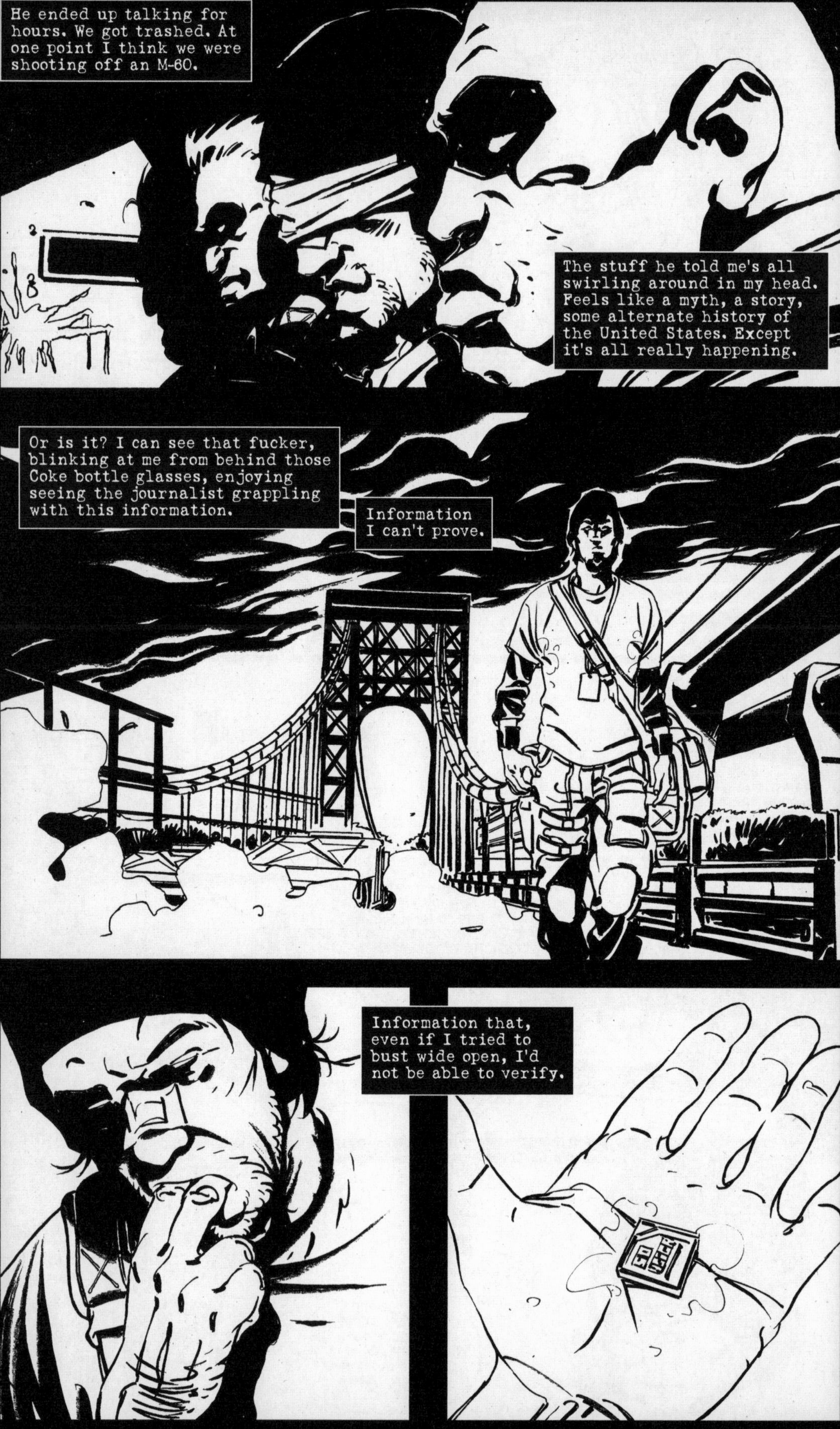
He ended up talking for hours. We got trashed. At one point I think we were shooting off an M-60.
The stuff he told me's all swirling around in my head. Feels like a myth, a story, some alternate history of the United States. Except it's all really happening.
Or is it? I can see that fucker, blinking at me from behind those Coke bottle glasses, enjoying seeing the journalist grappling with this information.
Information I can't prove.
Information that, even if I tried to bust wide open, I'd not be able to verify.

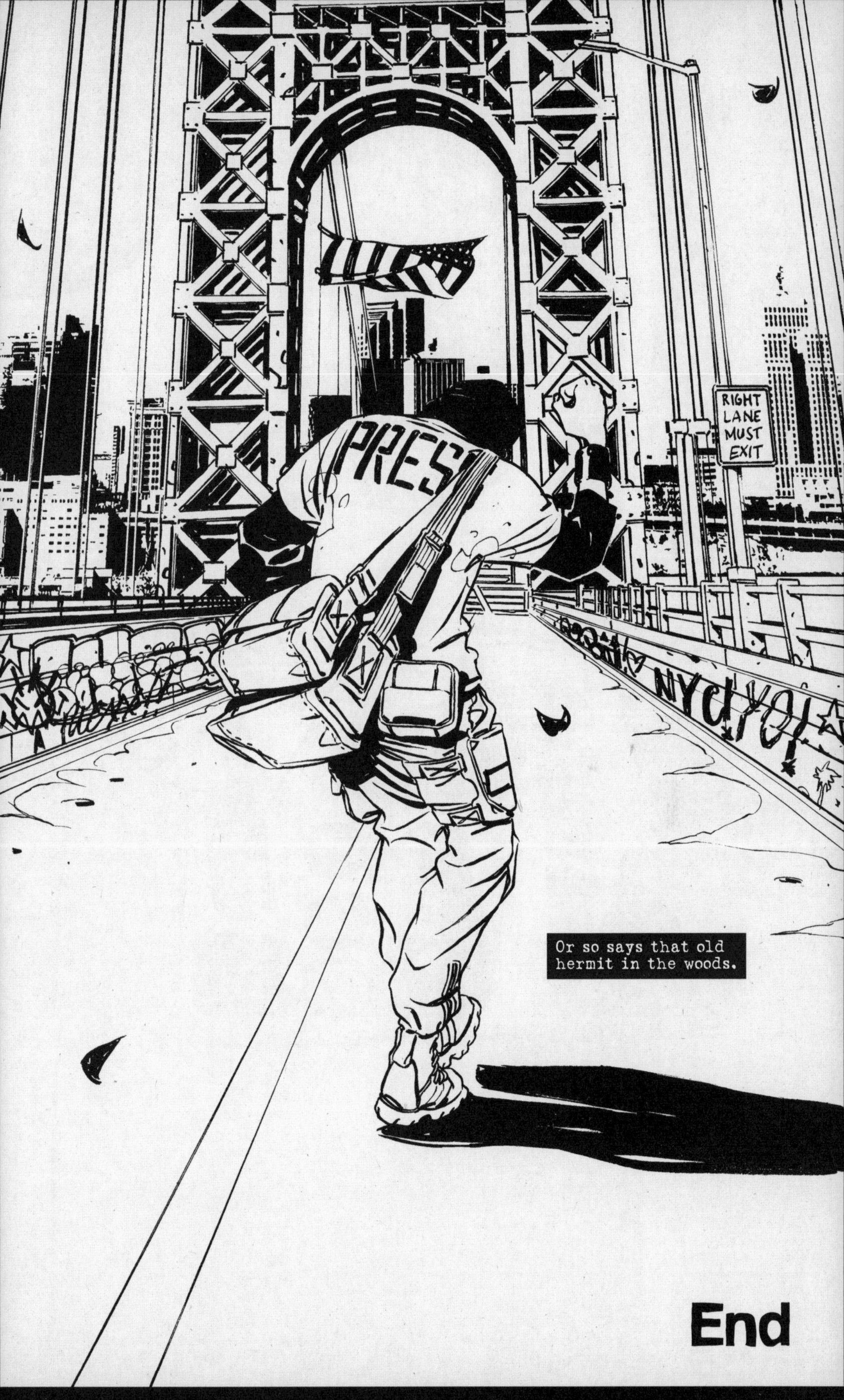
PRES
RIGHT LANE MUST EXIT
Or so says that old hermit in the woods.
End

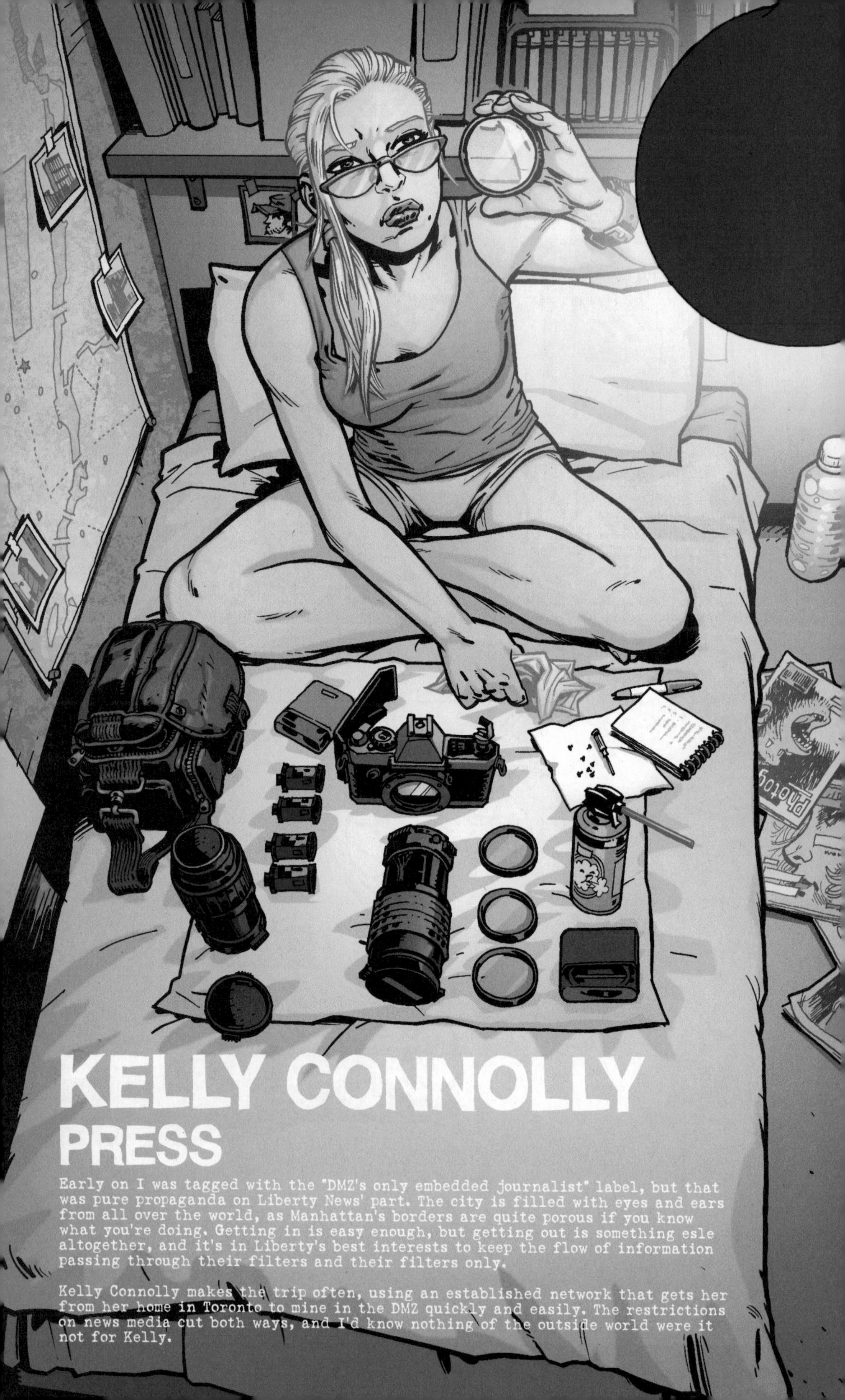

# KELLY CONNOLLY

## PRESS

Early on I was tagged with the "DMZ's only embedded journalist" label, but that was pure propaganda on Liberty News' part. The city is filled with eyes and ears from all over the world, as Manhattan's borders are quite porous if you know what you're doing. Getting in is easy enough, but getting out is something esle altogether, and it's in Liberty's best interests to keep the flow of information passing through their filters and their filters only.

Kelly Connolly makes the trip often, using an established network that gets her from her home in Toronto to mine in the DMZ quickly and easily. The restrictions on news media cut both ways, and I'd know nothing of the outside world were it not for Kelly.

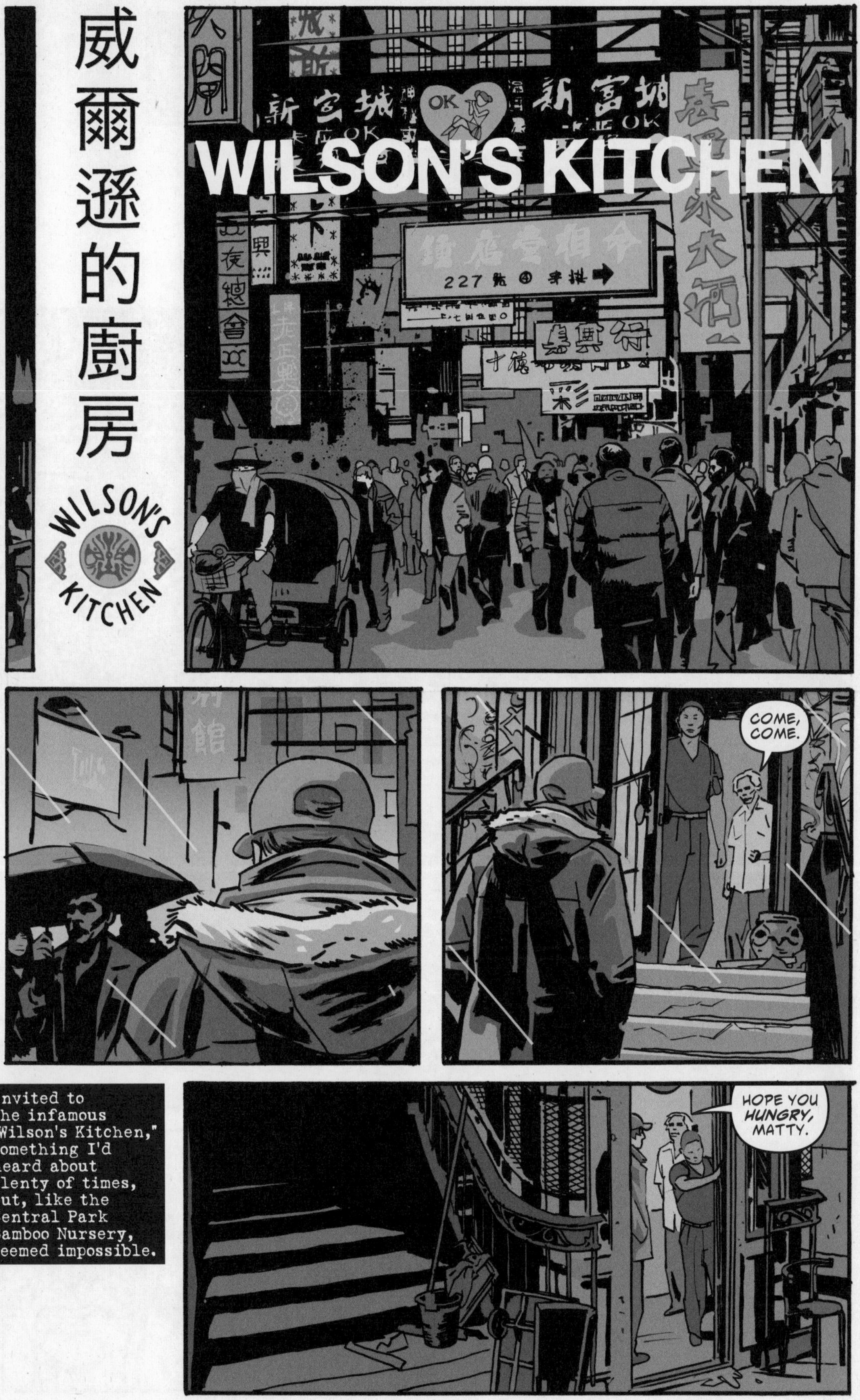
威爾遜的廚房
WILSON'S KITCHEN
WILSON'S KITCHEN
COME, COME.
Invited to the infamous "Wilson's Kitchen," something I'd heard about plenty of times, but, like the Central Park Bamboo Nursery, seemed impossible.
HOPE YOU HUNGRY, MATTY.

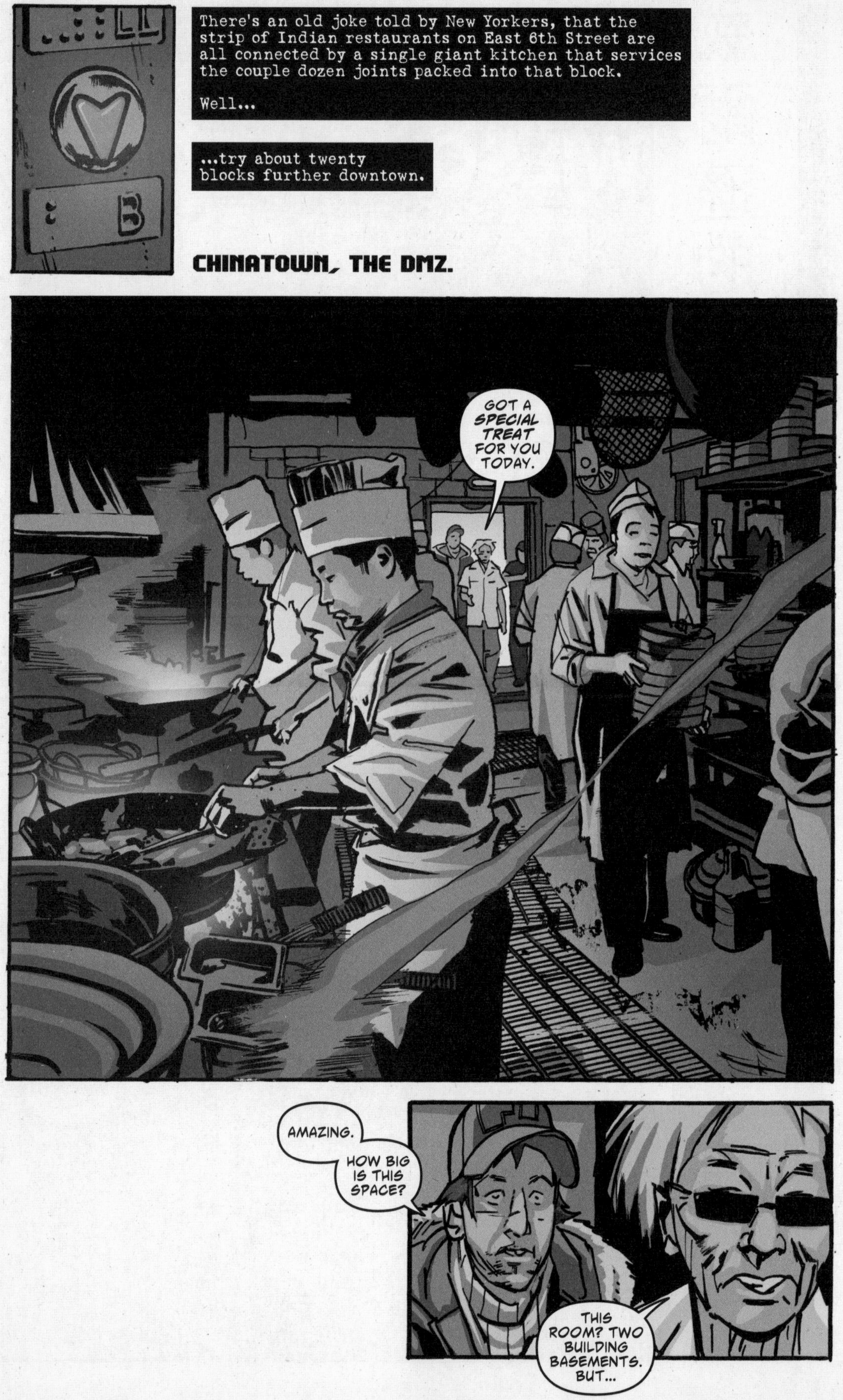
There's an old joke told by New Yorkers, that the strip of Indian restaurants on East 6th Street are all connected by a single giant kitchen that services the couple dozen joints packed into that block.
Well...
...try about twenty blocks further downtown.
CHINATOWN, THE DMZ.
GOT A SPECIAL TREAT FOR YOU TODAY.
AMAZING.
HOW BIG IS THIS SPACE?
THIS ROOM? TWO BUILDING BASEMENTS. BUT...

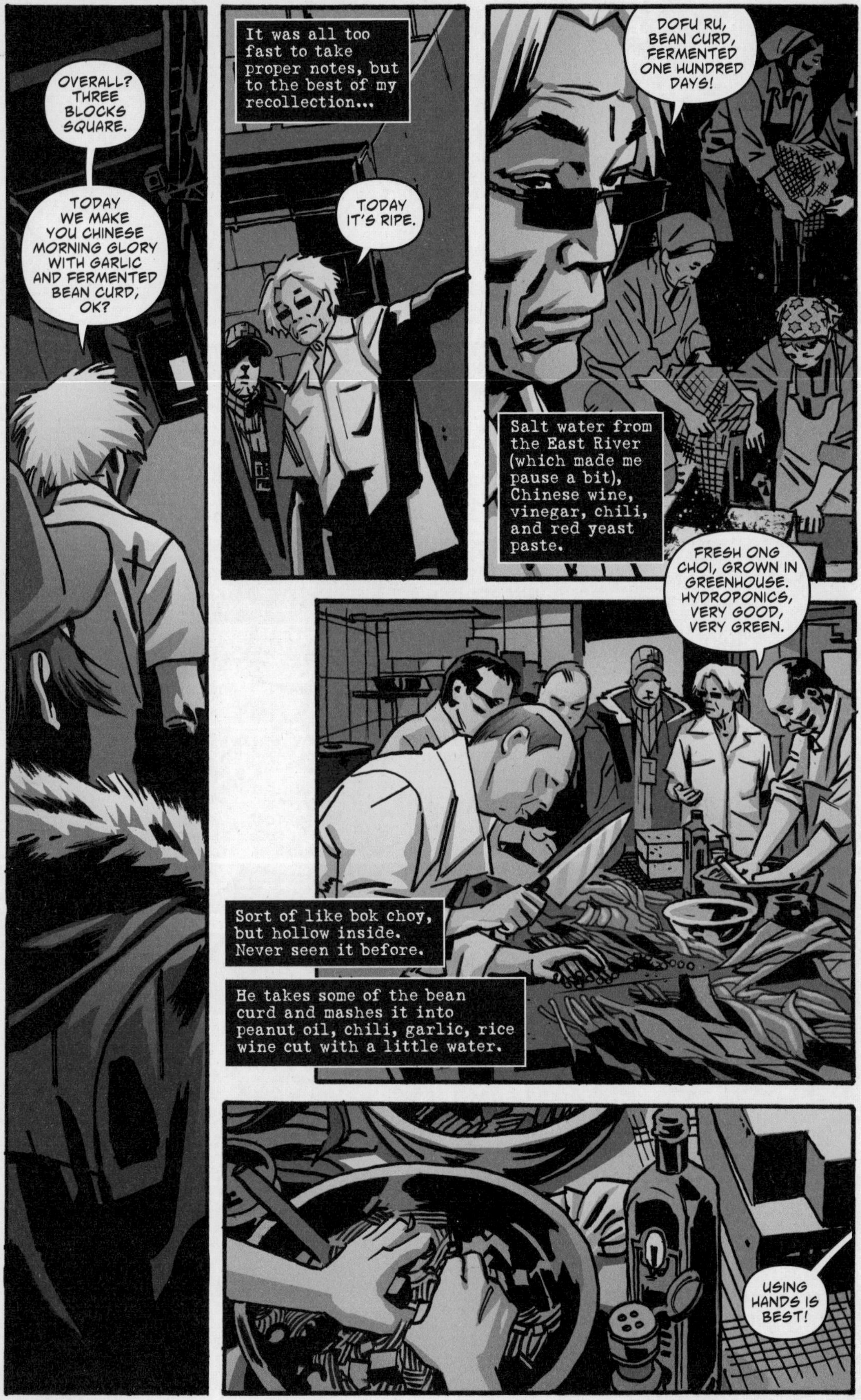

OVERALL? THREE BLOCKS SQUARE.
TODAY WE MAKE YOU CHINESE MORNING GLORY WITH GARLIC AND FERMENTED BEAN CURD, OK?
It was all too fast to take proper notes, but to the best of my recollection...
TODAY IT'S RIPE.
DOFU RU, BEAN CURD, FERMENTED ONE HUNDRED DAYS!
Salt water from the East River (which made me pause a bit), Chinese wine, vinegar, chili, and red yeast paste.
FRESH ONG CHOI, GROWN IN GREENHOUSE. HYDROPONICS, VERY GOOD, VERY GREEN.
Sort of like bok choy, but hollow inside. Never seen it before.
He takes some of the bean curd and mashes it into peanut oil, chili, garlic, rice wine cut with a little water.
USING HANDS IS BEST!

I can feel the heat across the room. The wok is heated and the mixture dumped in. Moments later, the greens were added, once some of the water cooked off.

WOOOSH

PERFECT AROMA!

Couldn't have been more than thirty seconds' cook time. The greens were crisp, the leaves soft but not soggy.

BEAN CURD FOR THE PLATE, TOO, NOT JUST THE SAUCE.

MY IMPROVISATION. BEAN CURD EASY TO MAKE, DOWN HERE. WE GOT LOTS.

PERFECT.

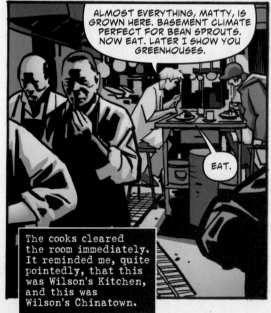

ALMOST EVERYTHING, MATTY, IS GROWN HERE. BASEMENT CLIMATE PERFECT FOR BEAN SPROUTS. NOW EAT. LATER I SHOW YOU GREENHOUSES.

EAT.

The cooks cleared the room immediately. It reminded me, quite pointedly, that this was Wilson's Kitchen, and this was Wilson's Chinatown.

And it's the rest of the world's loss.

WILSON'S KITCHEN

**End**

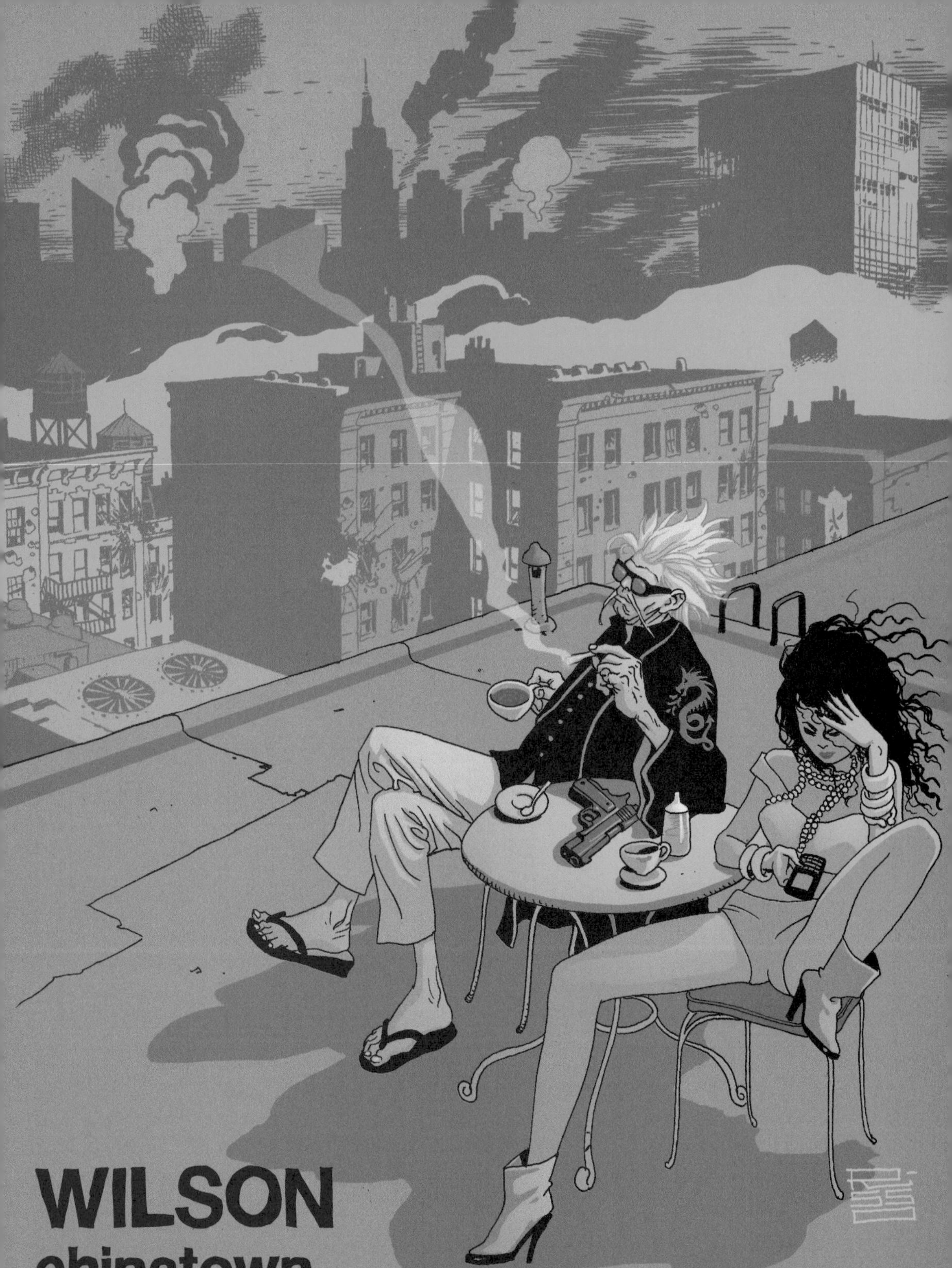

# WILSON
## chinatown

Where NYC had neighborhoods, the DMZ is all about its enclaves, zones of specific influence that sometimes are defined by neighborhood lines but more often than not have their own rules and borders. Keeping up with these conditions on the ground is a daily concern--often the lines on these "maps" are redrawn drastically after a night's fighting and in the morning you can find yourself living in a very different place than when you went to sleep the night before.

Wilson's Chinatown enclave is one of the few that has not only kept its name and identity, but more or less original borders. His influence is total--after surviving an assassination attempt, this "Ghost protector of Chinatown" has been untouchable, equal parts kind and cruel, and whatever power he uses to keep the glue of his dominion intact, it's practically invisible to outsiders.

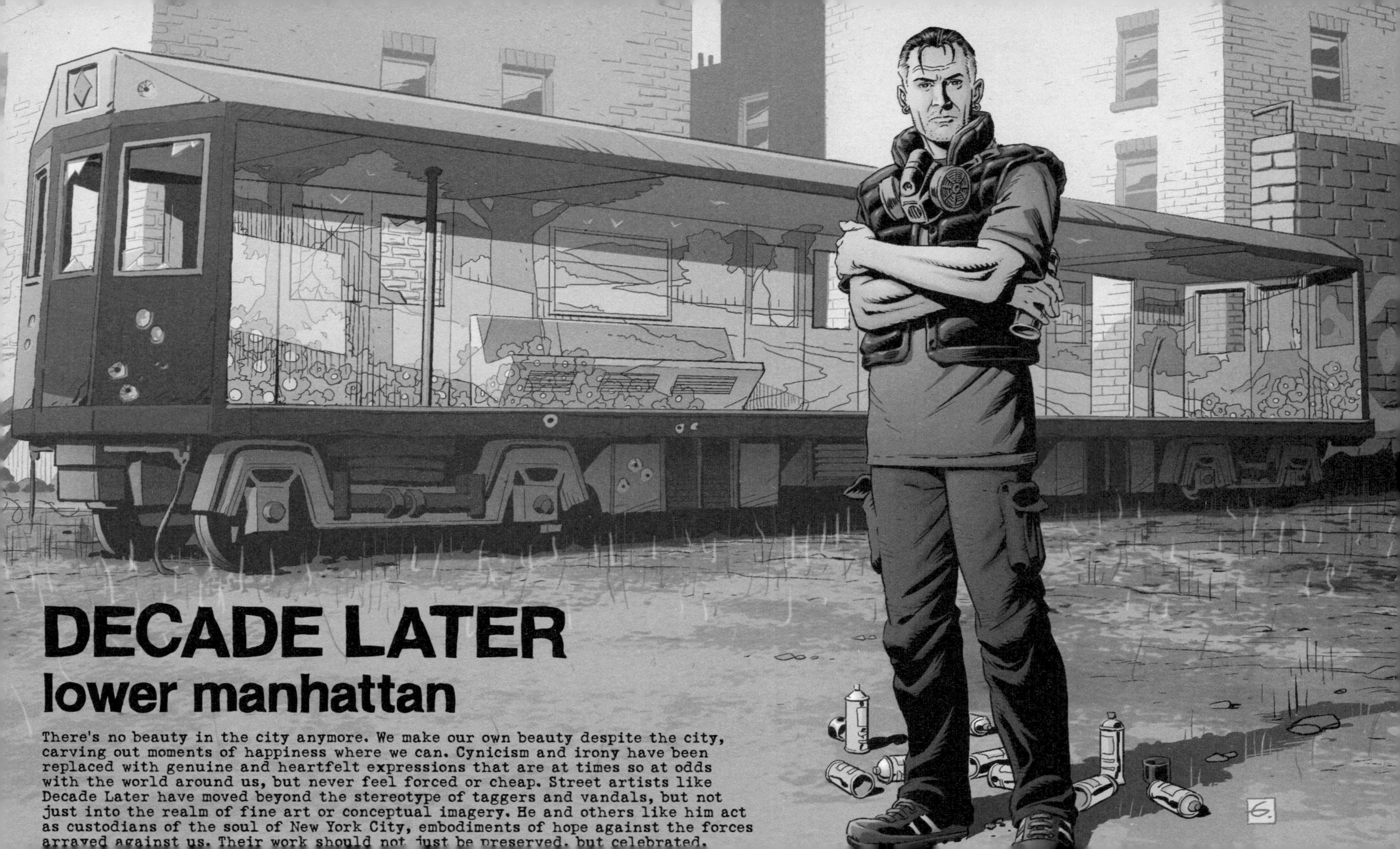

# DECADE LATER
## lower manhattan

There's no beauty in the city anymore. We make our own beauty despite the city, carving out moments of happiness where we can. Cynicism and irony have been replaced with genuine and heartfelt expressions that are at times so at odds with the world around us, but never feel forced or cheap. Street artists like Decade Later have moved beyond the stereotype of taggers and vandals, but not just into the realm of fine art or conceptual imagery. He and others like him act as custodians of the soul of New York City, embodiments of hope against the forces arrayed against us. Their work should not just be preserved, but celebrated.

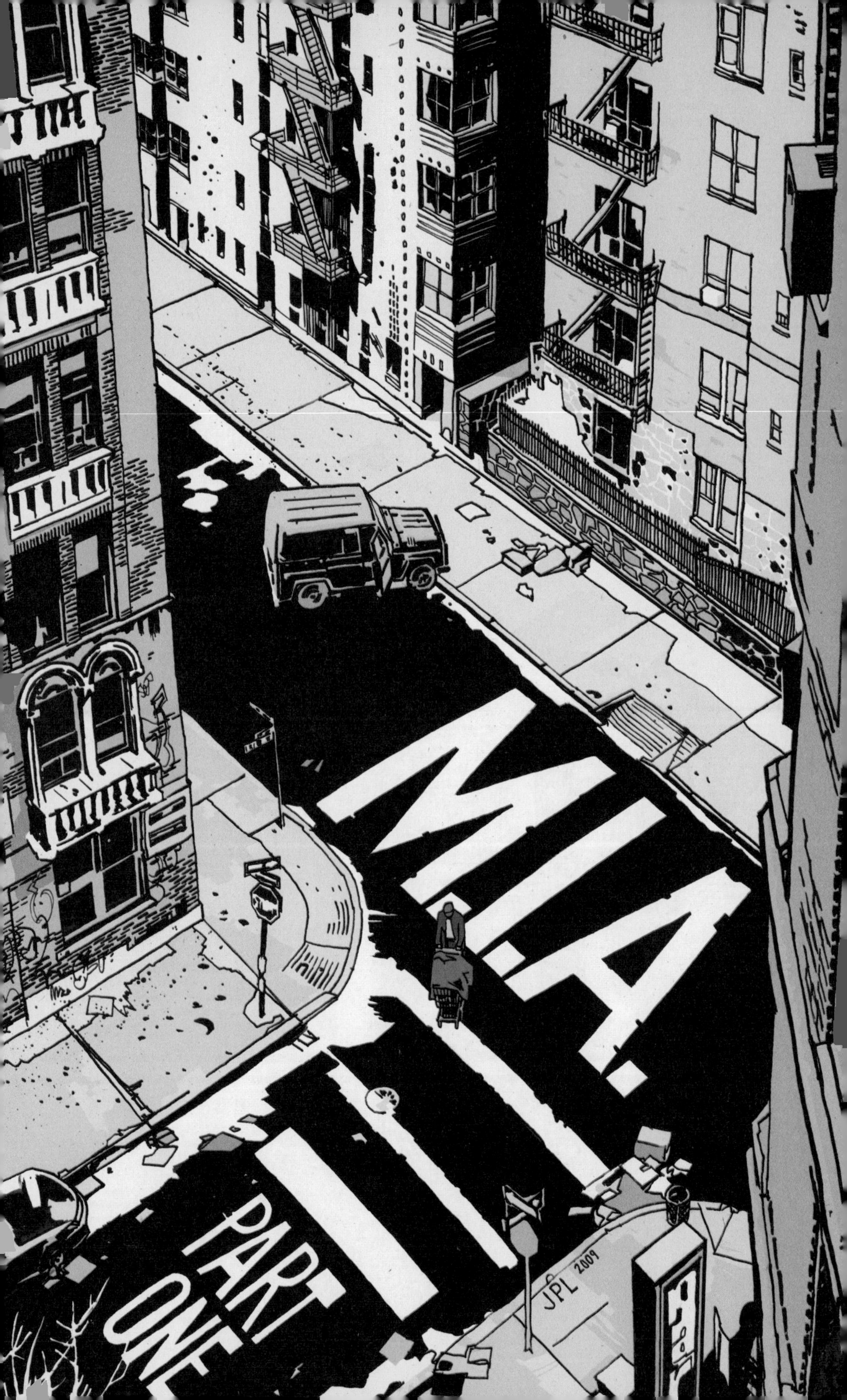
M.I.A.
II
PART ONE
JPL 2009

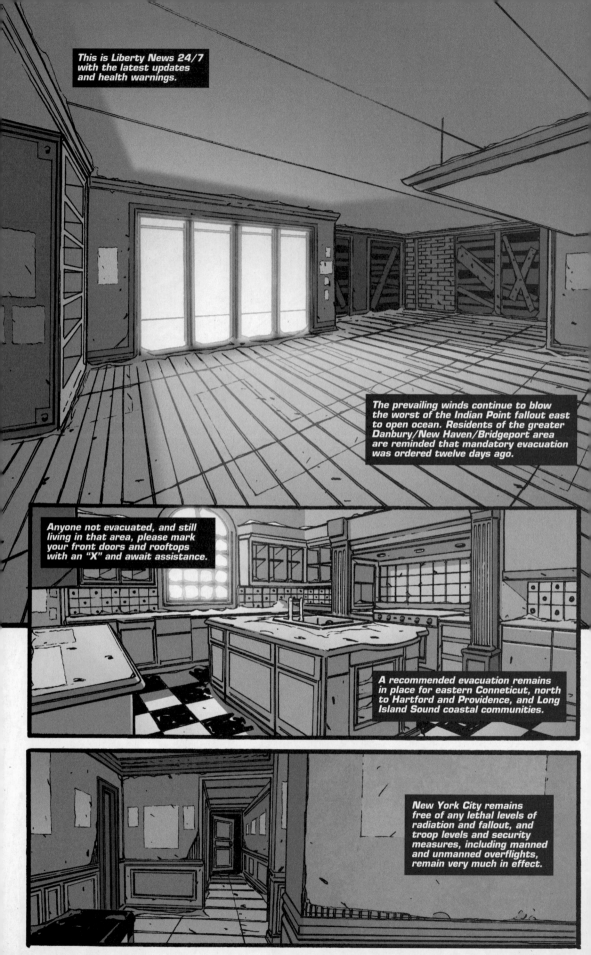

This is Liberty News 24/7 with the latest updates and health warnings.

The prevailing winds continue to blow the worst of the Indian Point fallout east to open ocean. Residents of the greater Danbury/New Haven/Bridgeport area are reminded that mandatory evacuation was ordered twelve days ago.

Anyone not evacuated, and still living in that area, please mark your front doors and rooftops with an "X" and await assistance.

A recommended evacuation remains in place for eastern Conneticut, north to Hartford and Providence, and Long Island Sound coastal communities.

New York City remains free of any lethal levels of radiation and fallout, and troop levels and security measures, including manned and unmanned overflights, remain very much in effect.

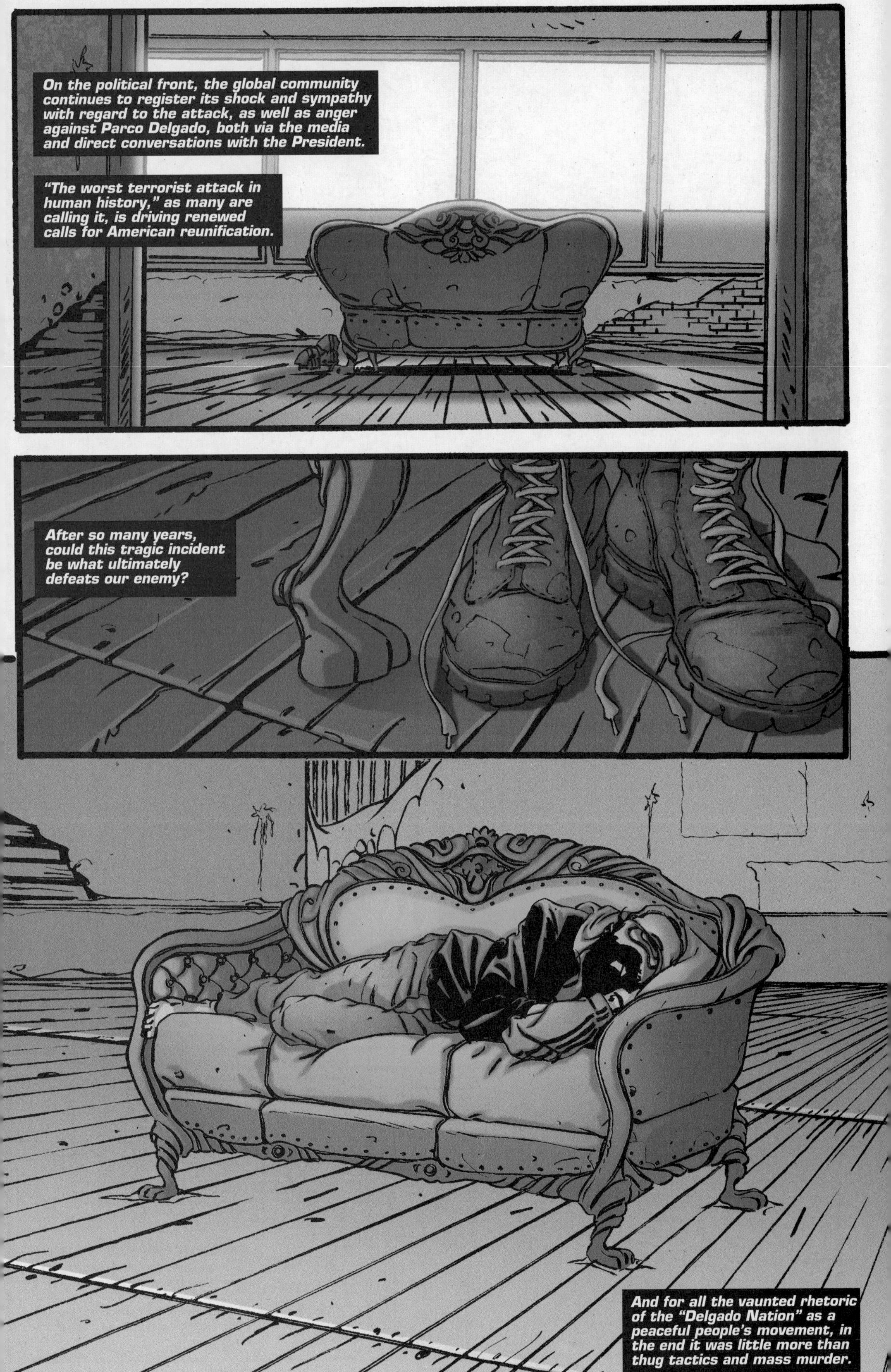
On the political front, the global community continues to register its shock and sympathy with regard to the attack, as well as anger against Parco Delgado, both via the media and direct conversations with the President.
"The worst terrorist attack in human history," as many are calling it, is driving renewed calls for American reunification.
After so many years, could this tragic incident be what ultimately defeats our enemy?
And for all the vaunted rhetoric of the "Delgado Nation" as a peaceful people's movement, in the end it was little more than thug tactics and mass murder.

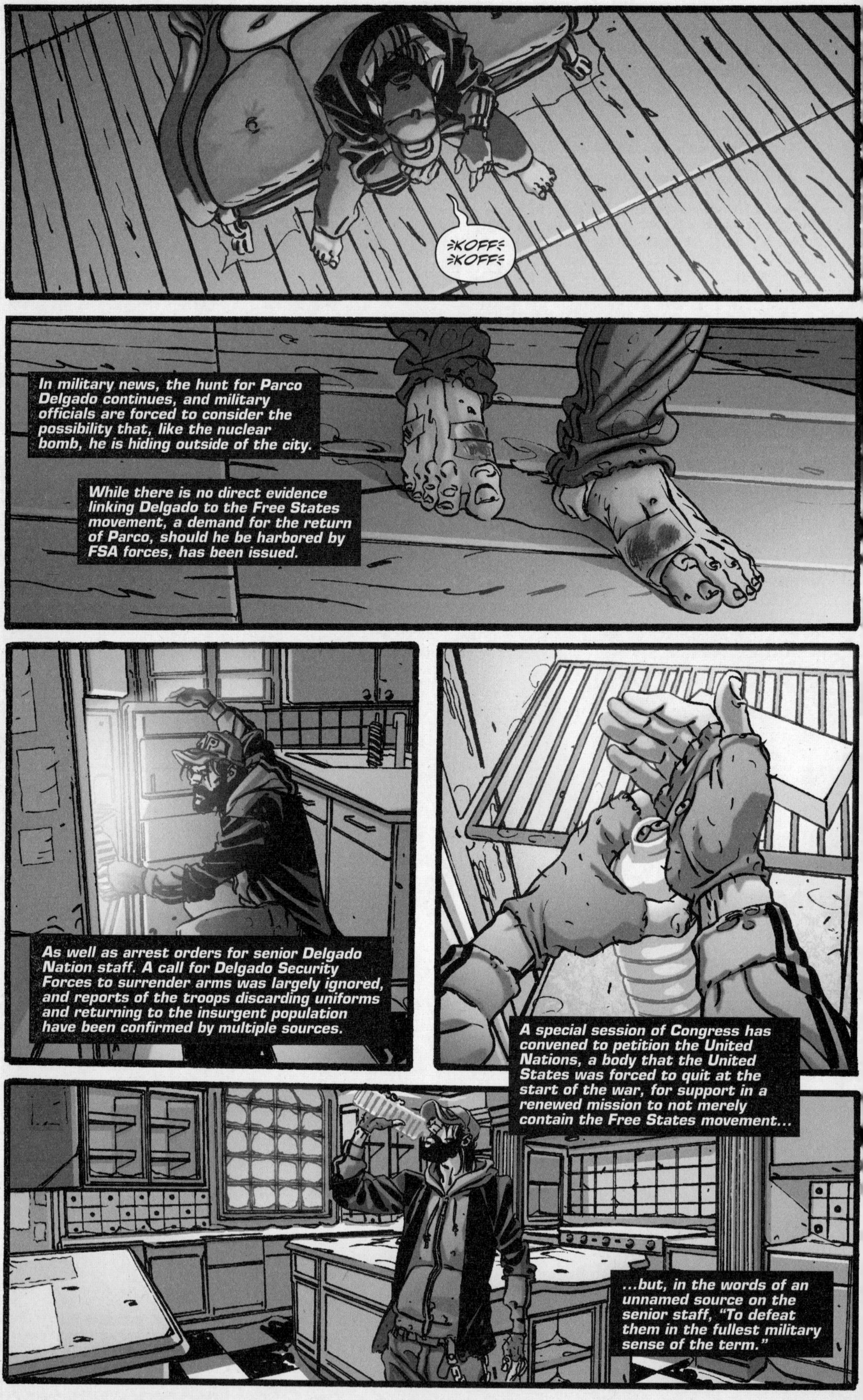
KOFF KOFF
In military news, the hunt for Parco Delgado continues, and military officials are forced to consider the possibility that, like the nuclear bomb, he is hiding outside of the city.
While there is no direct evidence linking Delgado to the Free States movement, a demand for the return of Parco, should he be harbored by FSA forces, has been issued.
As well as arrest orders for senior Delgado Nation staff. A call for Delgado Security Forces to surrender arms was largely ignored, and reports of the troops discarding uniforms and returning to the insurgent population have been confirmed by multiple sources.
A special session of Congress has convened to petition the United Nations, a body that the United States was forced to quit at the start of the war, for support in a renewed mission to not merely contain the Free States movement...
...but, in the words of an unnamed source on the senior staff, "To defeat them in the fullest military sense of the term."

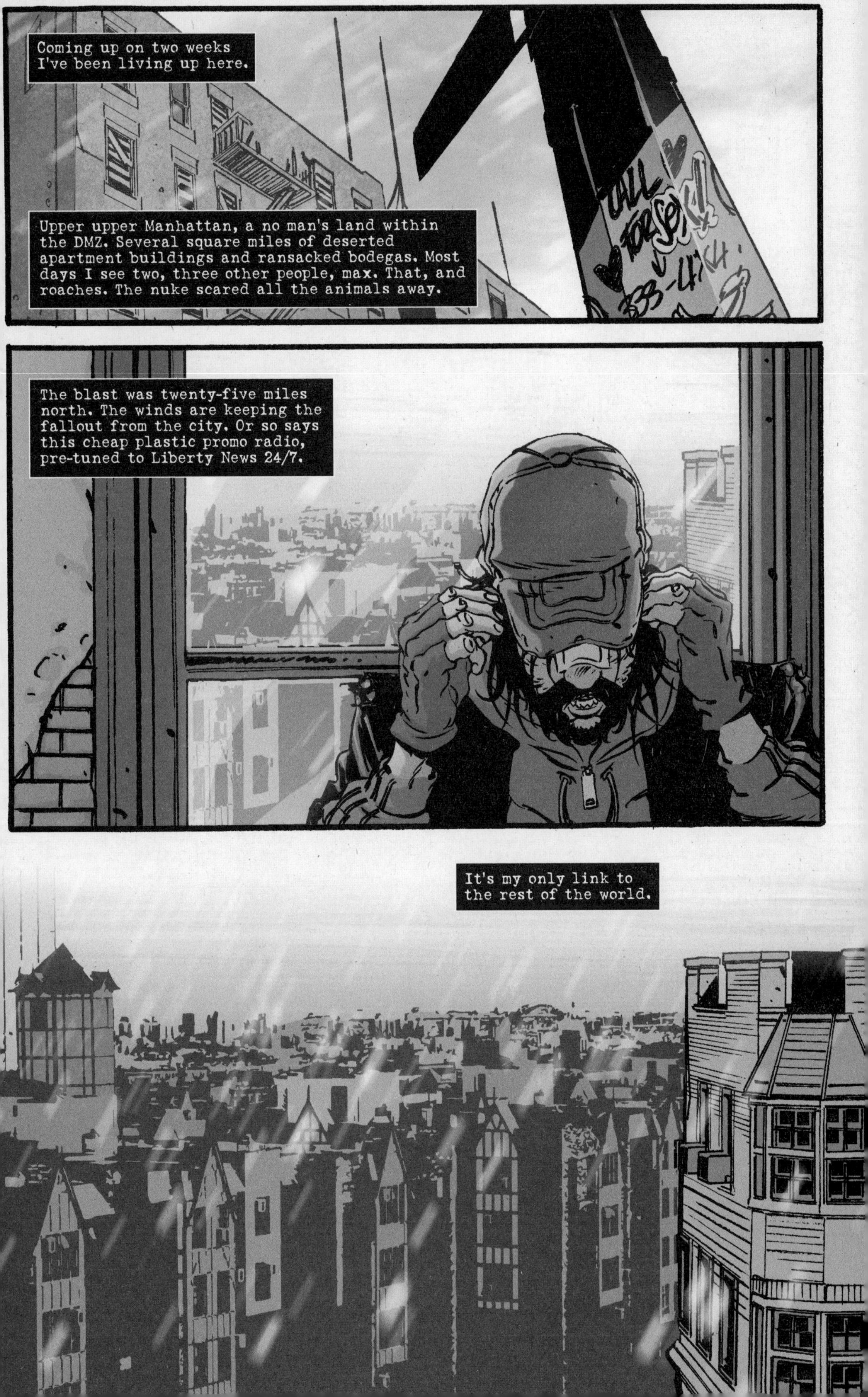
Coming up on two weeks I've been living up here.
Upper upper Manhattan, a no man's land within the DMZ. Several square miles of deserted apartment buildings and ransacked bodegas. Most days I see two, three other people, max. That, and roaches. The nuke scared all the animals away.
The blast was twenty-five miles north. The winds are keeping the fallout from the city. Or so says this cheap plastic promo radio, pre-tuned to Liberty News 24/7.
It's my only link to the rest of the world.

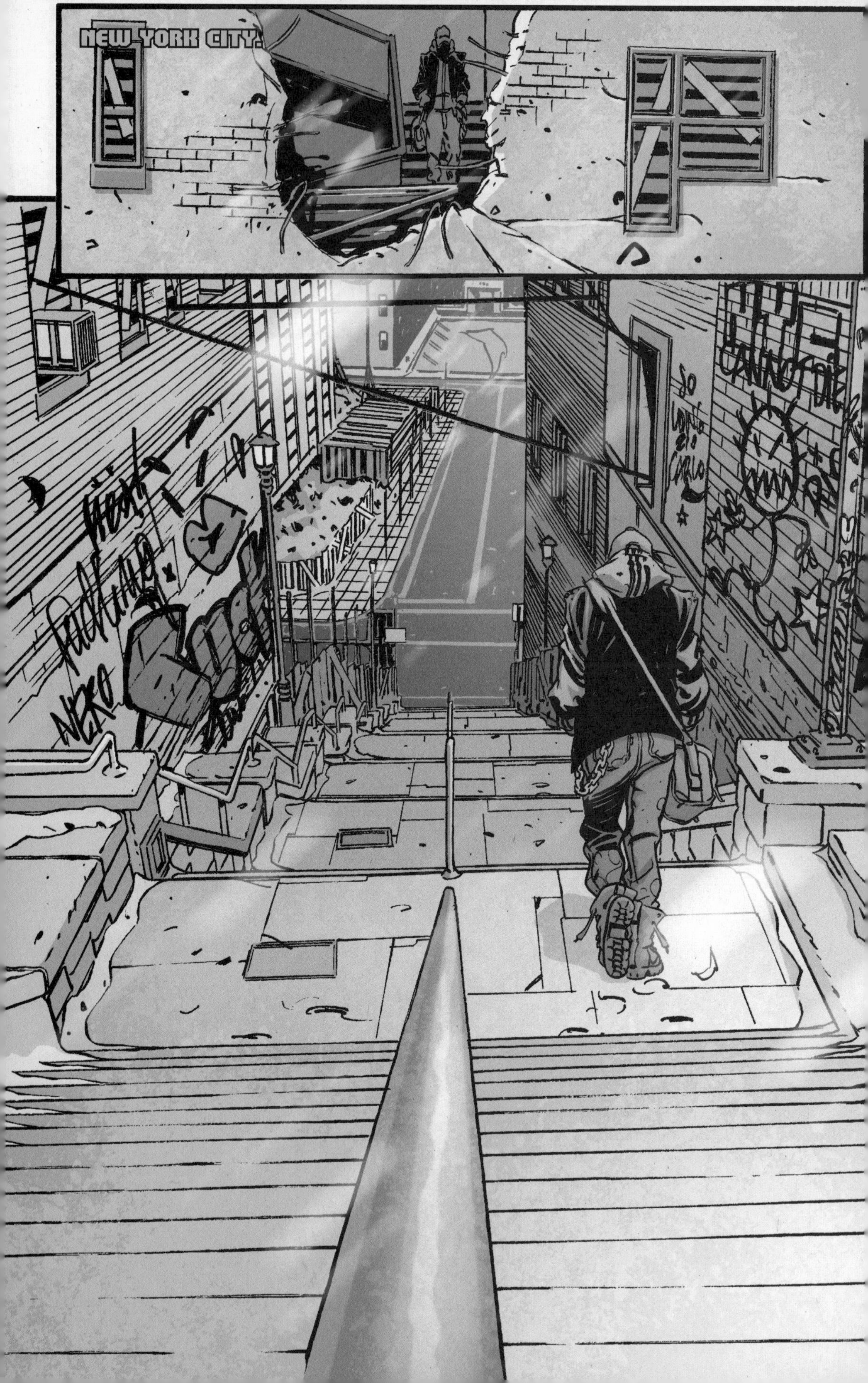
NEW YORK CITY.

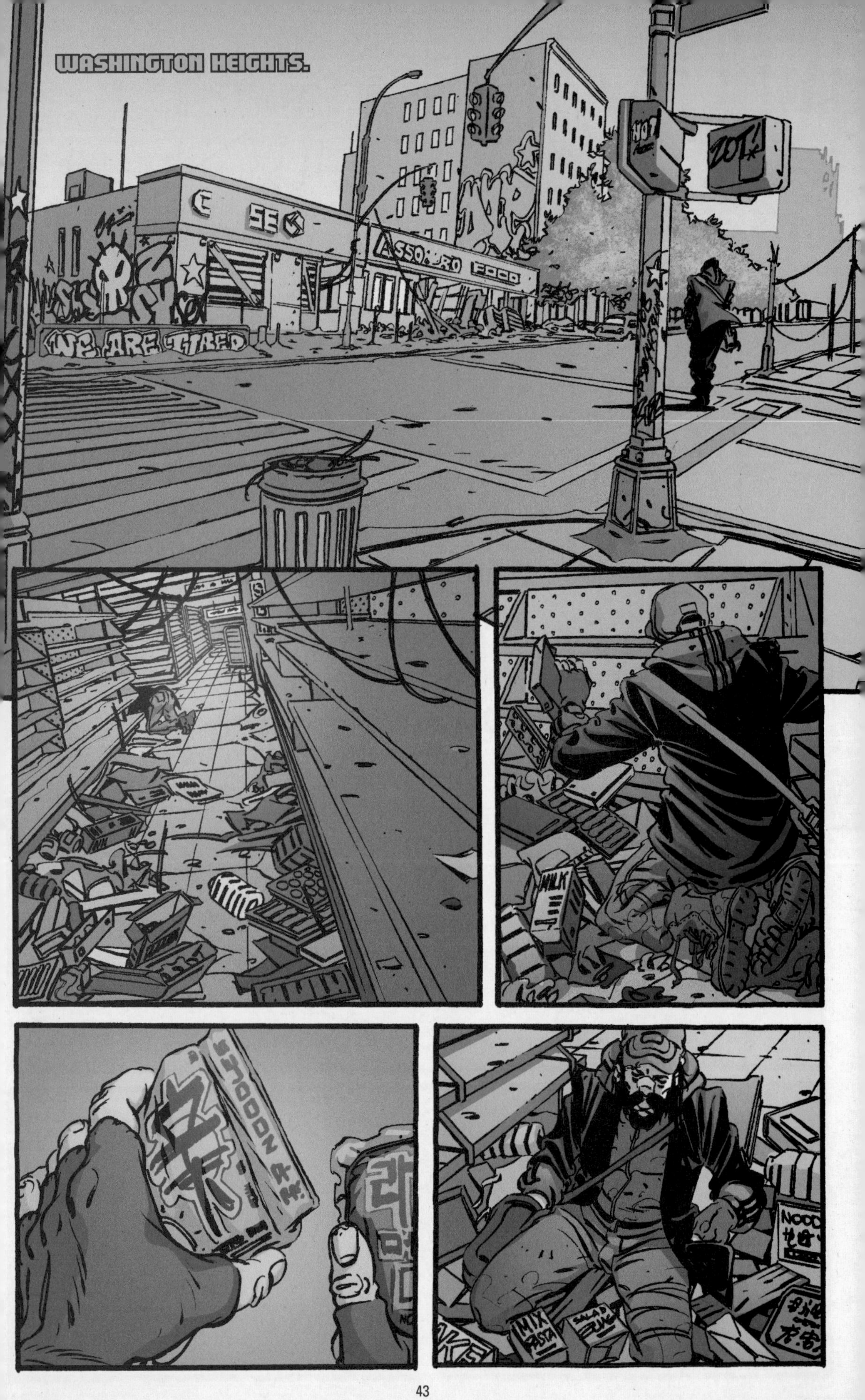
WASHINGTON HEIGHTS.
WE ARE TIRED
FOOD
MILK
MIX
PASTA
SALAD

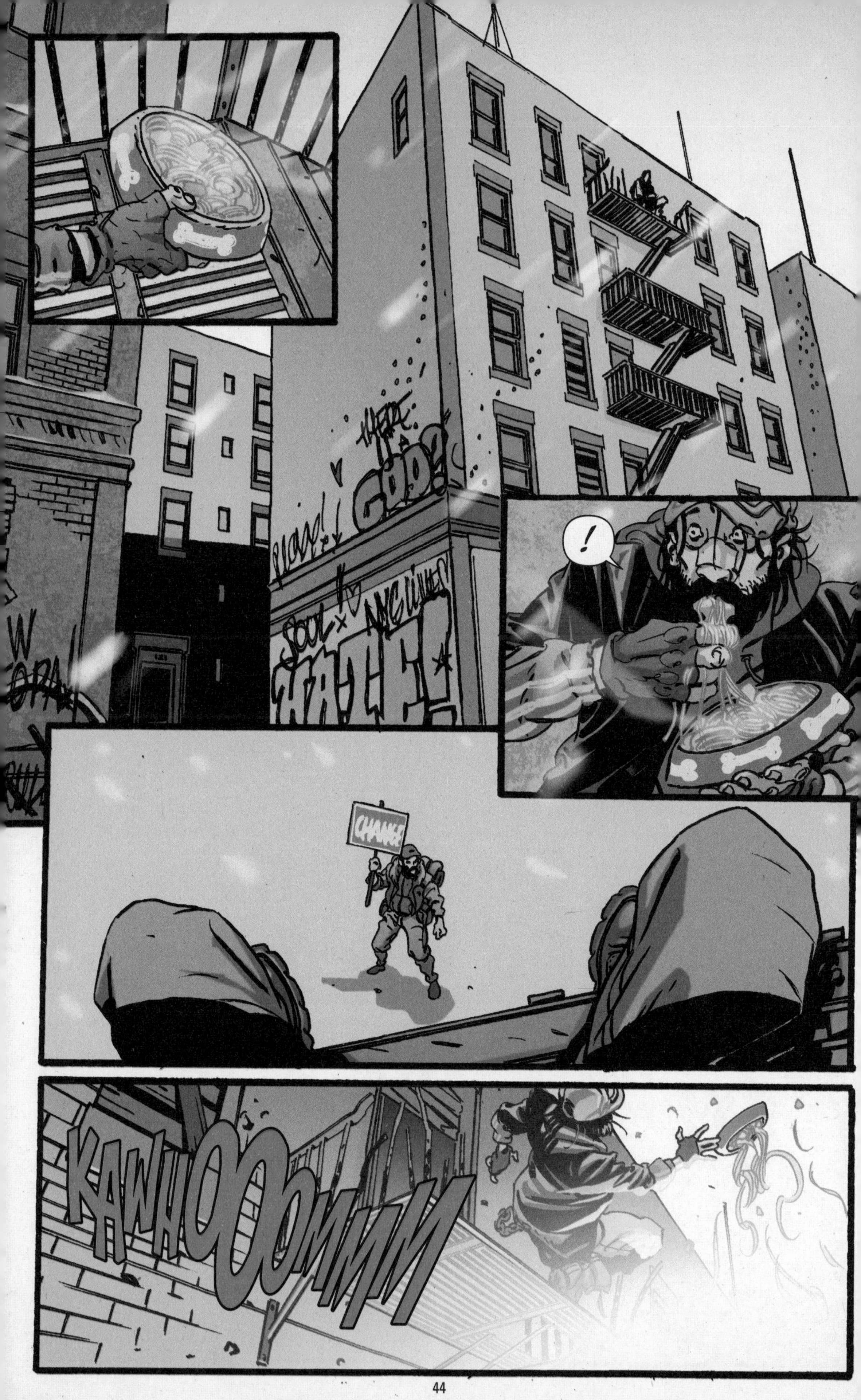
!
CHANGE
KAWHOOOMMMM

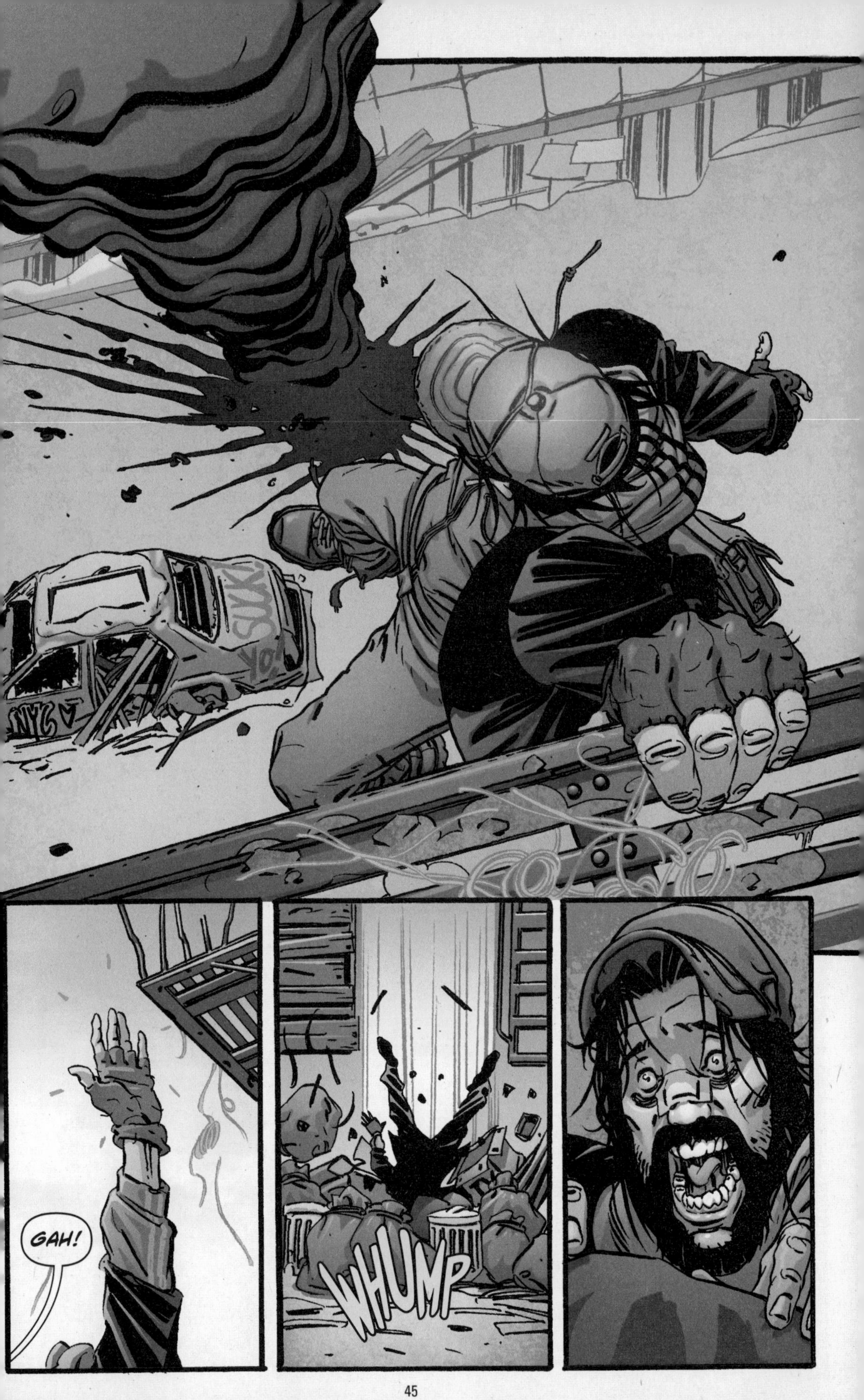
SUCK!
YO!
NYC
GAH!
WHUMP

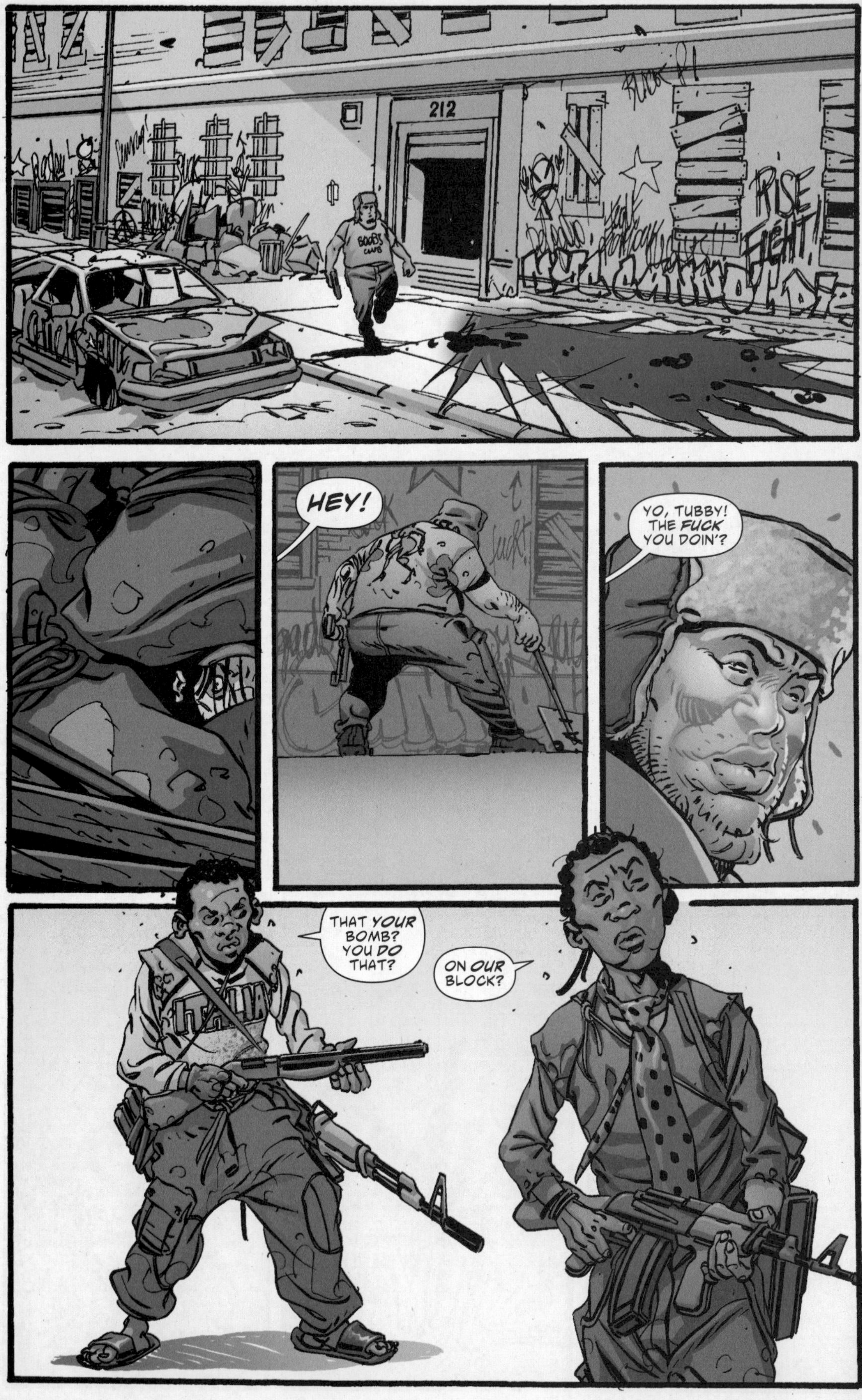
212
RISE
FIGHT
HEY!
YO, TUBBY! THE FUCK YOU DOIN'?
THAT YOUR BOMB? YOU DO THAT?
ON OUR BLOCK?

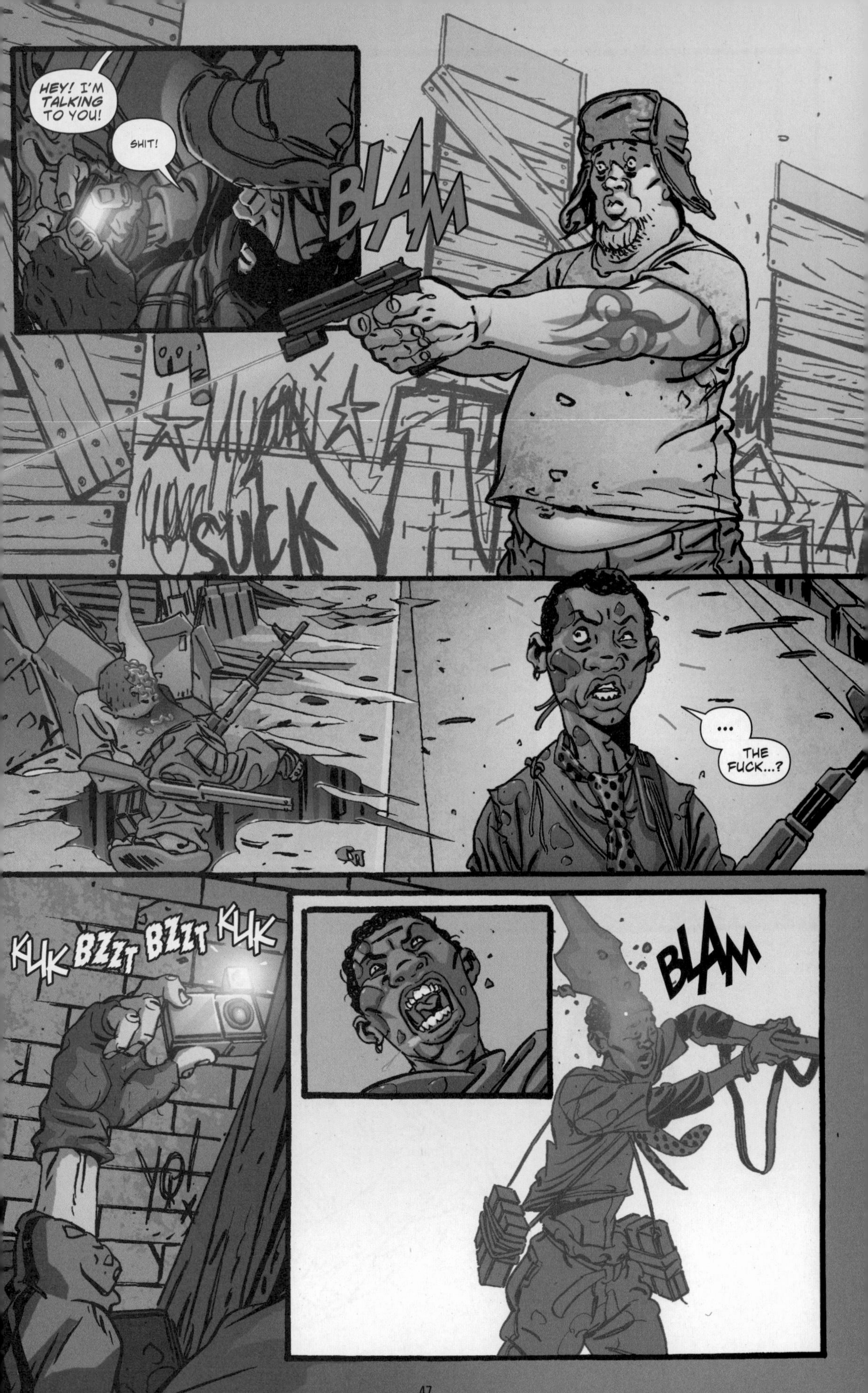
HEY! I'M TALKING TO YOU!
SHIT!
BLAM
YOU SUCK
... THE FUCK...?
KLIK BZZT BZZT KLIK
BLAM
YO!

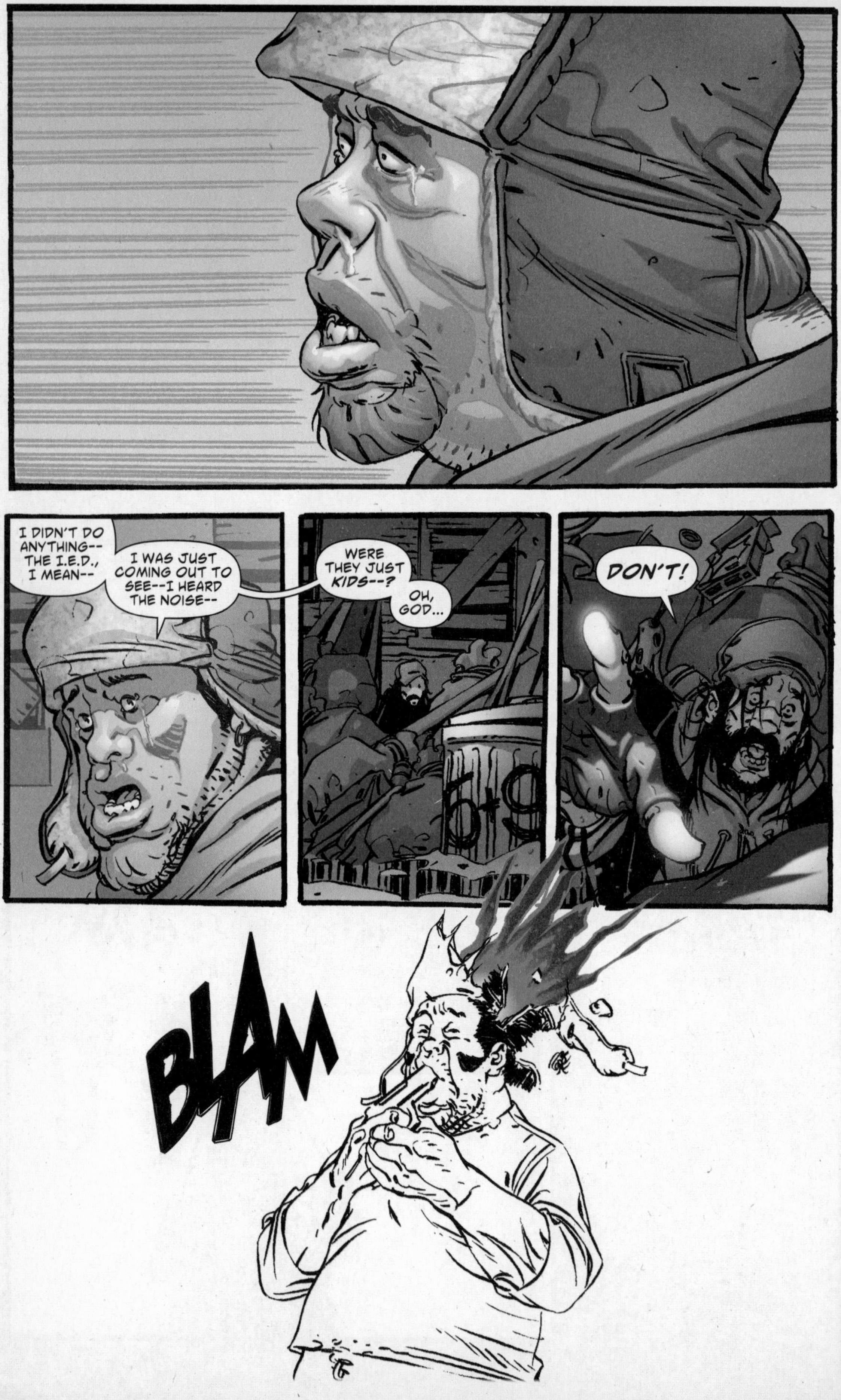

I DIDN'T DO ANYTHING-- THE I.E.D., I MEAN--
I WAS JUST COMING OUT TO SEE--I HEARD THE NOISE--
WERE THEY JUST *KIDS*--?
OH, GOD...
*DON'T!*
BLAM

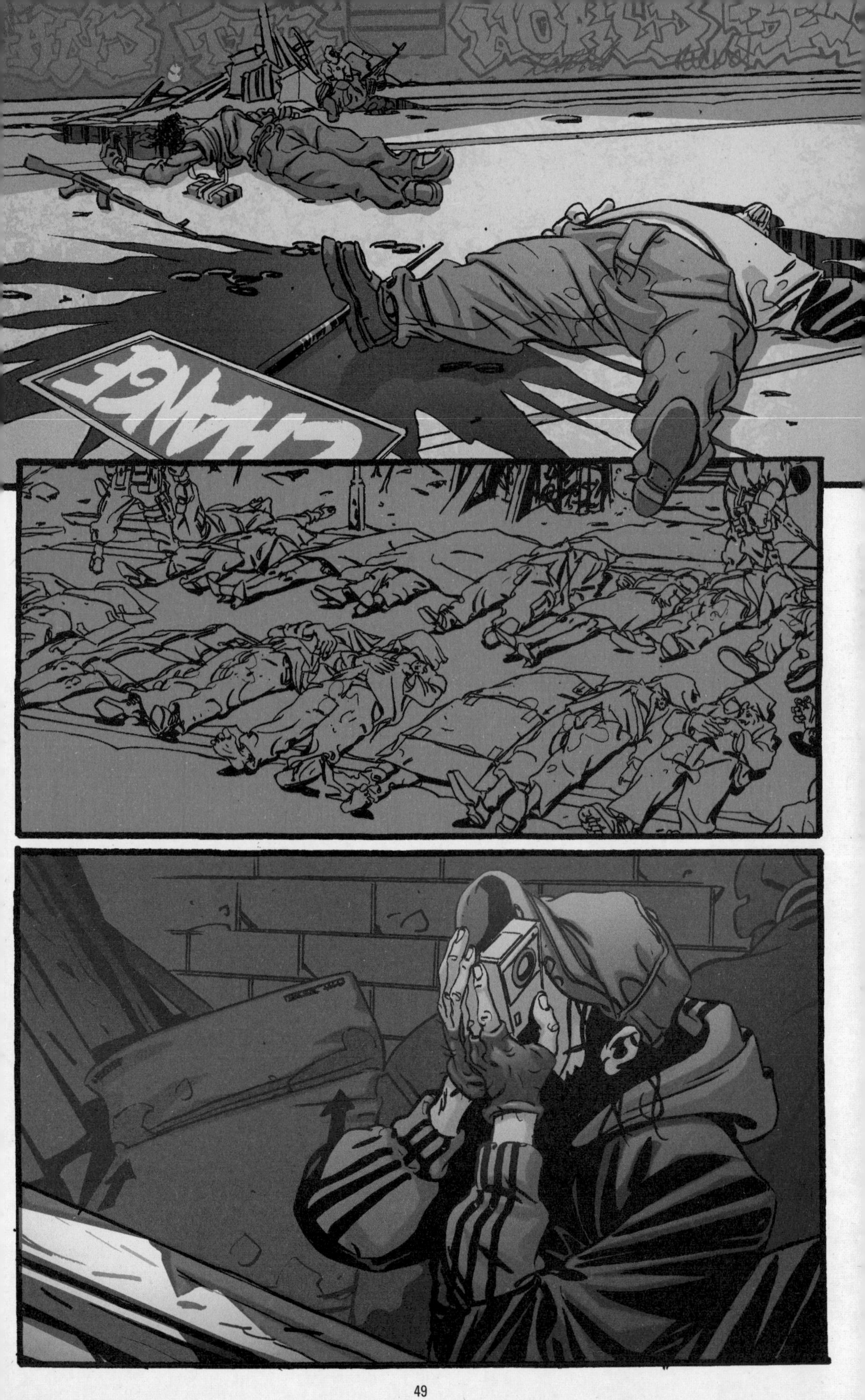

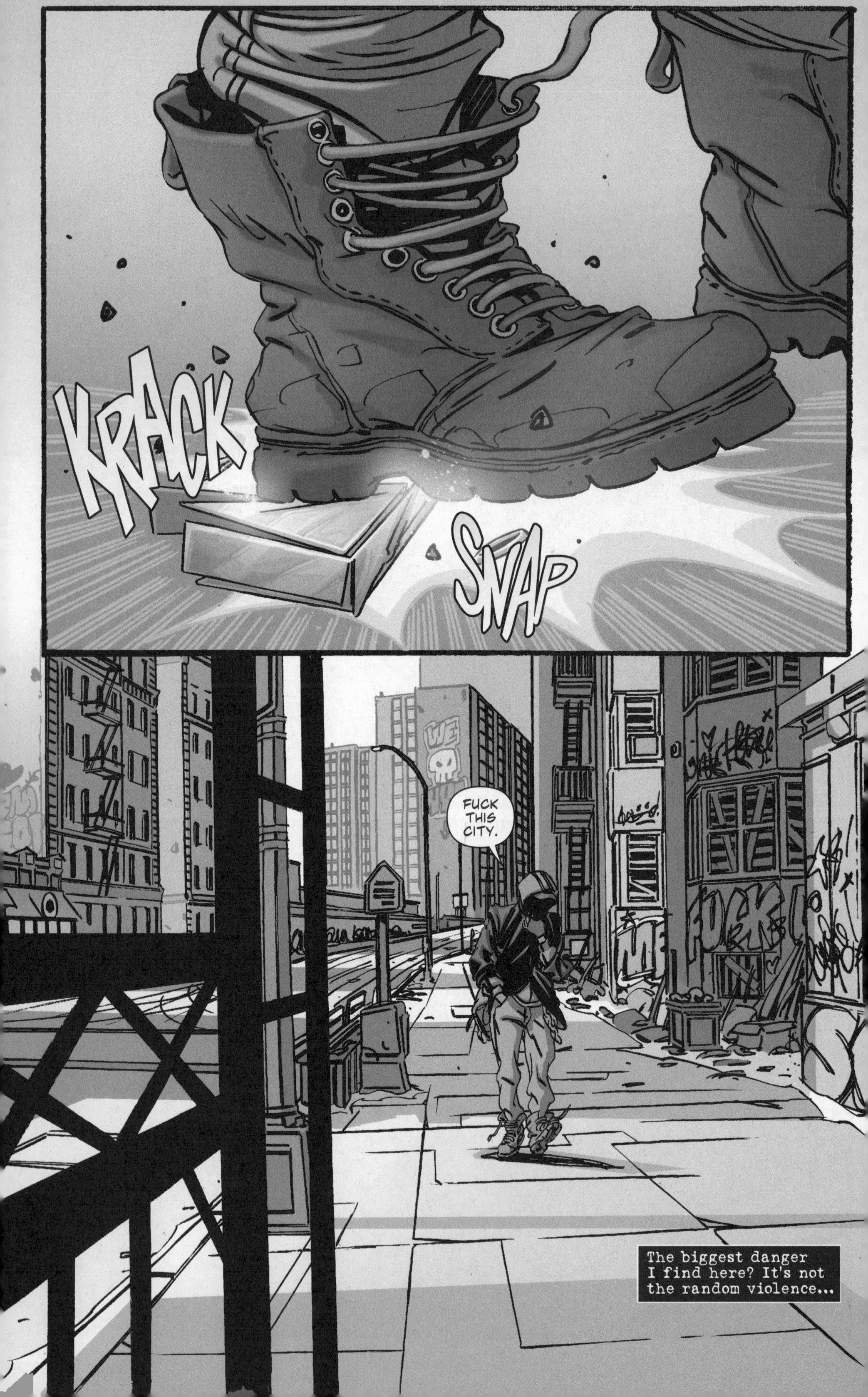
KRACK
SNAP
FUCK THIS CITY.
The biggest danger I find here? It's not the random violence...

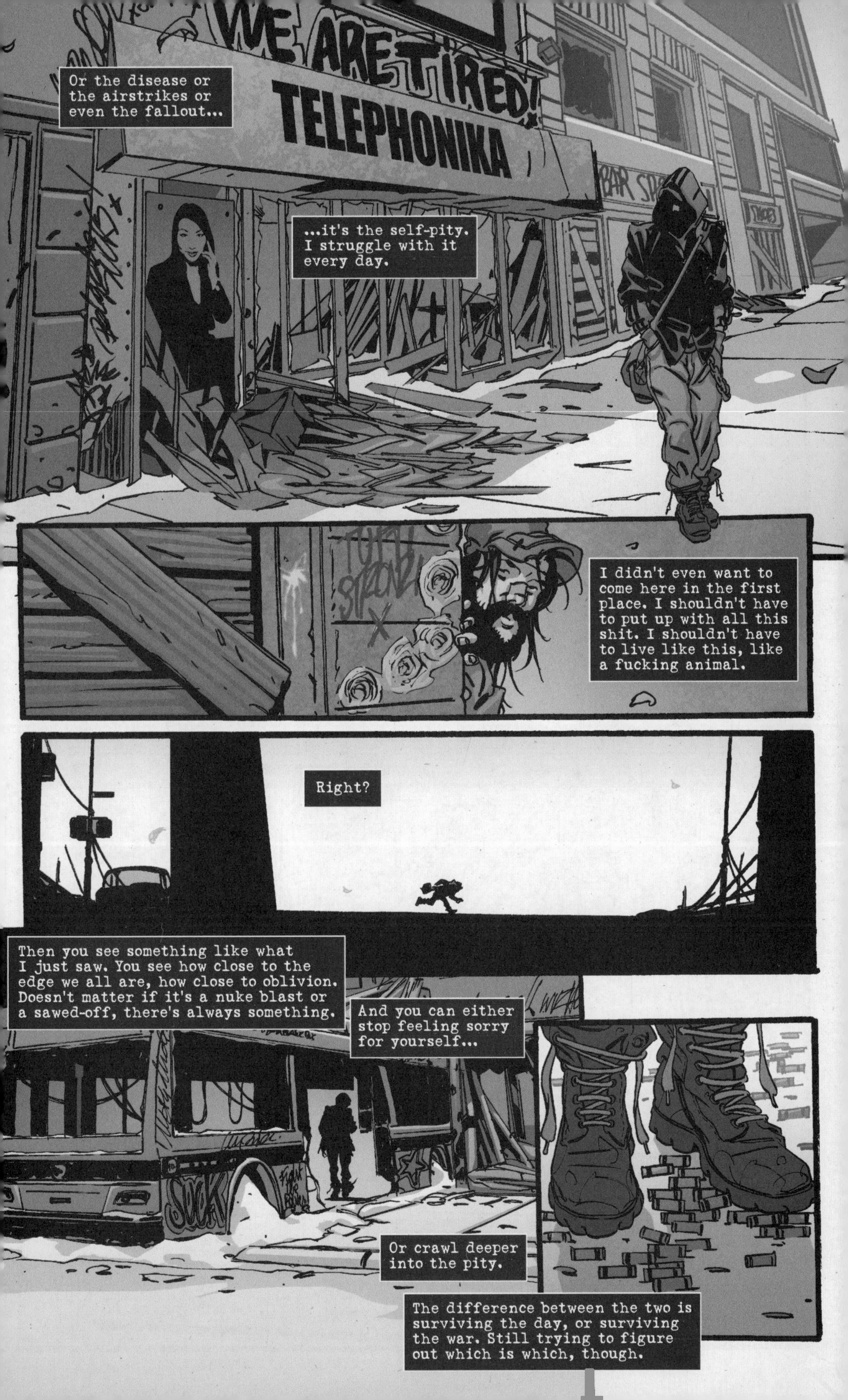
WE ARE TIRED!
TELEPHONIKA
Or the disease or the airstrikes or even the fallout...
...it's the self-pity. I struggle with it every day.
I didn't even want to come here in the first place. I shouldn't have to put up with all this shit. I shouldn't have to live like this, like a fucking animal.
Right?
Then you see something like what I just saw. You see how close to the edge we all are, how close to oblivion. Doesn't matter if it's a nuke blast or a sawed-off, there's always something.
And you can either stop feeling sorry for yourself...
Or crawl deeper into the pity.
The difference between the two is surviving the day, or surviving the war. Still trying to figure out which is which, though.

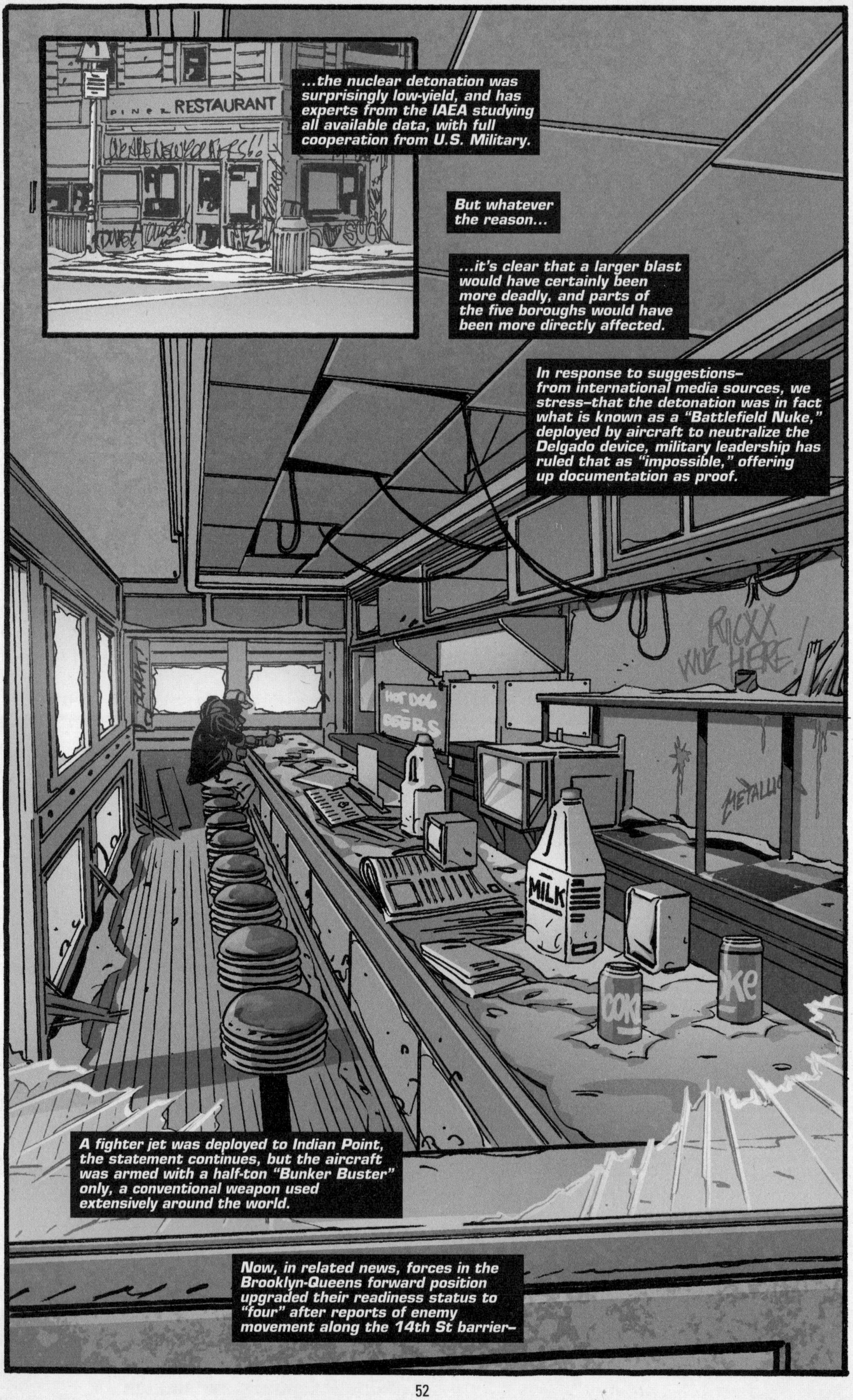

RESTAURANT
...the nuclear detonation was surprisingly low-yield, and has experts from the IAEA studying all available data, with full cooperation from U.S. Military.
But whatever the reason...
...it's clear that a larger blast would have certainly been more deadly, and parts of the five boroughs would have been more directly affected.
In response to suggestions–from international media sources, we stress–that the detonation was in fact what is known as a "Battlefield Nuke," deployed by aircraft to neutralize the Delgado device, military leadership has ruled that as "impossible," offering up documentation as proof.
MILK
A fighter jet was deployed to Indian Point, the statement continues, but the aircraft was armed with a half-ton "Bunker Buster" only, a conventional weapon used extensively around the world.
Now, in related news, forces in the Brooklyn-Queens forward position upgraded their readiness status to "four" after reports of enemy movement along the 14th St barrier–

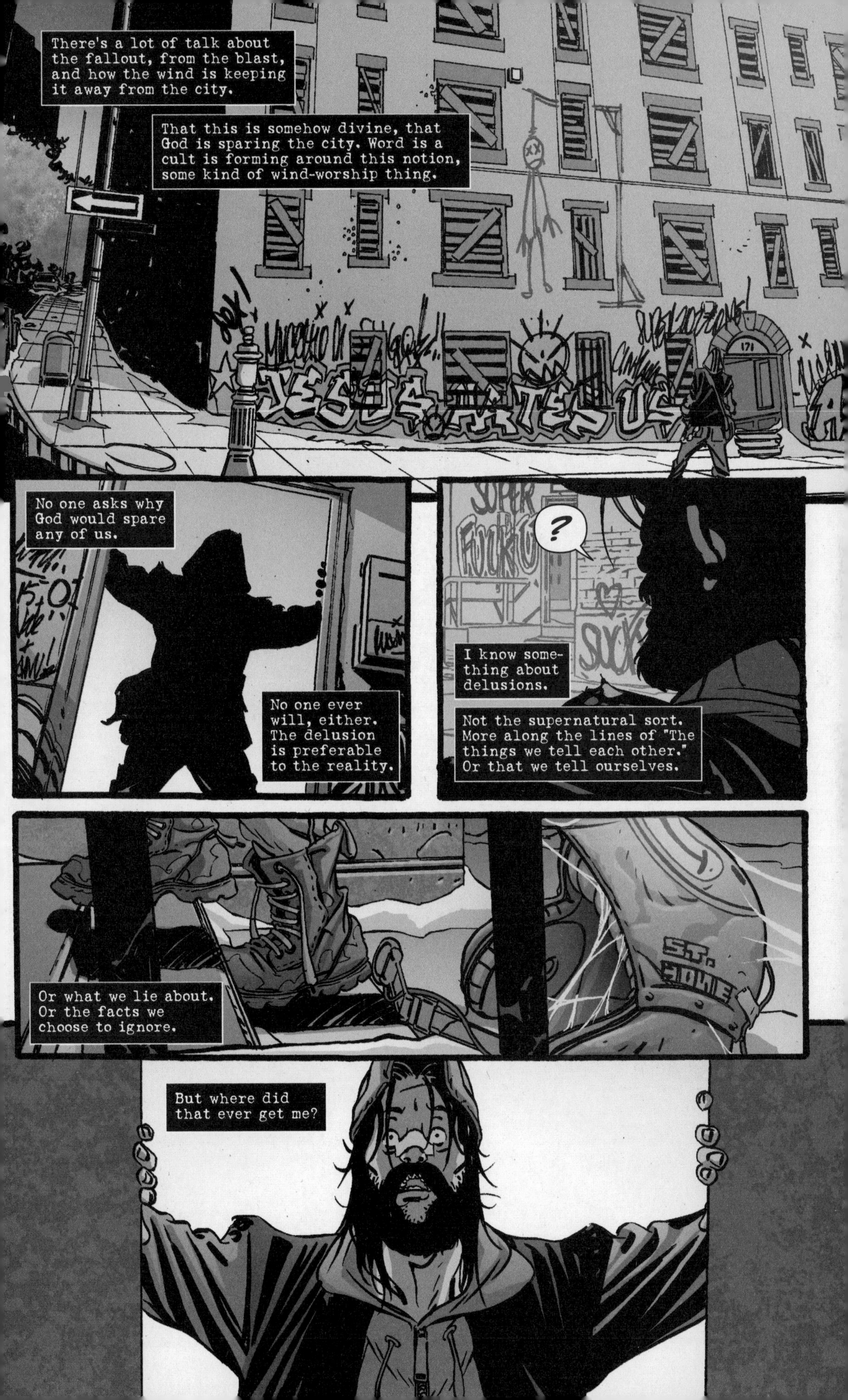
There's a lot of talk about the fallout, from the blast, and how the wind is keeping it away from the city.
That this is somehow divine, that God is sparing the city. Word is a cult is forming around this notion, some kind of wind-worship thing.
No one asks why God would spare any of us.
No one ever will, either. The delusion is preferable to the reality.
?
I know something about delusions.
Not the supernatural sort. More along the lines of "The things we tell each other." Or that we tell ourselves.
Or what we lie about. Or the facts we choose to ignore.
But where did that ever get me?

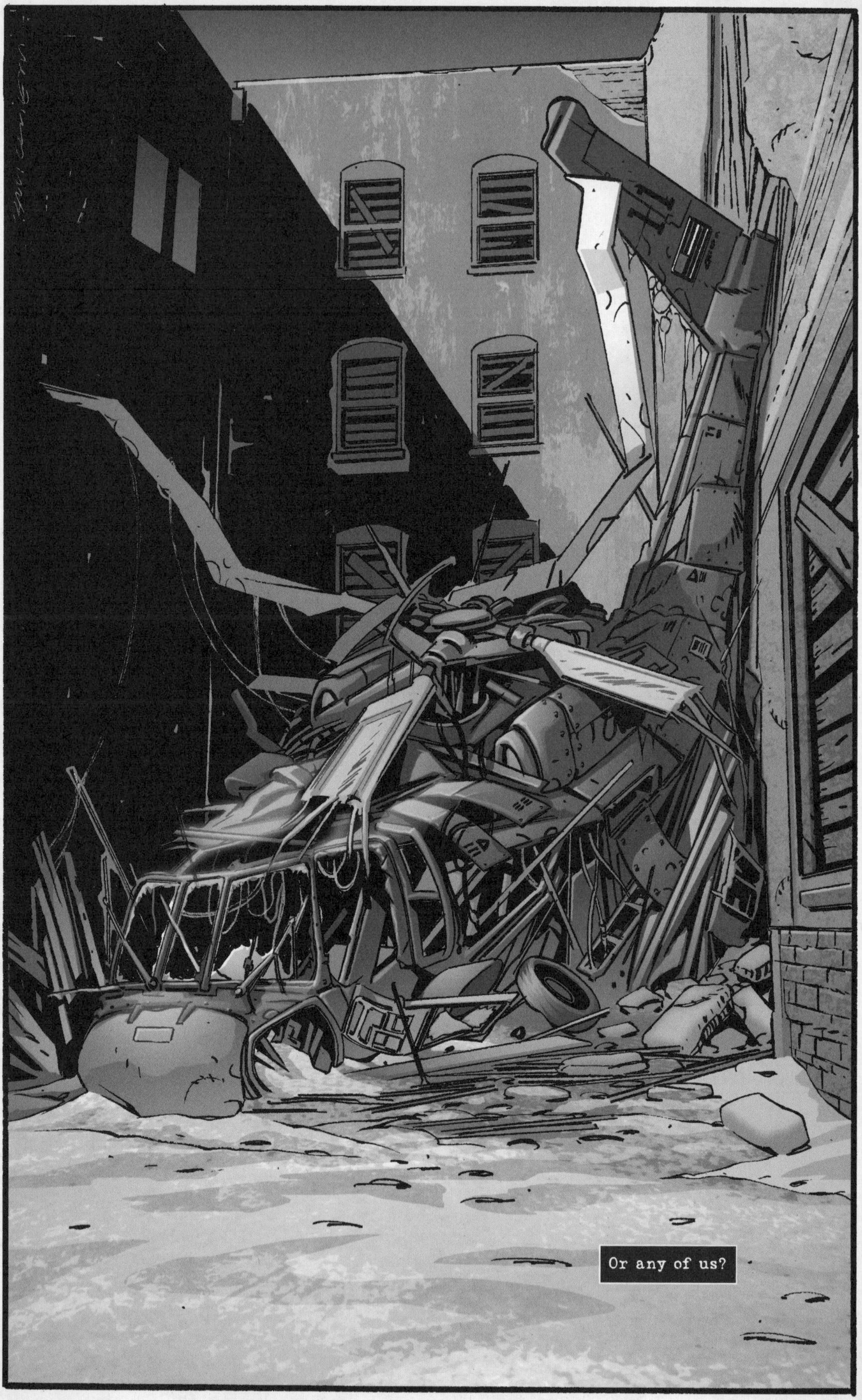
Or any of us?

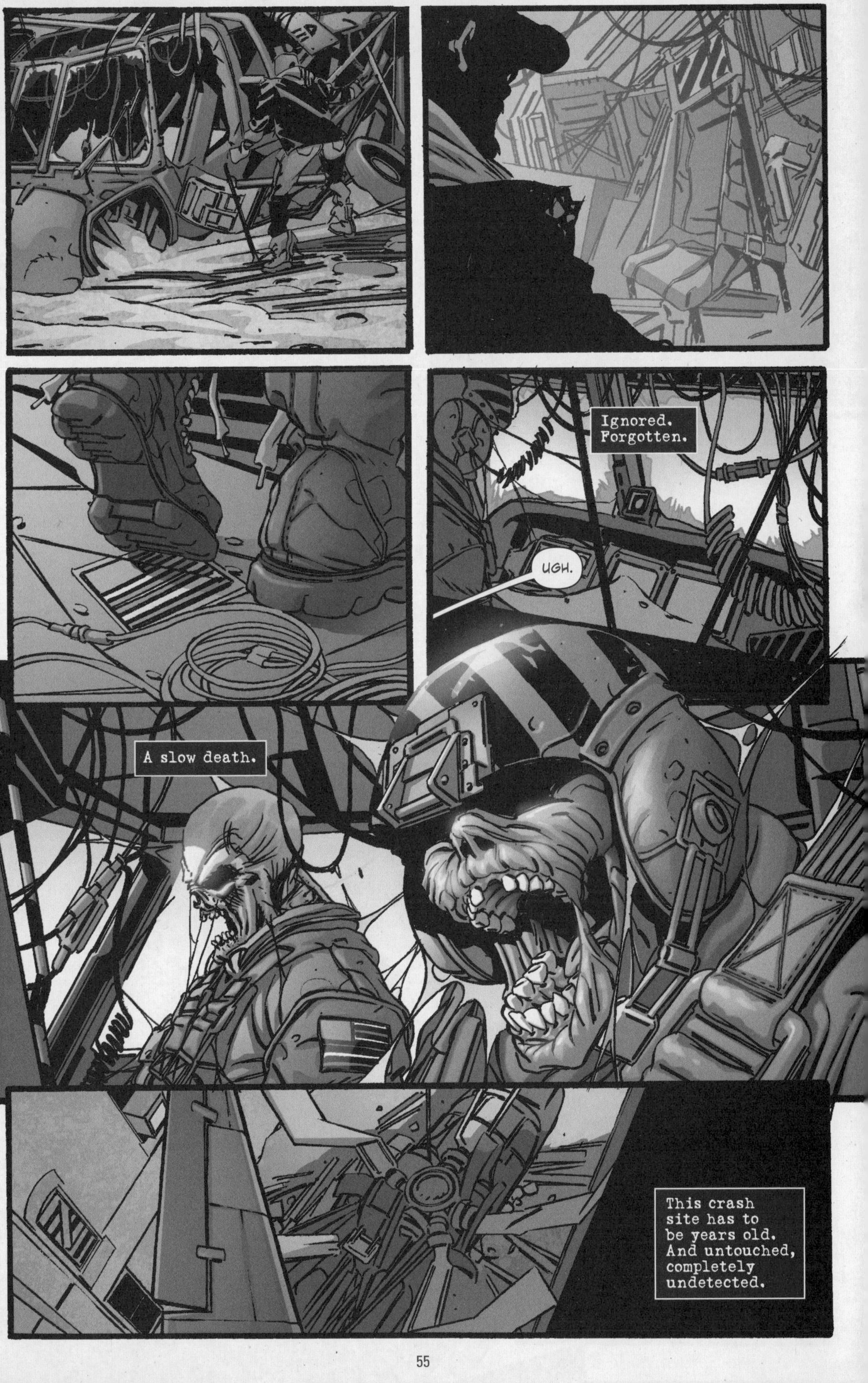
Ignored.
Forgotten.
UGH.
A slow death.
This crash site has to be years old. And untouched, completely undetected.

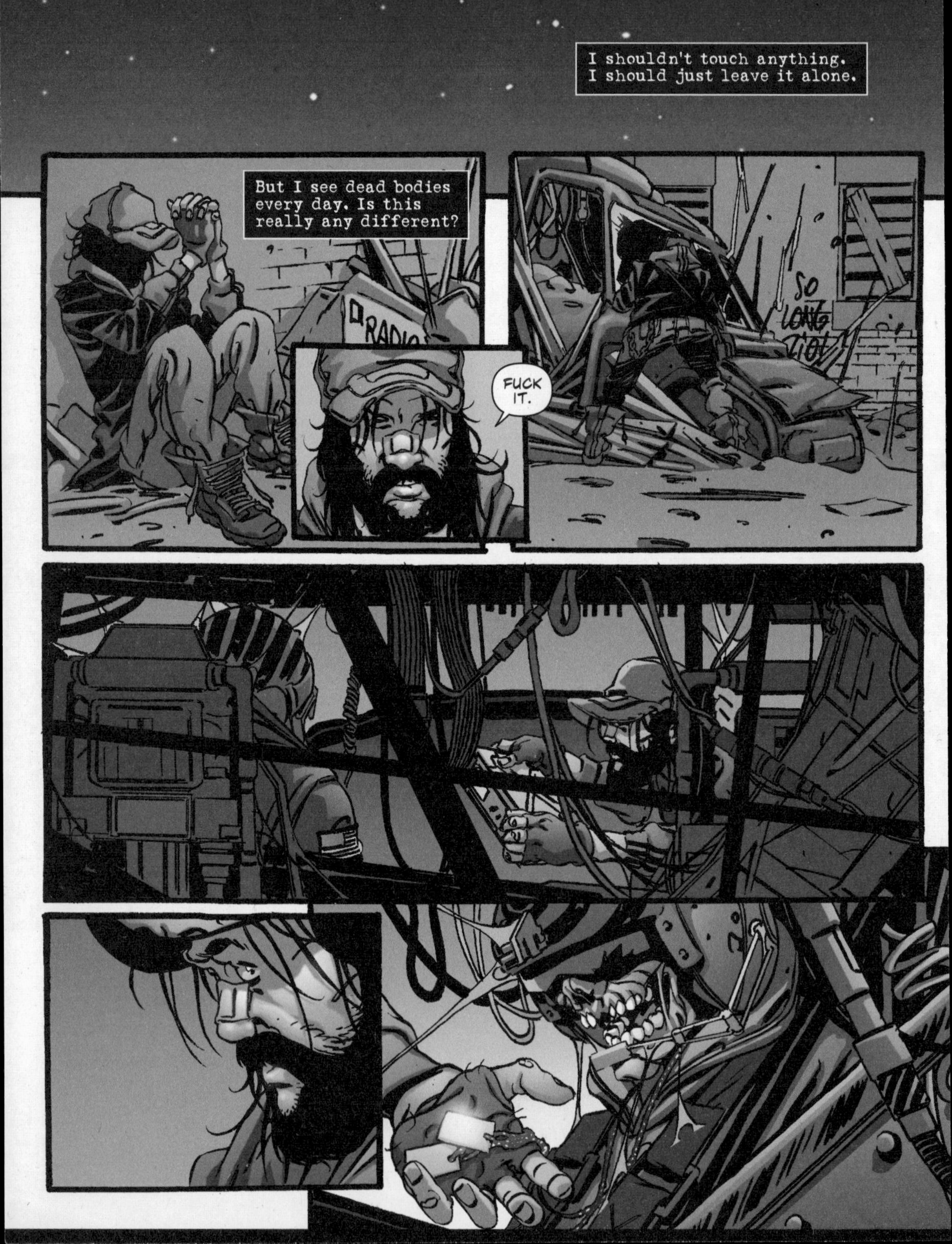
I shouldn't touch anything. I should just leave it alone.
But I see dead bodies every day. Is this really any different?
RADIO
FUCK IT.
SO LONG

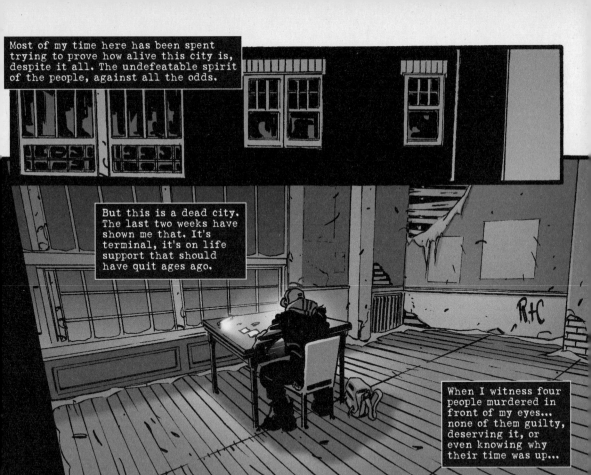

Most of my time here has been spent trying to prove how alive this city is, despite it all. The undefeatable spirit of the people, against all the odds.

But this is a dead city. The last two weeks have shown me that. It's terminal, it's on life support that should have quit ages ago.

When I witness four people murdered in front of my eyes... none of them guilty, deserving it, or even knowing why their time was up...

...and I walk away and have a cup of coffee?

This is a dead city, and every time I get up and walk away from something I'm killing it all over again.

Staring at the paper trail left by those two pilots won't help any.

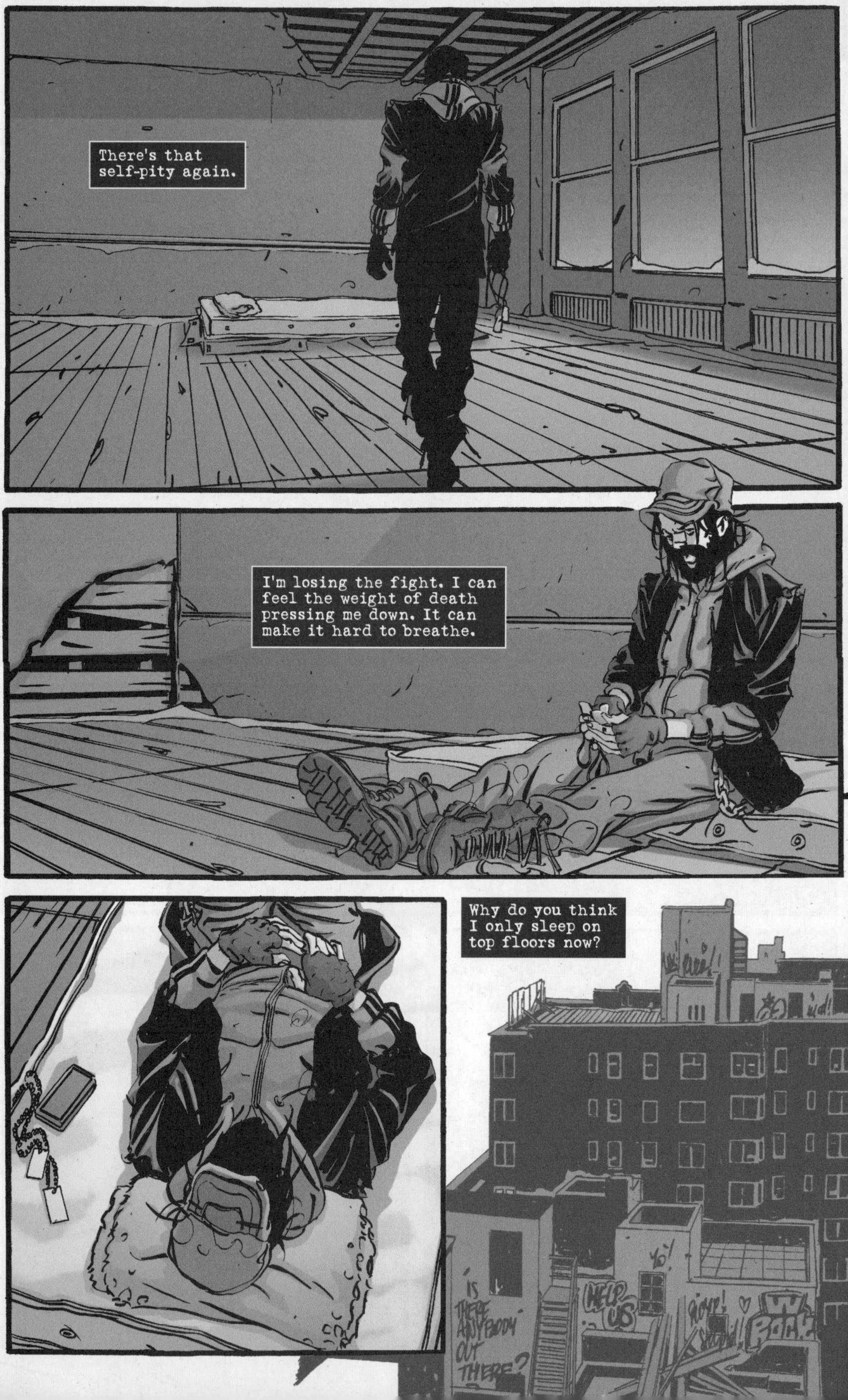
There's that self-pity again.
I'm losing the fight. I can feel the weight of death pressing me down. It can make it hard to breathe.
Why do you think I only sleep on top floors now?
IS THERE ANYBODY OUT THERE?
HELP US

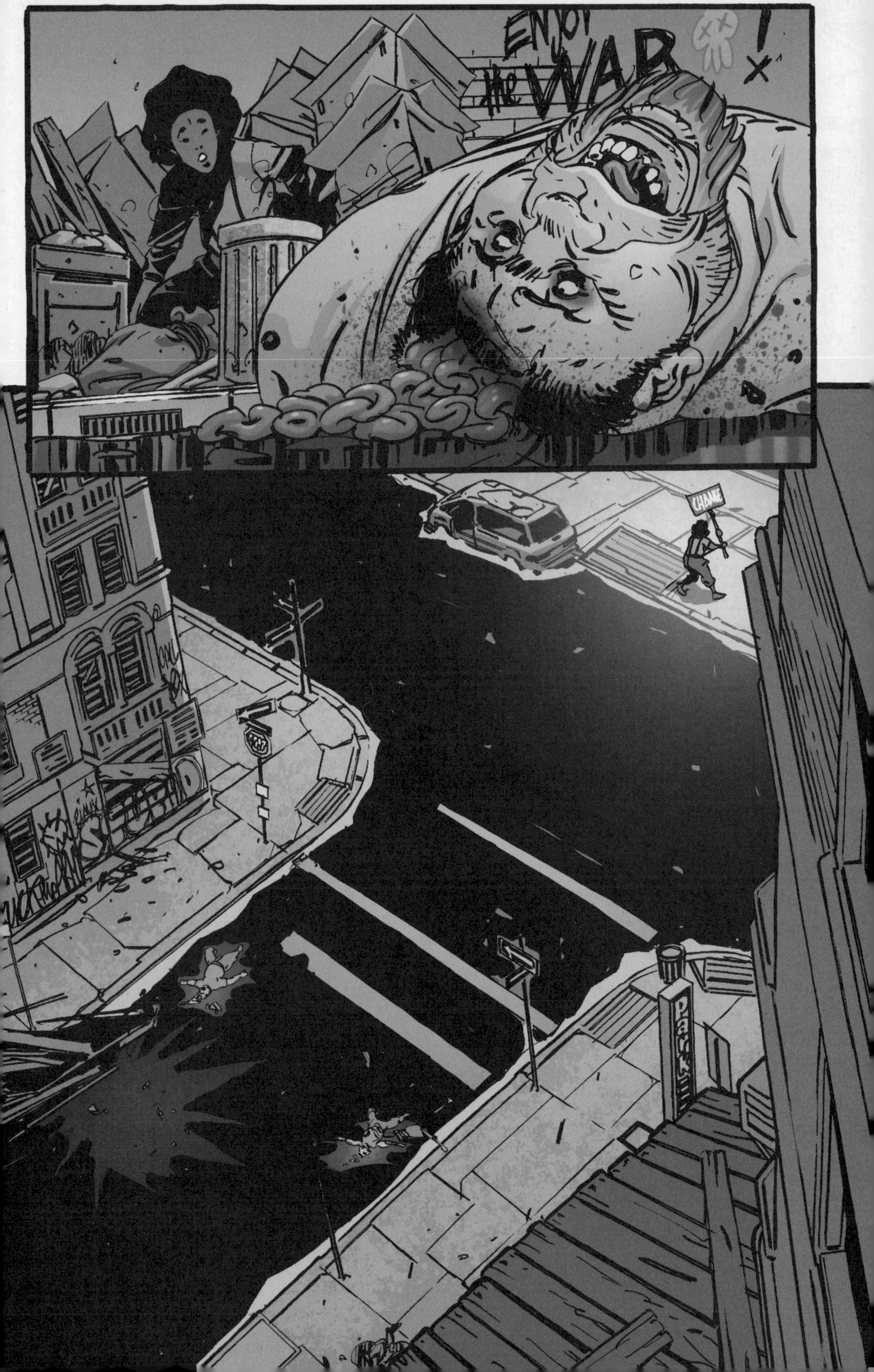
ENJOY the WAR
CHANGE

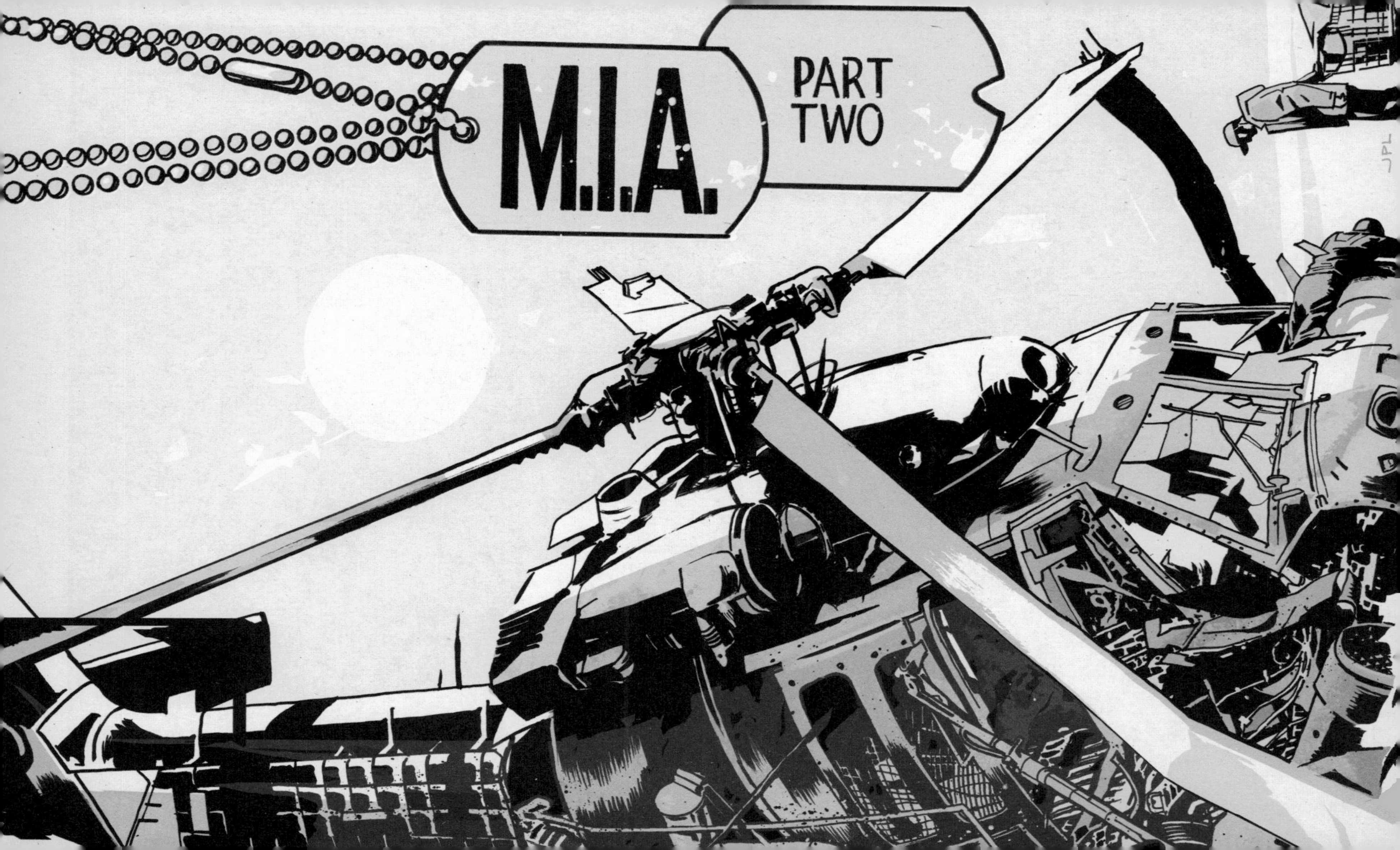
M.I.A.
PART TWO
JPL

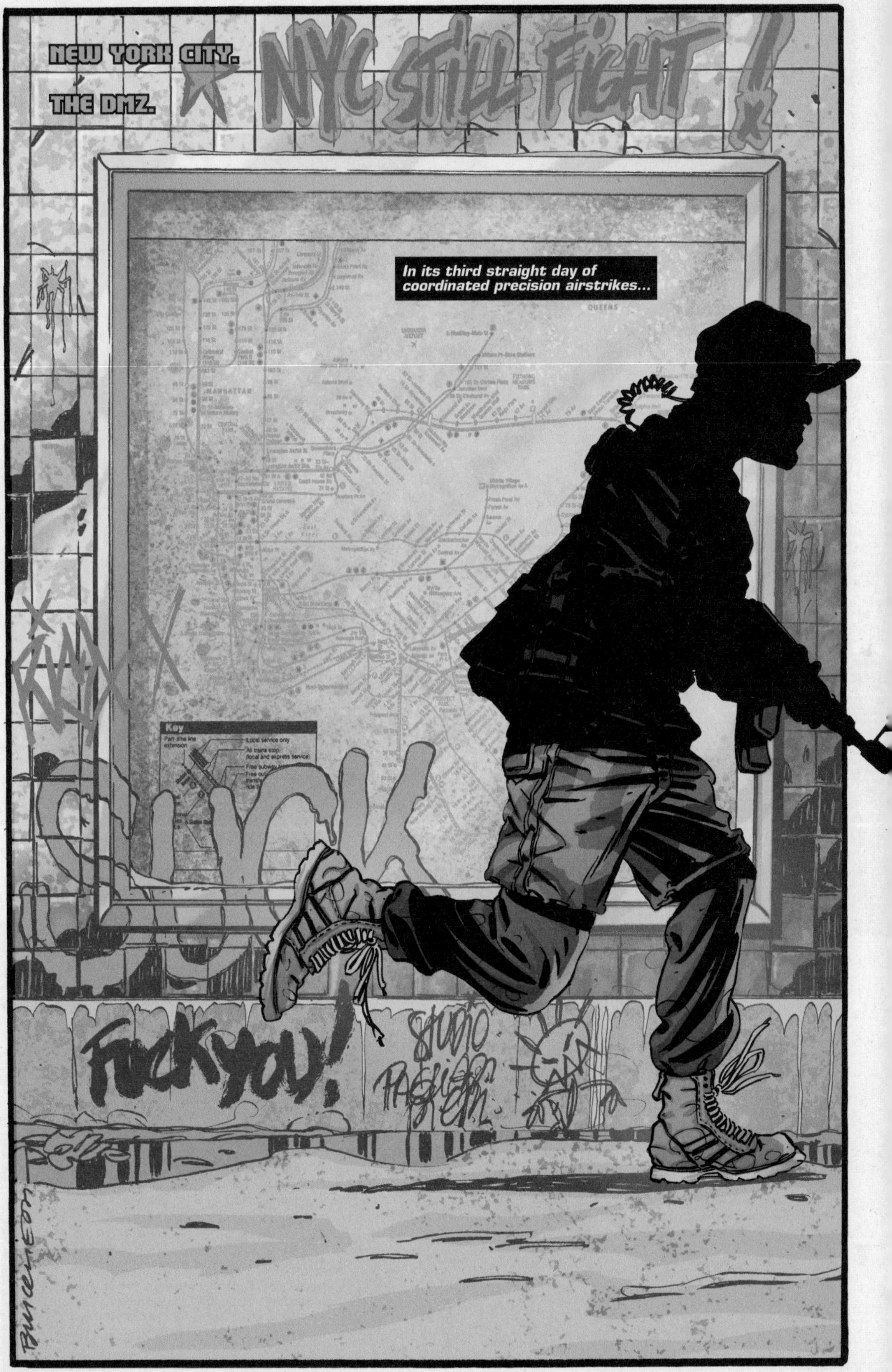
NEW YORK CITY.
THE DMZ.
NYC STILL FIGHT!
In its third straight day of coordinated precision airstrikes...
FUCK YOU!

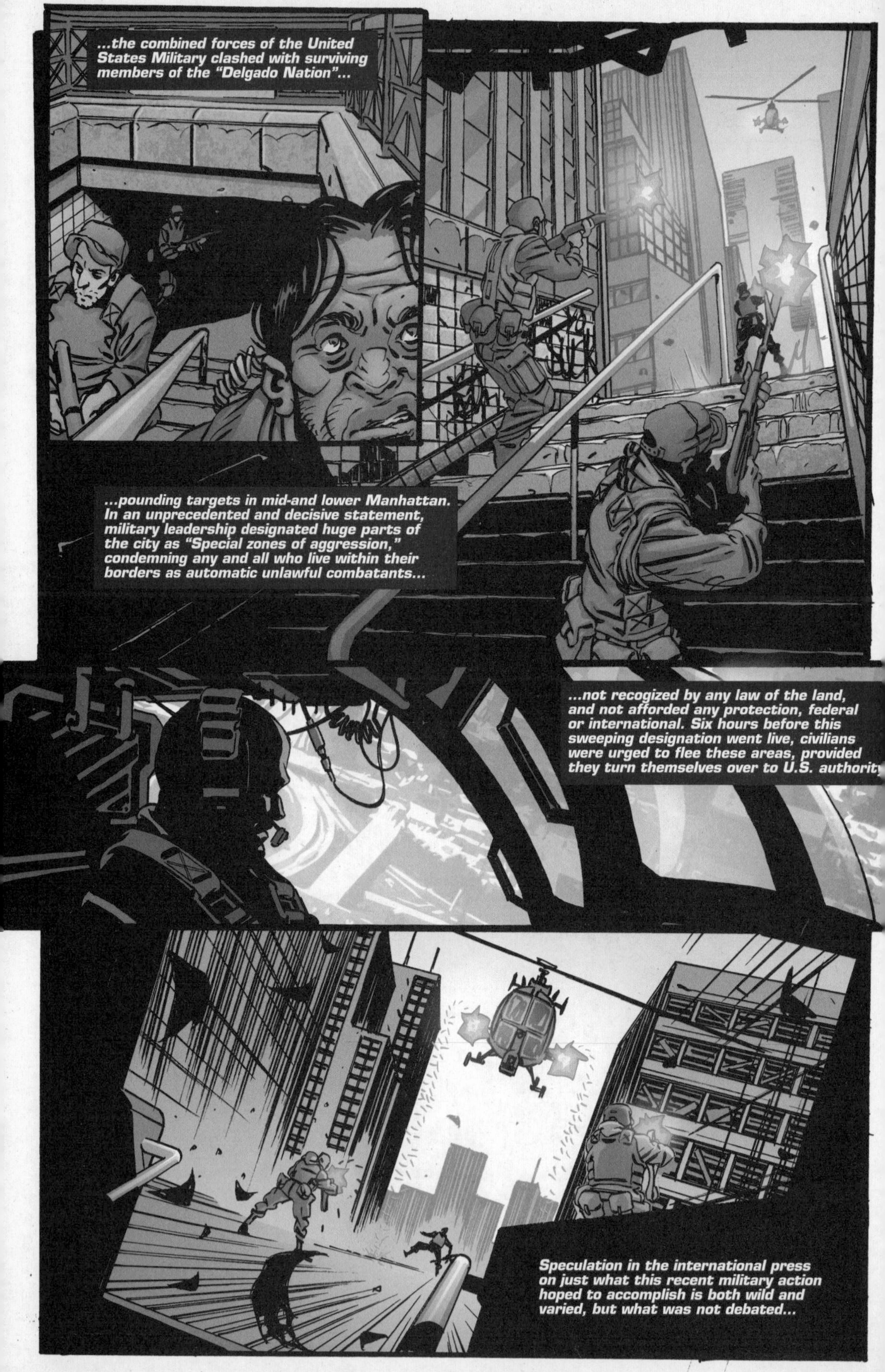
...the combined forces of the United States Military clashed with surviving members of the "Delgado Nation"...
...pounding targets in mid-and lower Manhattan. In an unprecedented and decisive statement, military leadership designated huge parts of the city as "Special zones of aggression," condemning any and all who live within their borders as automatic unlawful combatants...
...not recogized by any law of the land, and not afforded any protection, federal or international. Six hours before this sweeping designation went live, civilians were urged to flee these areas, provided they turn themselves over to U.S. authorit
Speculation in the international press on just what this recent military action hoped to accomplish is both wild and varied, but what was not debated...

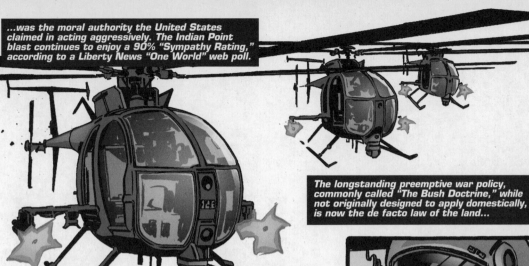

...was the moral authority the United States claimed in acting aggressively. The Indian Point blast continues to enjoy a 90% "Sympathy Rating," according to a Liberty News "One World" web poll.

The longstanding preemptive war policy, commonly called "The Bush Doctrine," while not originally designed to apply domestically, is now the de facto law of the land...

"To defeat them in the purest military sense of the term." is the soundbite on every pundit's lips these recent days.

How this will play out in the days and weeks to come remains to be seen.

With the military flying hundreds of sorties per twelve-hour period...

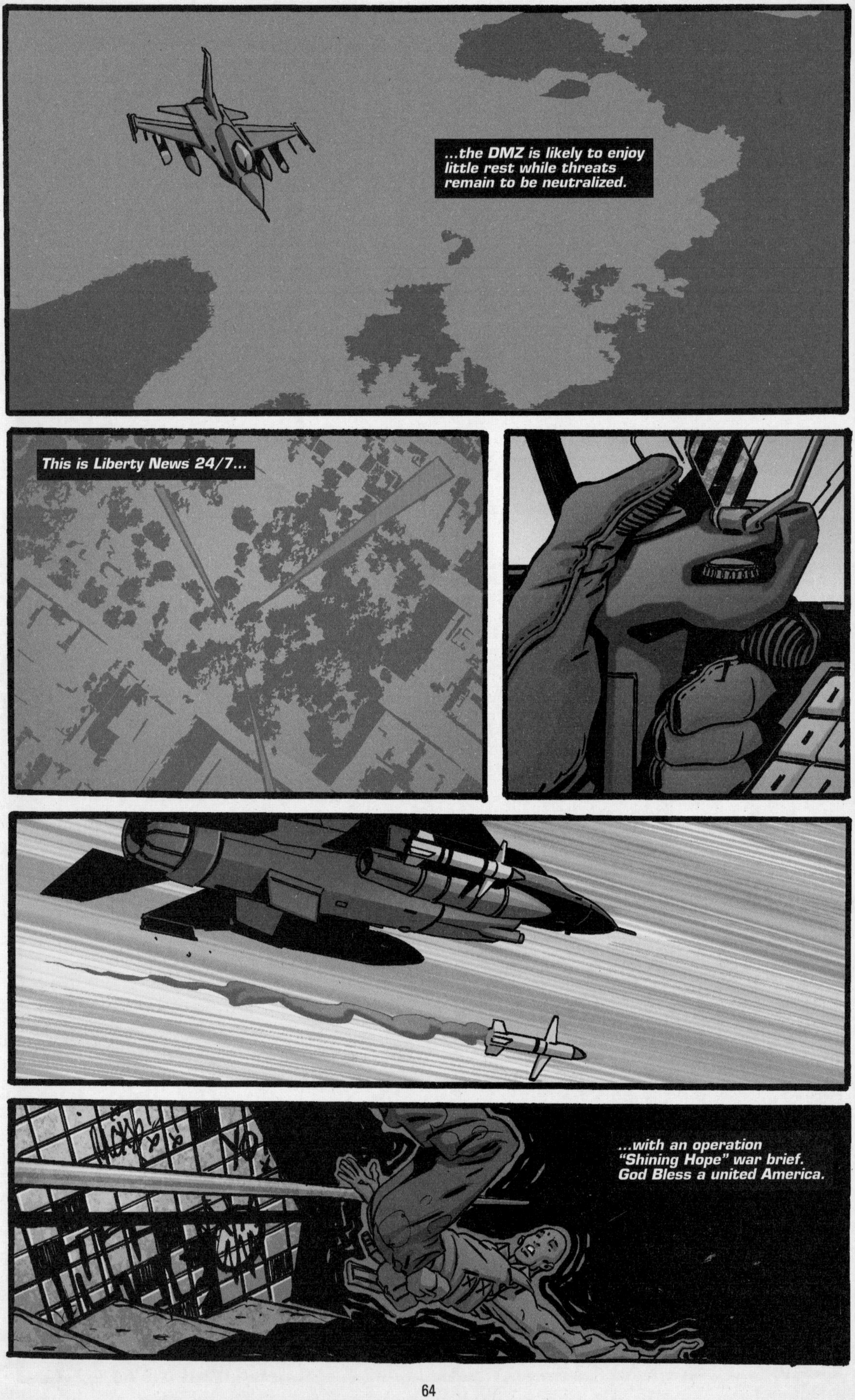
...the DMZ is likely to enjoy little rest while threats remain to be neutralized.
This is Liberty News 24/7...
...with an operation "Shining Hope" war brief. God Bless a united America.

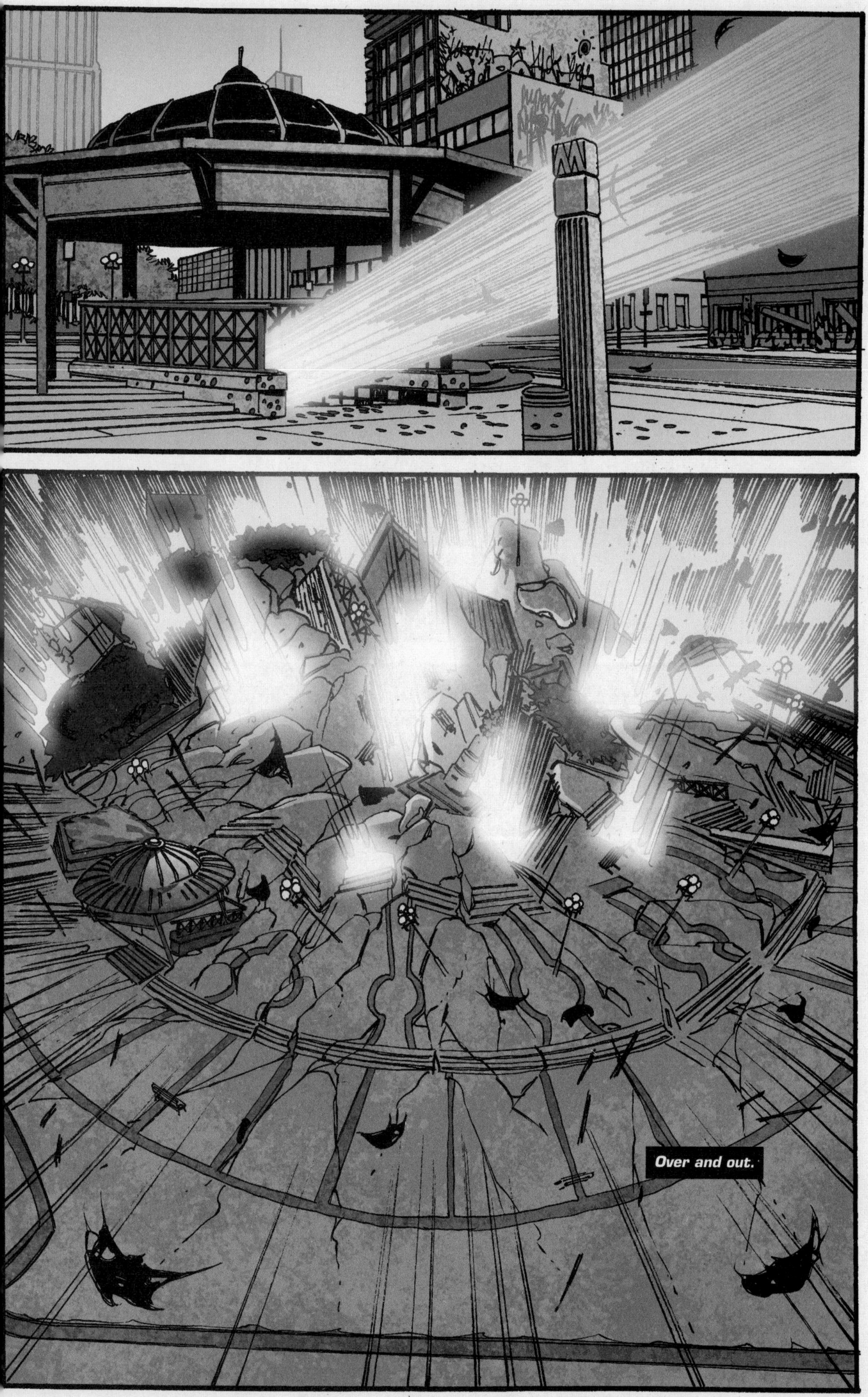
Over and out.

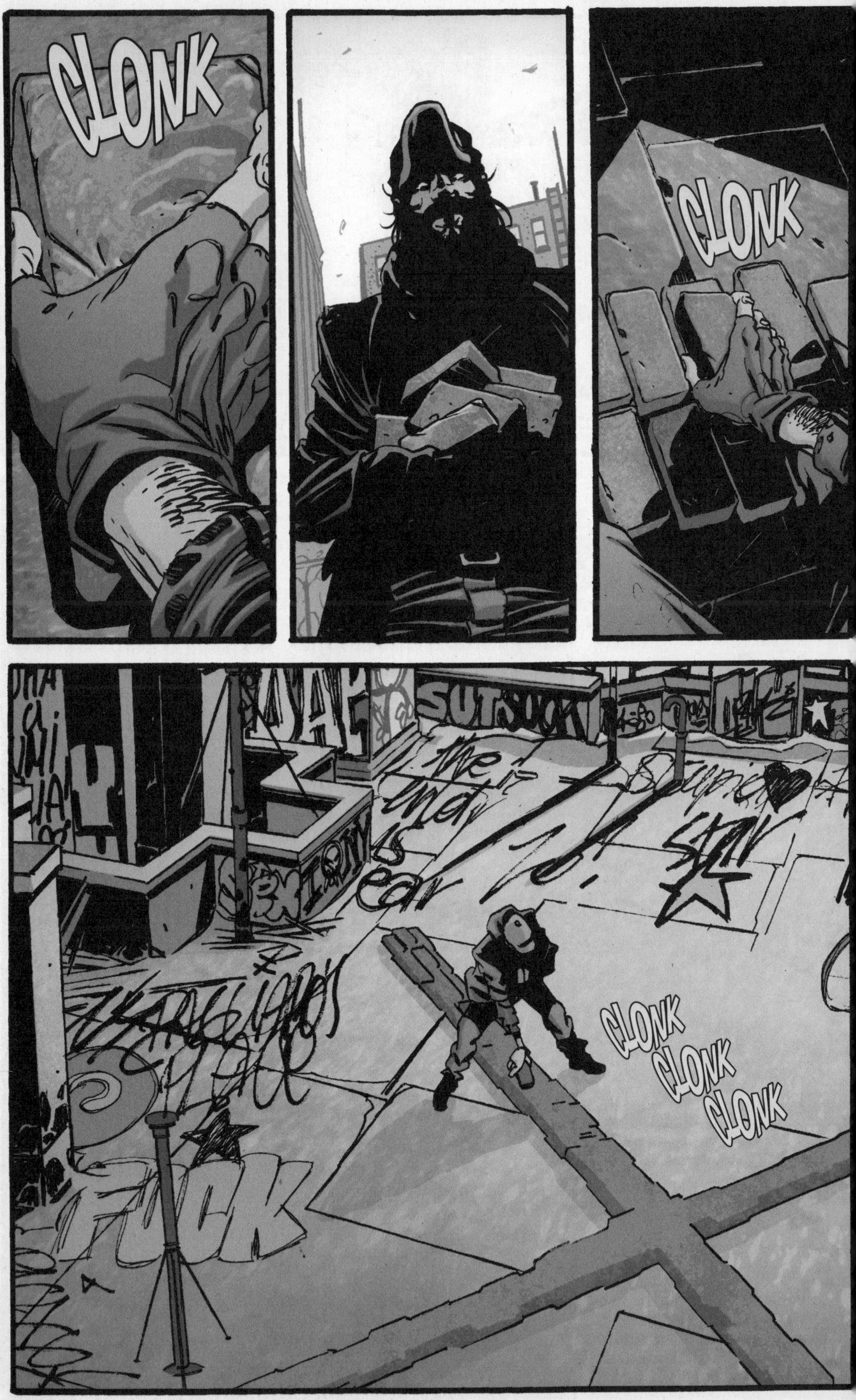
CLONK
CLONK
SUTSUCK
CLONK
CLONK
CLONK

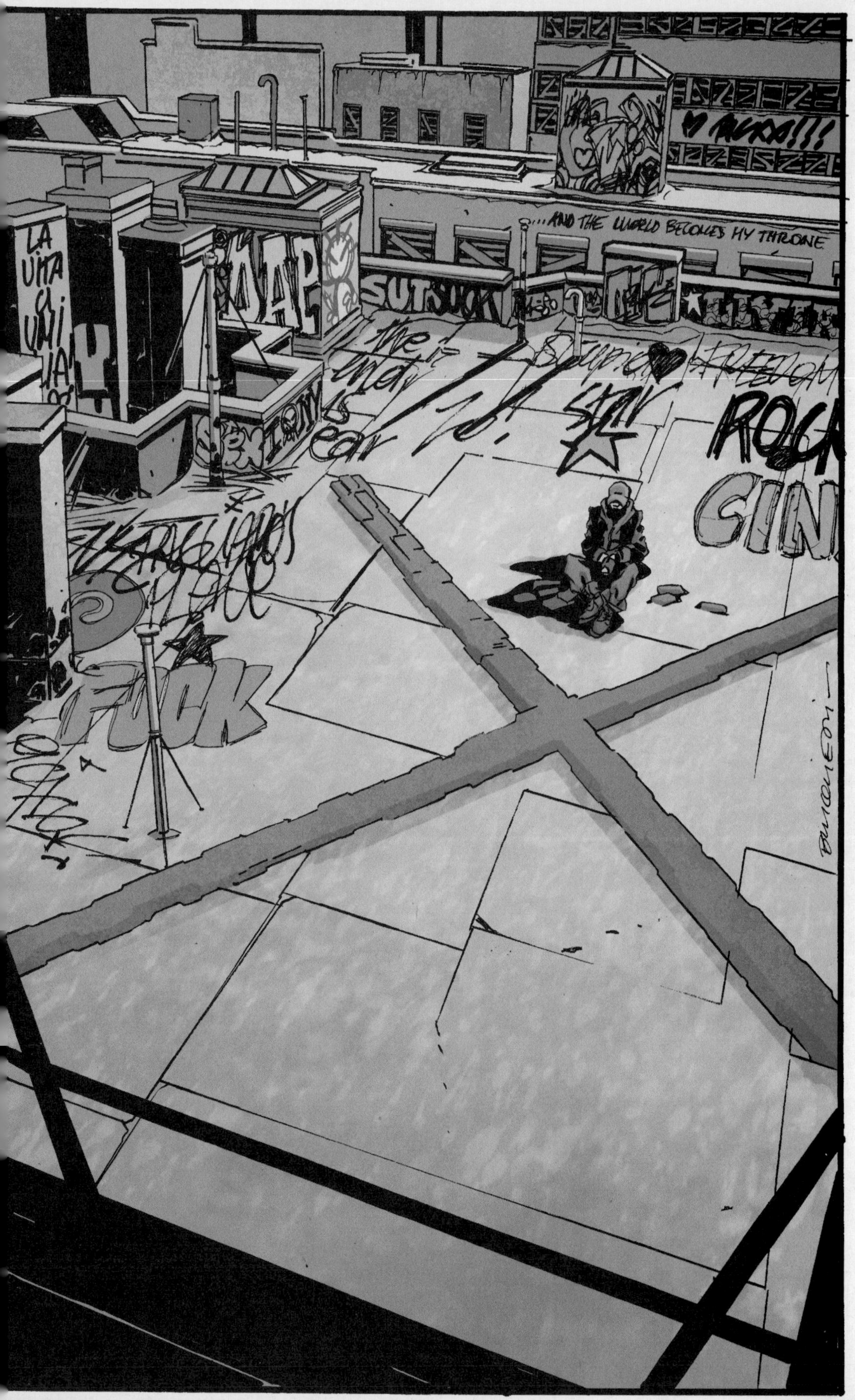
...AND THE WORLD BECOMES MY THRONE.
SUTSUCK
FUCK

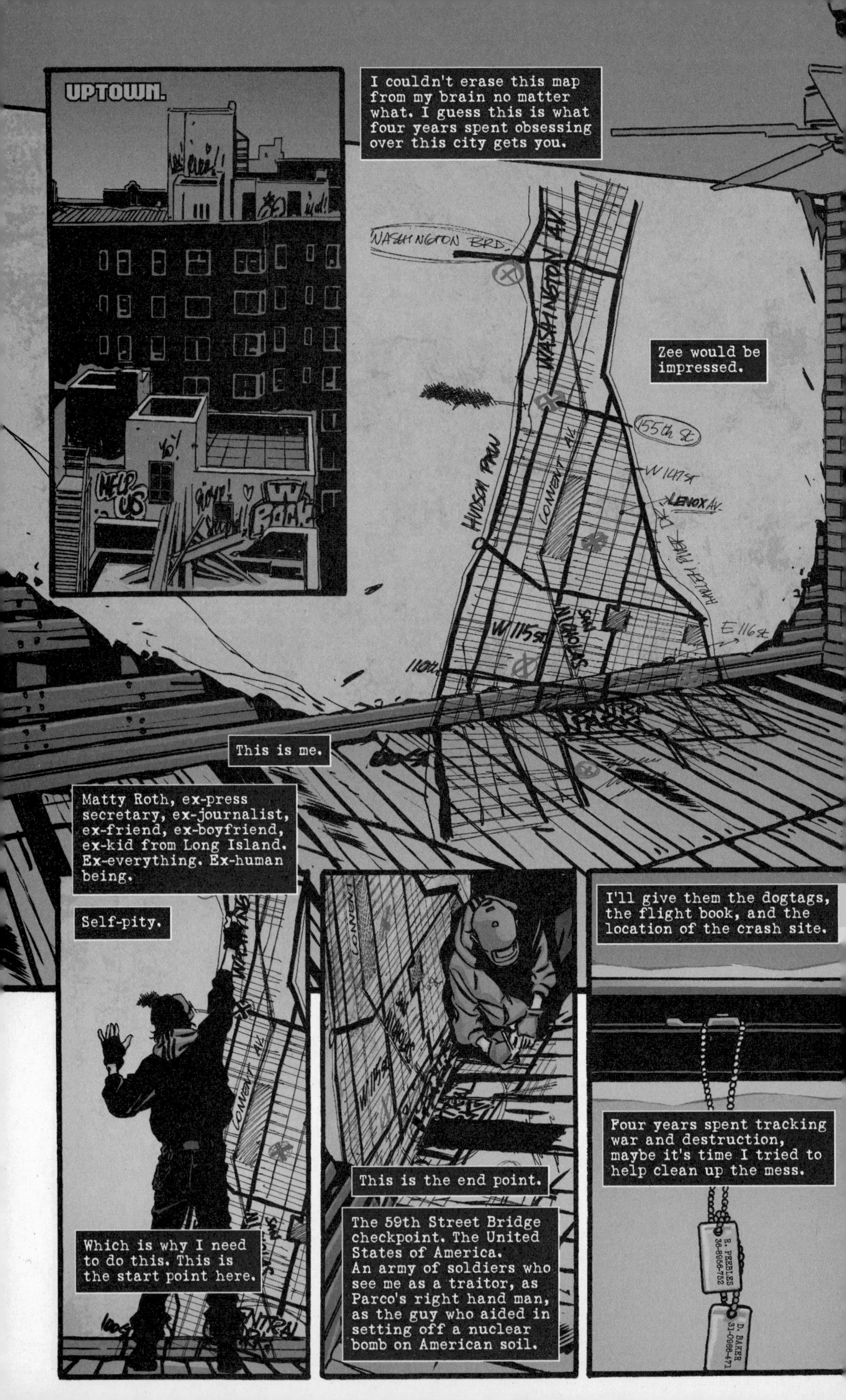
UPTOWN.
I couldn't erase this map from my brain no matter what. I guess this is what four years spent obsessing over this city gets you.
WASHINGTON AV.
155th St
W 147 St
LENOX AV.
CONVENT AV.
W 115 St
E 116 St
Zee would be impressed.
This is me.
Matty Roth, ex-press secretary, ex-journalist, ex-friend, ex-boyfriend, ex-kid from Long Island. Ex-everything. Ex-human being.
Self-pity.
Which is why I need to do this. This is the start point here.
This is the end point.
The 59th Street Bridge checkpoint. The United States of America.
An army of soldiers who see me as a traitor, as Parco's right hand man, as the guy who aided in setting off a nuclear bomb on American soil.
I'll give them the dogtags, the flight book, and the location of the crash site.
Four years spent tracking war and destruction, maybe it's time I tried to help clean up the mess.
R. PEEBLES 38-8658-752
D. BAKER 31-0986-471

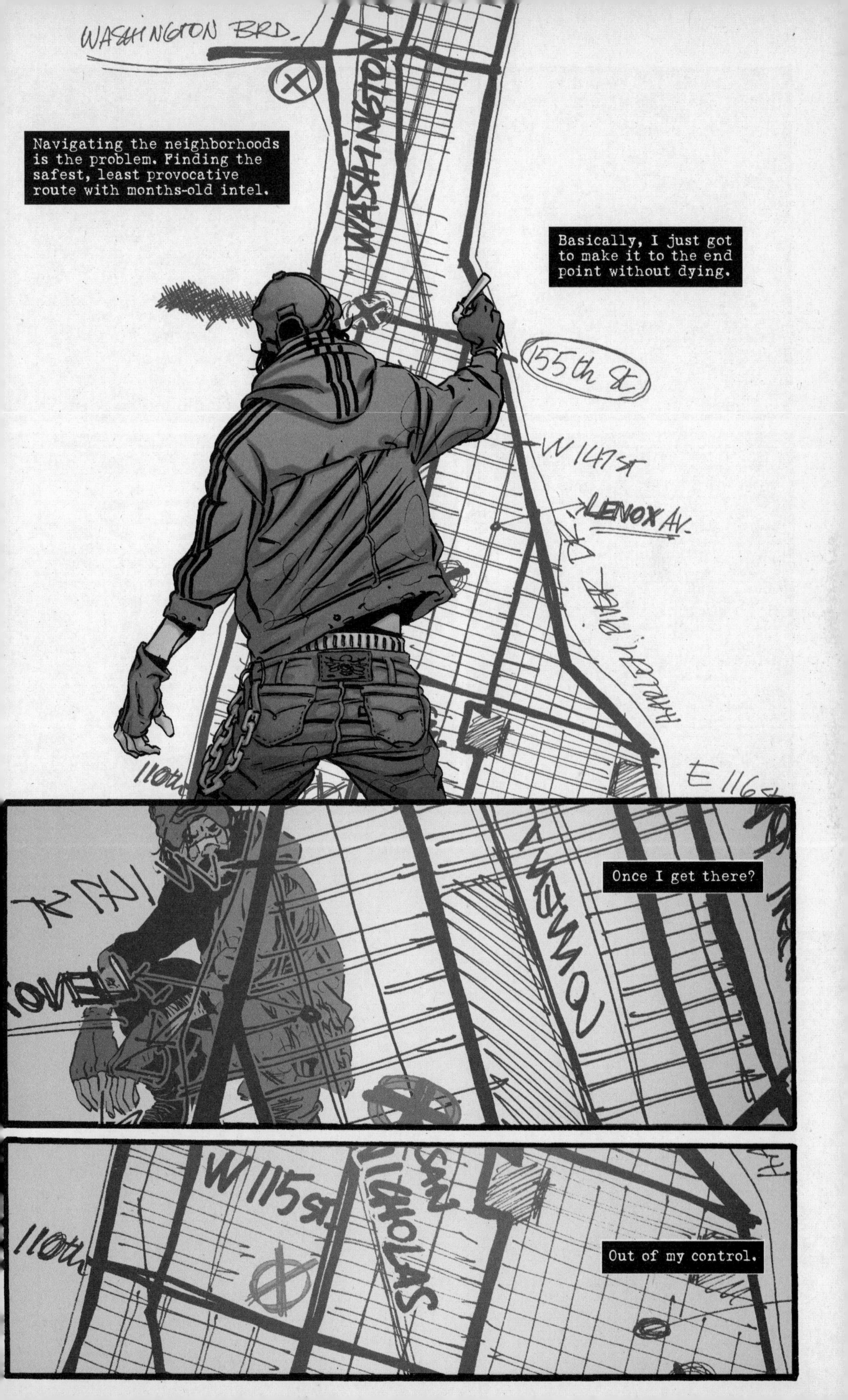
WASHINGTON BRD.
WASHINGTON
Navigating the neighborhoods is the problem. Finding the safest, least provocative route with months-old intel.
Basically, I just got to make it to the end point without dying.
155th St
W 147 St
LENOX AV.
HARLEM RIVER
110th
E 116
Once I get there?
W 115 St.
ST. NICHOLAS
110th
Out of my control.

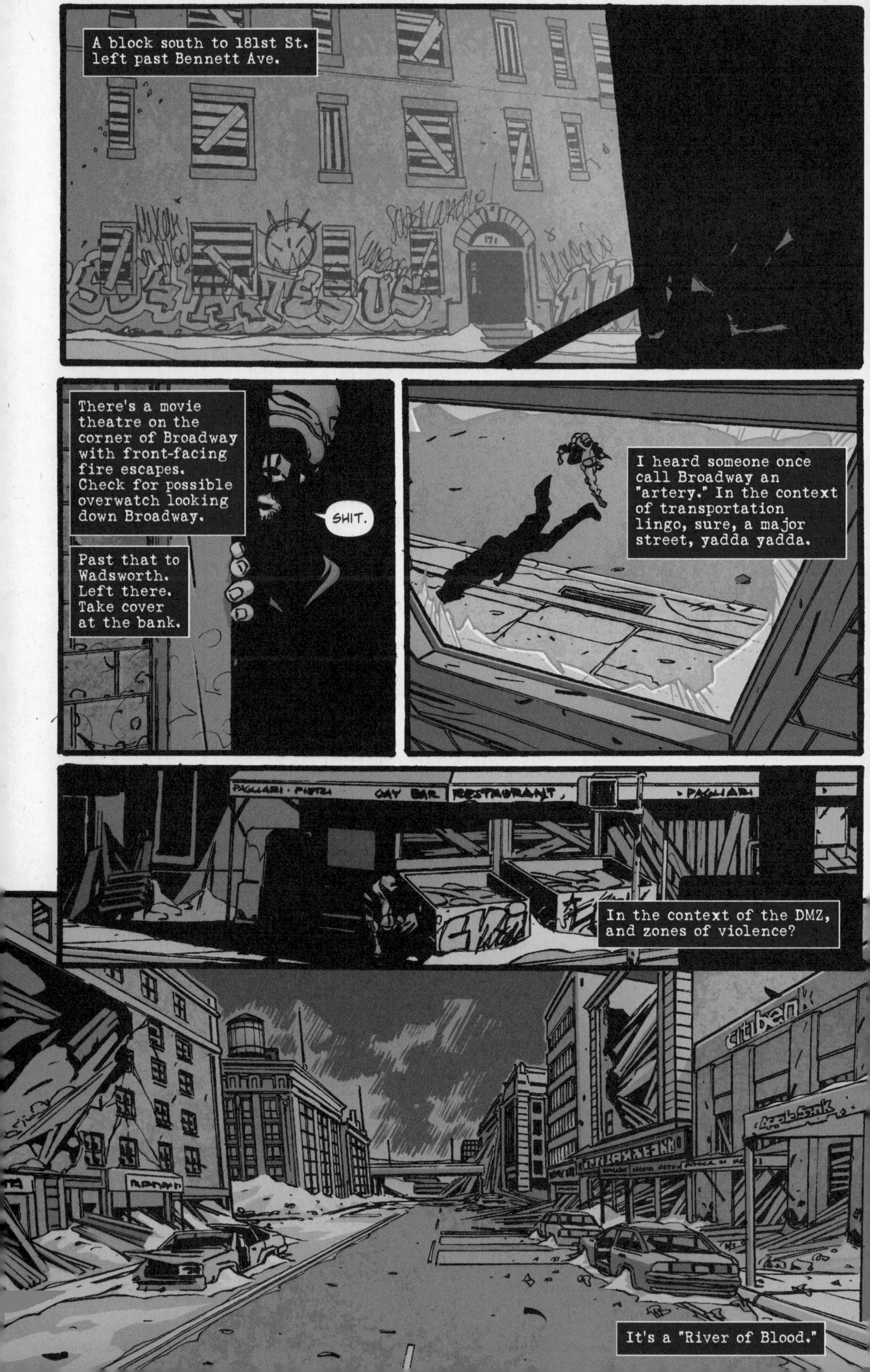

A block south to 181st St. left past Bennett Ave.
There's a movie theatre on the corner of Broadway with front-facing fire escapes. Check for possible overwatch looking down Broadway.
Past that to Wadsworth. Left there. Take cover at the bank.
SHIT.
I heard someone once call Broadway an "artery." In the context of transportation lingo, sure, a major street, yadda yadda.
RESTAURANT
In the context of the DMZ, and zones of violence?
citibank
It's a "River of Blood."

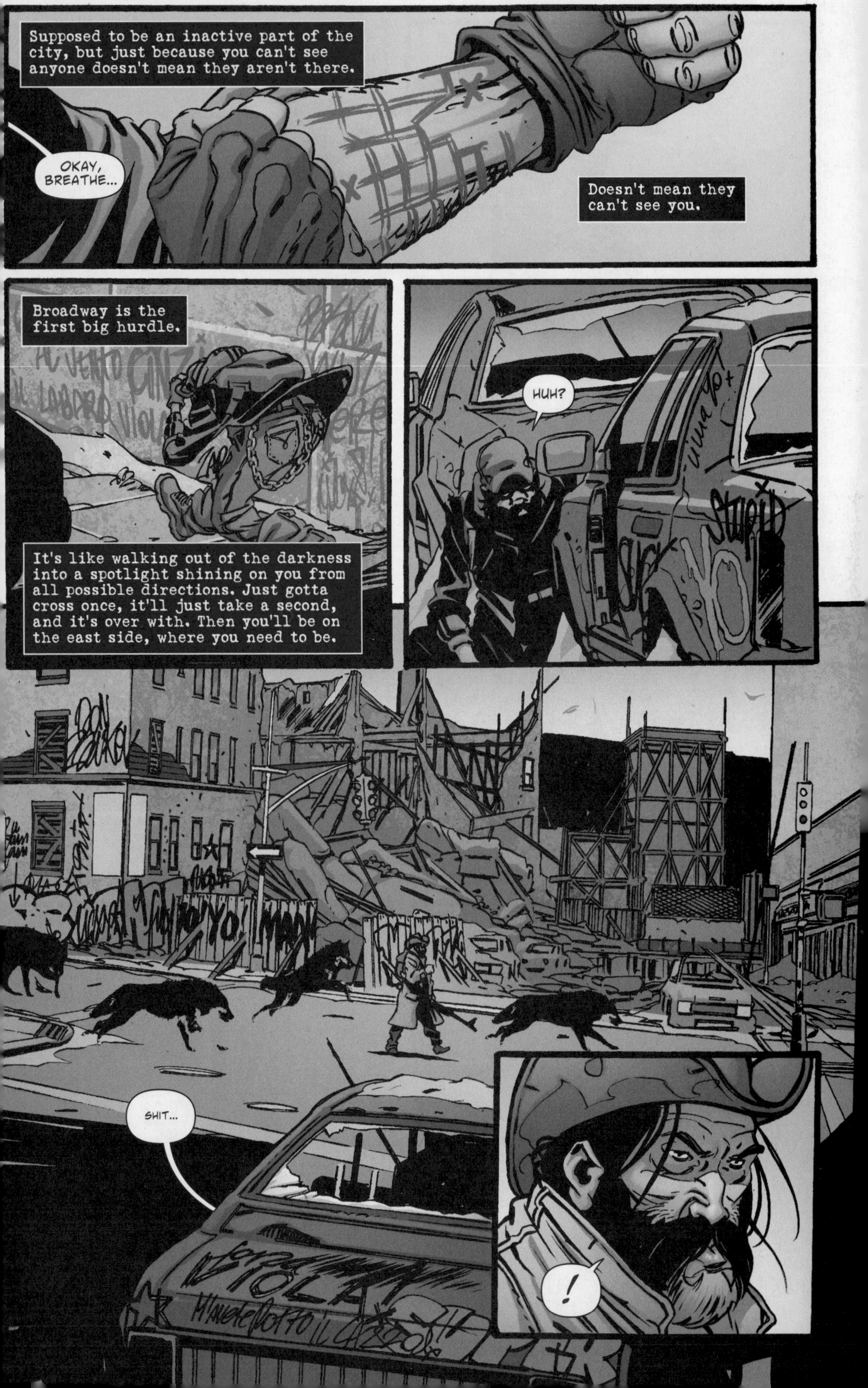
Supposed to be an inactive part of the city, but just because you can't see anyone doesn't mean they aren't there.
OKAY, BREATHE...
Doesn't mean they can't see you.
Broadway is the first big hurdle.
It's like walking out of the darkness into a spotlight shining on you from all possible directions. Just gotta cross once, it'll just take a second, and it's over with. Then you'll be on the east side, where you need to be.
HUH?
SHIT...
!

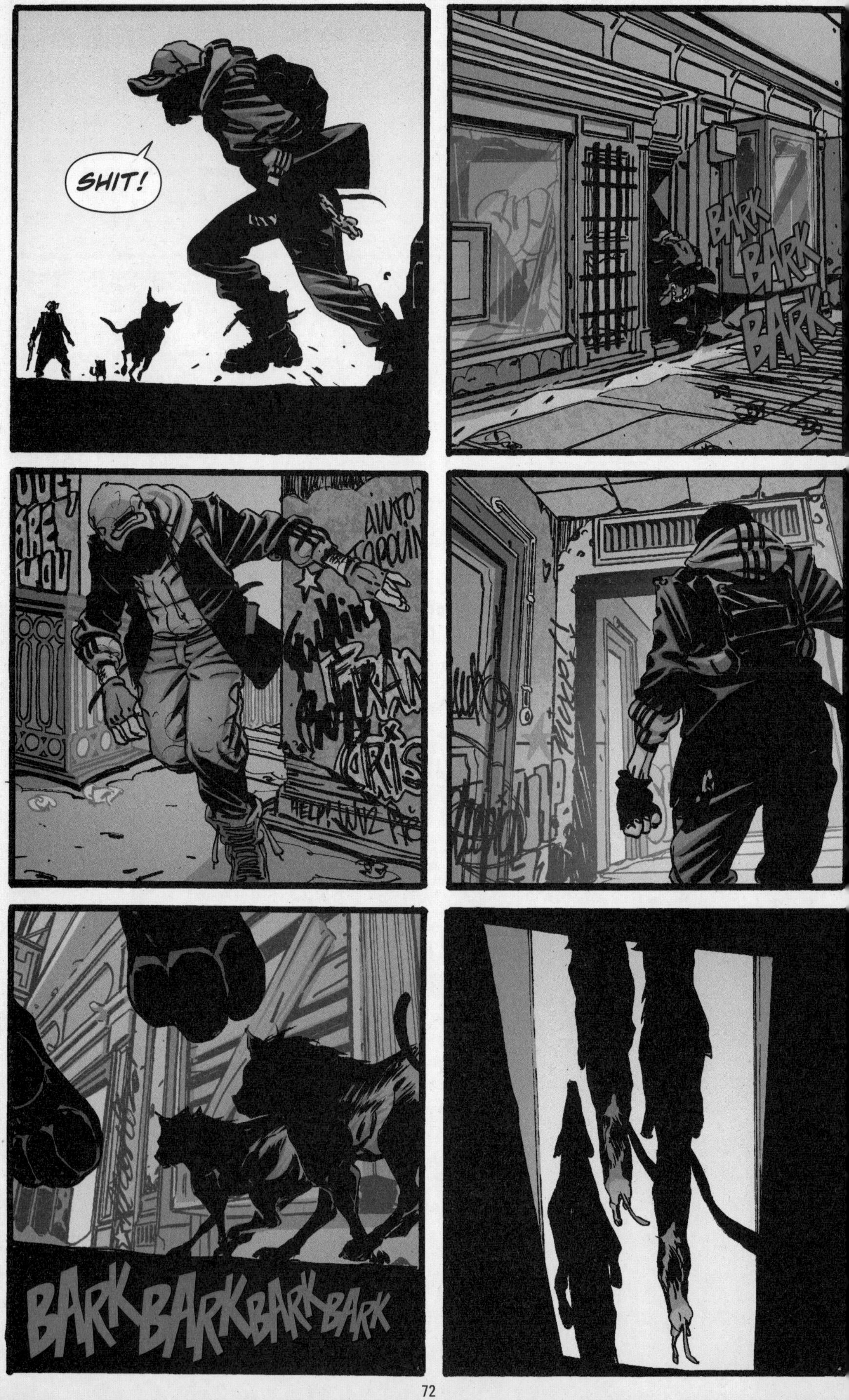
SHIT!
BARK
BARK
BARK
BARK BARK BARK BARK

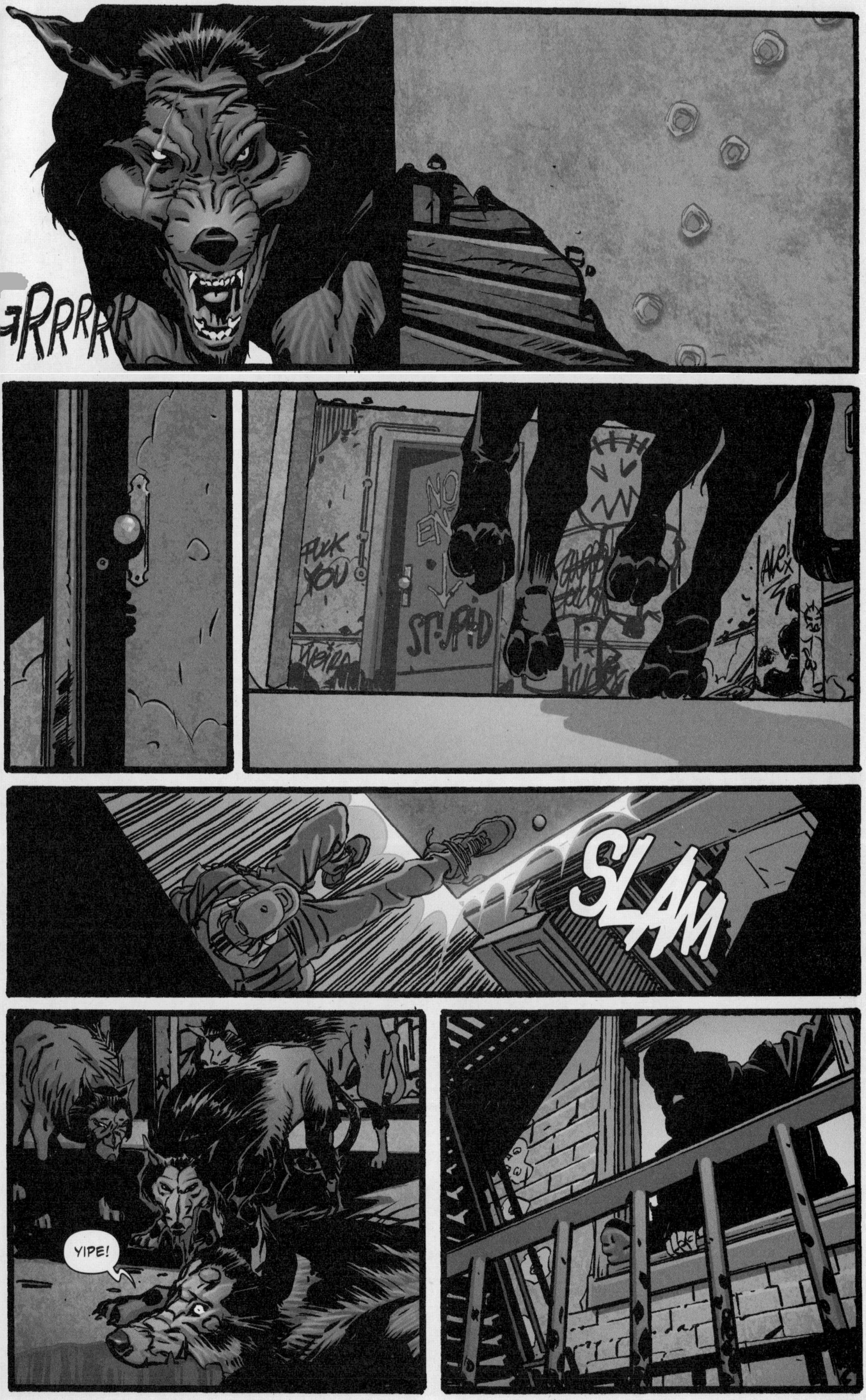
GRRRRR
FUCK YOU
SLAM
YIPE!

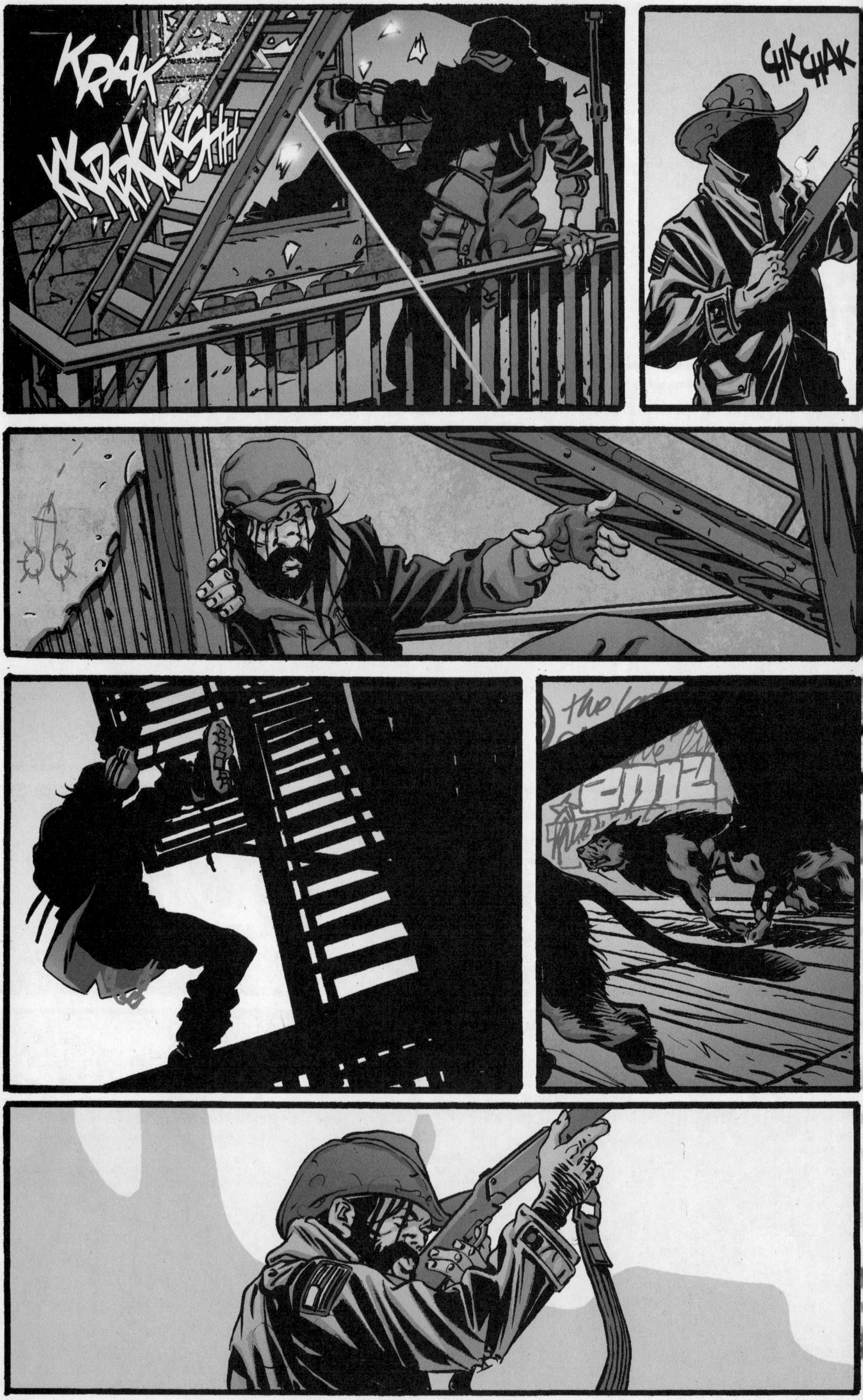
KRAK
KKRAKKKSHH
CHK CHAK

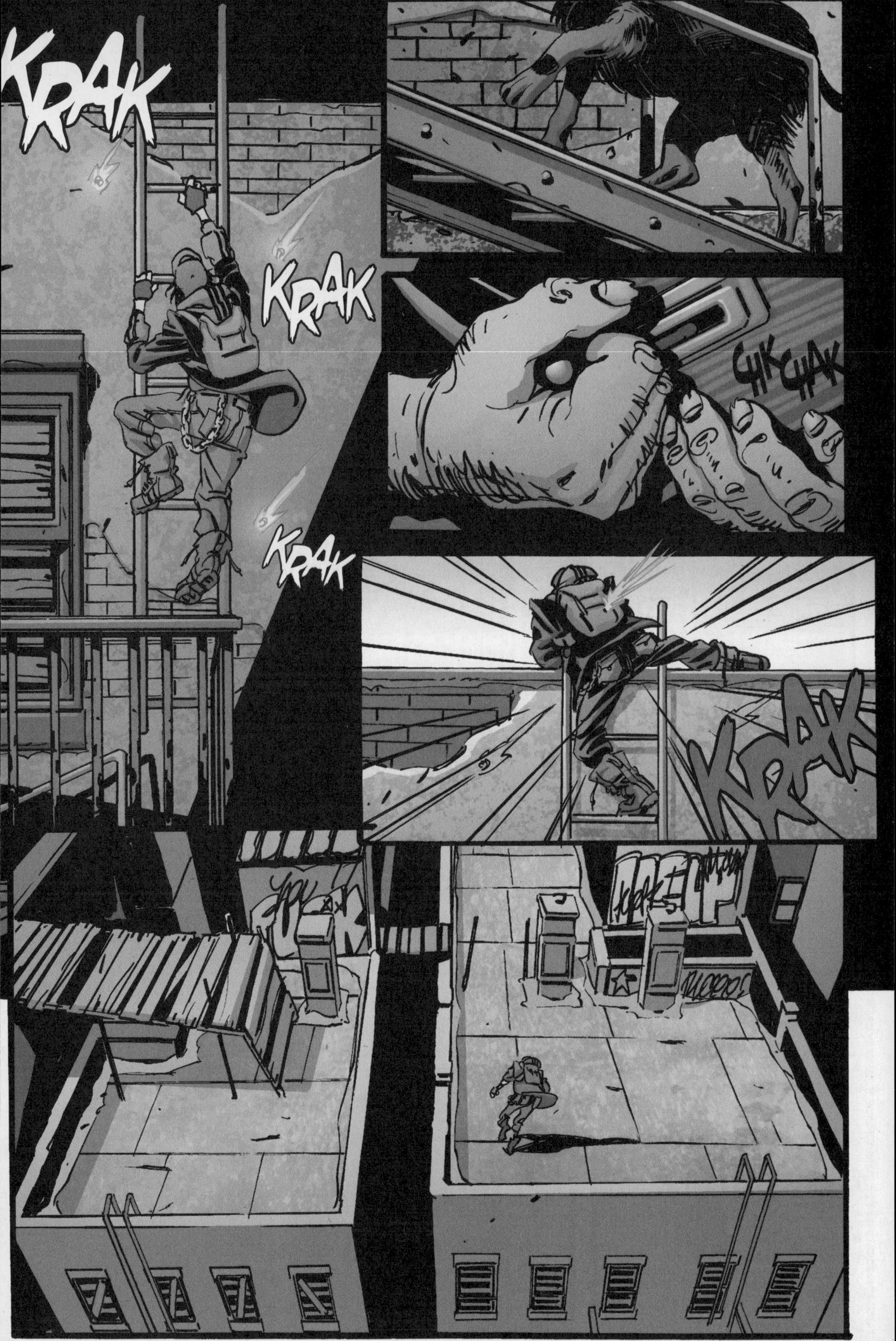
KRAK
KRAK
KRAK
CHK CHAK
KRAK

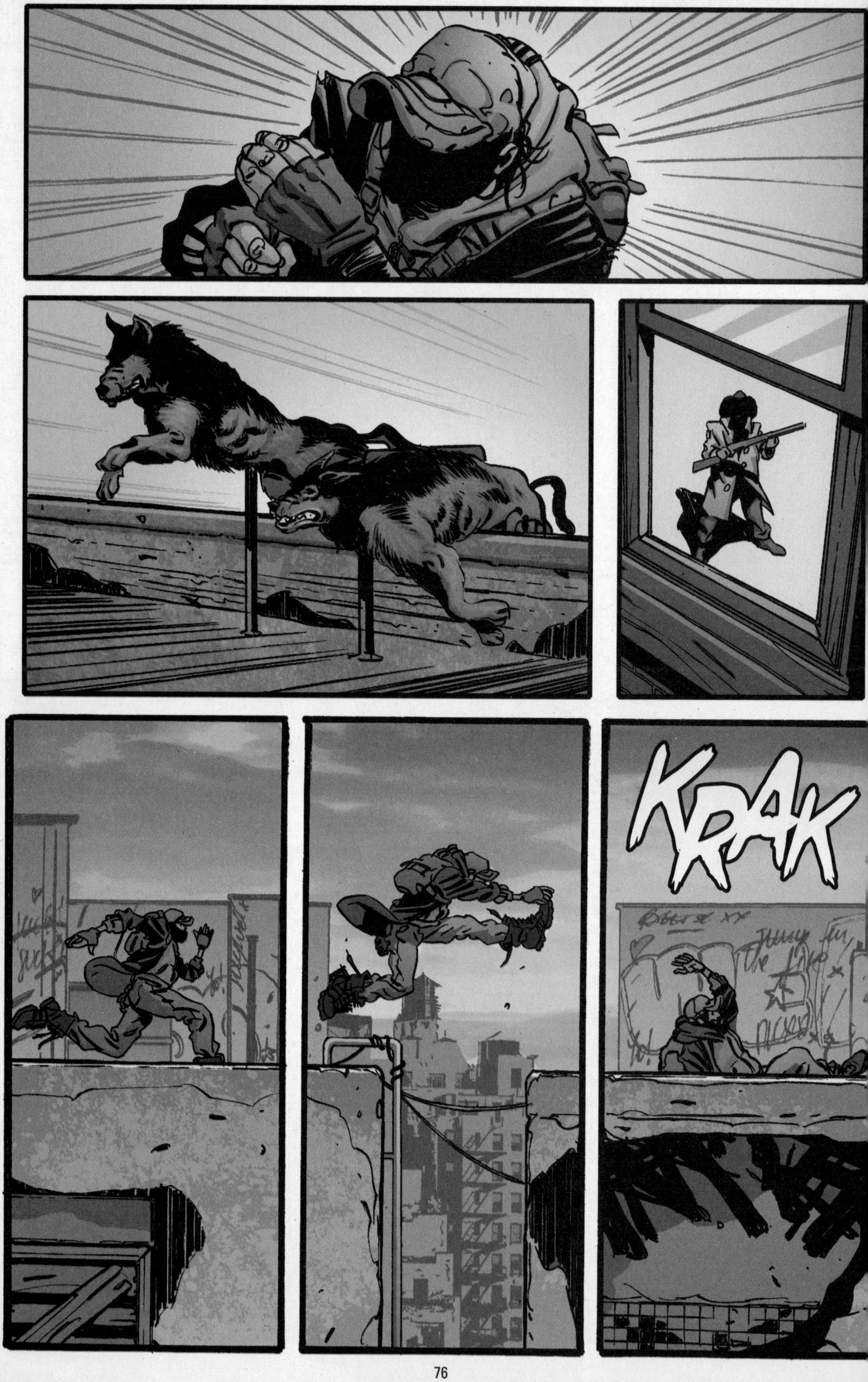
KRAK

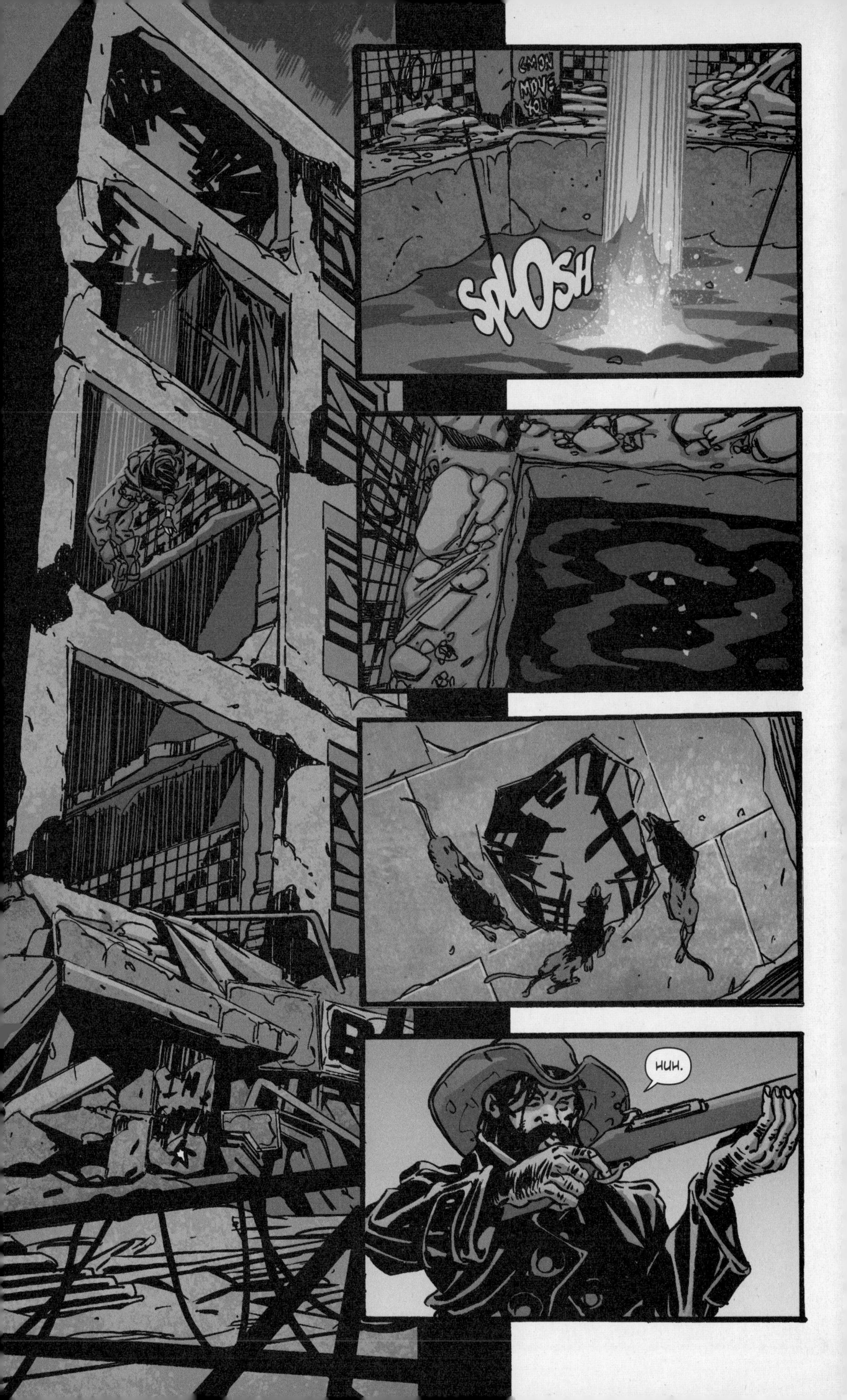
YO!
C'MON MOVE YO!
SPLOSH
HUH.

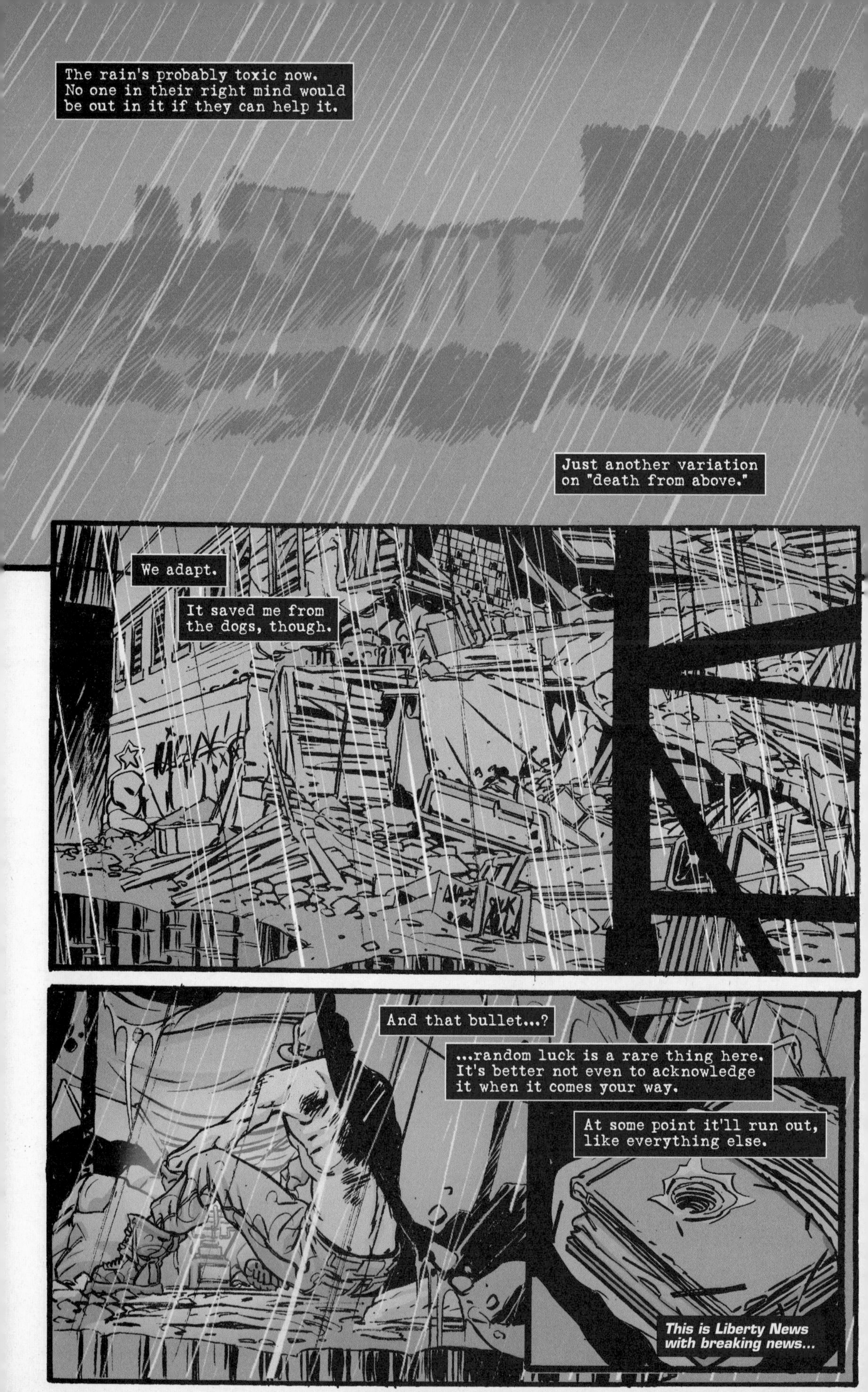

The rain's probably toxic now. No one in their right mind would be out in it if they can help it.
Just another variation on "death from above."
We adapt.
It saved me from the dogs, though.
And that bullet...?
...random luck is a rare thing here. It's better not even to acknowledge it when it comes your way.
At some point it'll run out, like everything else.
This is Liberty News with breaking news...

Military forensics have recovered what is being tentatively described as "Parco's escape vehicle," a Delgado Nation-designated civilian Humvee...

...half-submerged in the Hudson River off the West Side Highway and West 24th St.

Technicians were able to date the vehicle's entry into the water at no more than seven days ago, and personal effects still inside indicate that Parco Delgado did indeed use this particular Humvee.

Further tests are under way to determine if he was a driver or a passenger at the time of the accident.

Because of the proximity to the New Jersey coastline, and the urgent need to process the scene for any information indicating the status of the war criminal Delgado...

*EEDOM OR DEATH OR NEW JERSEY !*

...military leadership authorized suppressive bombings of the Jersey coastal defenses. Free States leadership was notified thirty minutes prior

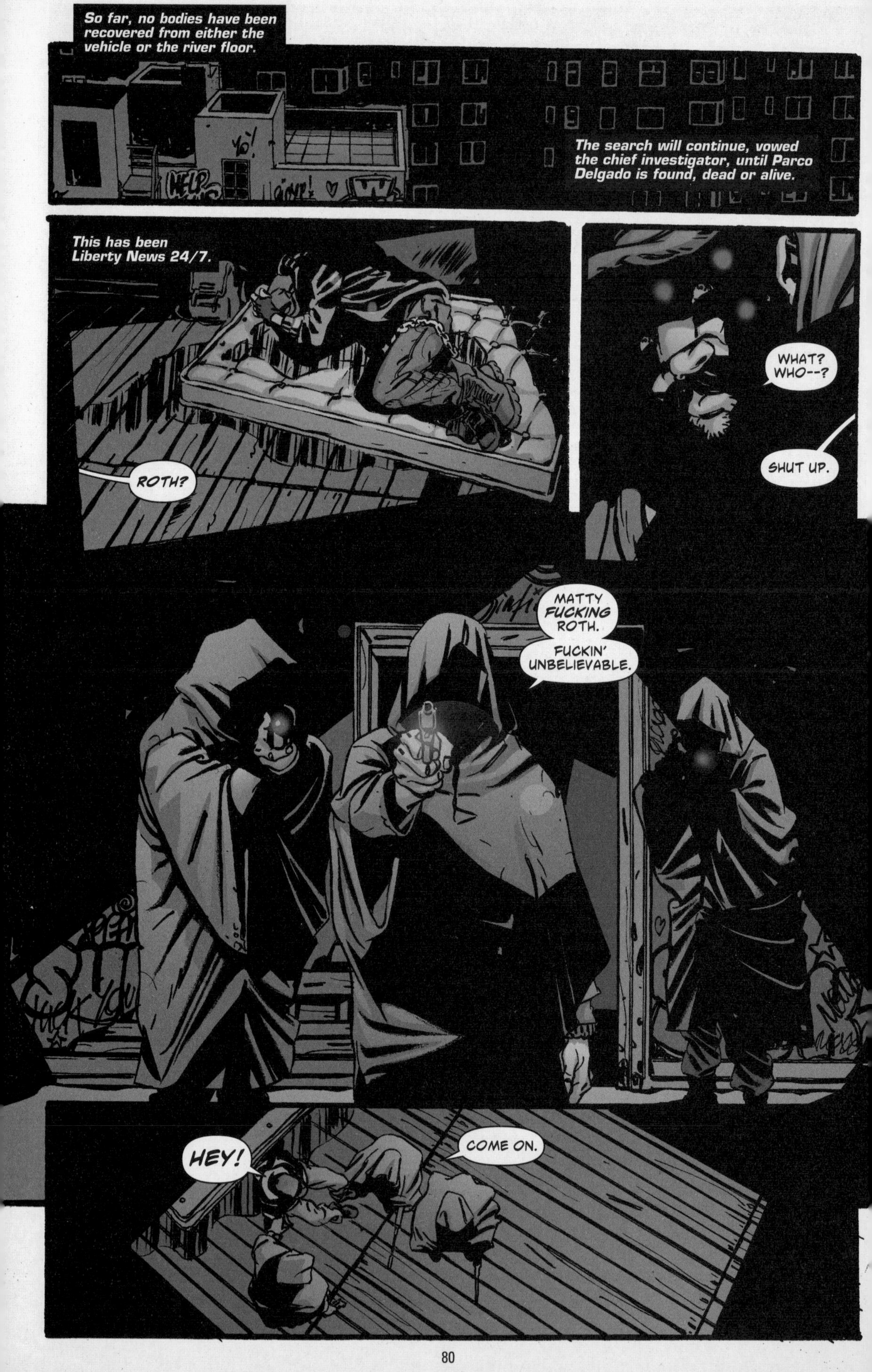
So far, no bodies have been recovered from either the vehicle or the river floor.
The search will continue, vowed the chief investigator, until Parco Delgado is found, dead or alive.
This has been Liberty News 24/7.
ROTH?
WHAT? WHO--?
SHUT UP.
MATTY FUCKING ROTH.
FUCKIN' UNBELIEVABLE.
HEY!
COME ON.

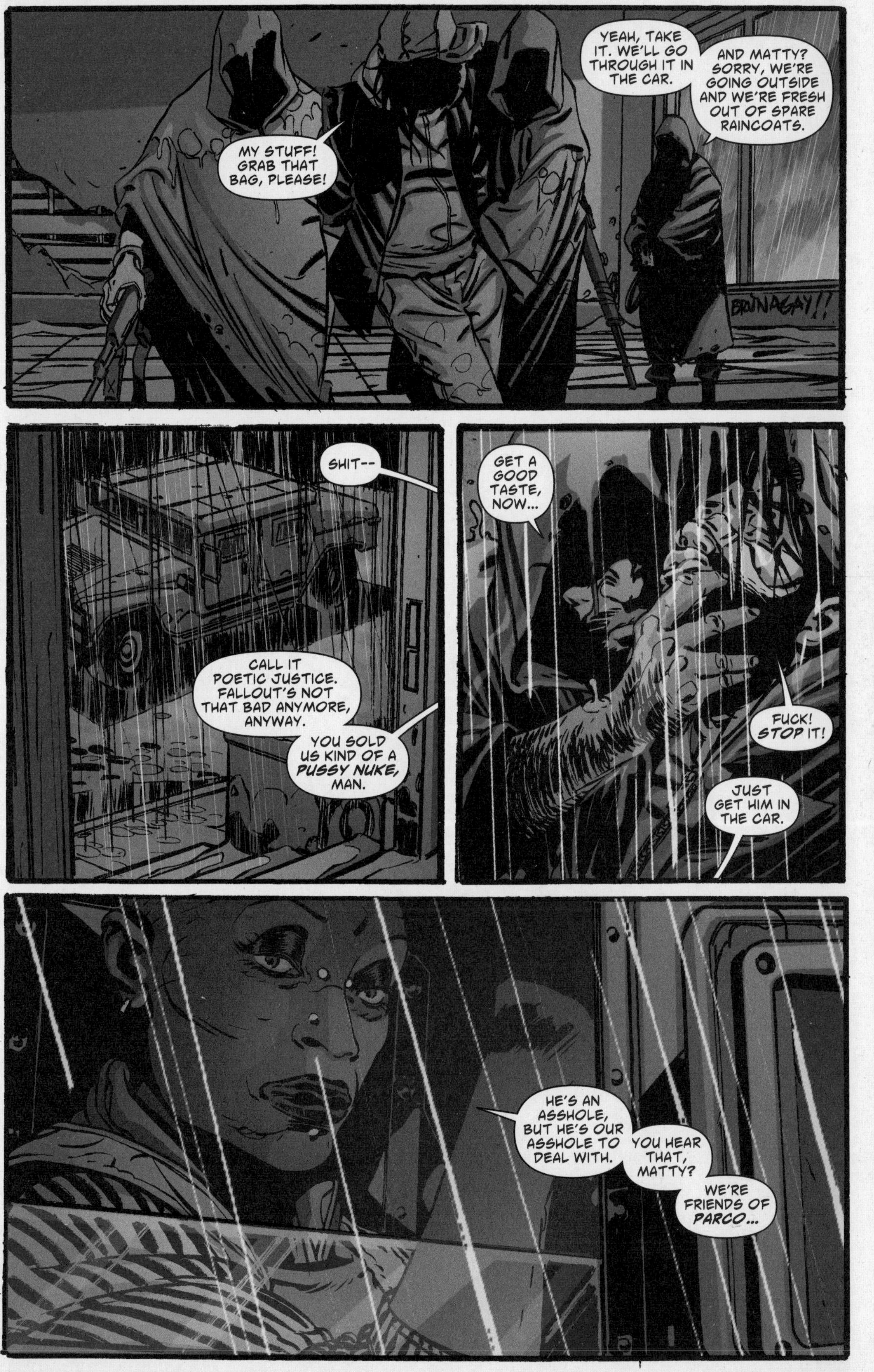

MY STUFF! GRAB THAT BAG, PLEASE!
YEAH, TAKE IT. WE'LL GO THROUGH IT IN THE CAR.
AND MATTY? SORRY, WE'RE GOING OUTSIDE AND WE'RE FRESH OUT OF SPARE RAINCOATS.
SHIT--
CALL IT POETIC JUSTICE. FALLOUT'S NOT THAT BAD ANYMORE, ANYWAY.
YOU SOLD US KIND OF A *PUSSY NUKE*, MAN.
GET A GOOD TASTE, NOW...
FUCK! *STOP* IT!
JUST GET HIM IN THE CAR.
HE'S AN ASSHOLE, BUT HE'S OUR ASSHOLE TO DEAL WITH.
YOU HEAR THAT, MATTY?
WE'RE FRIENDS OF *PARCO*...

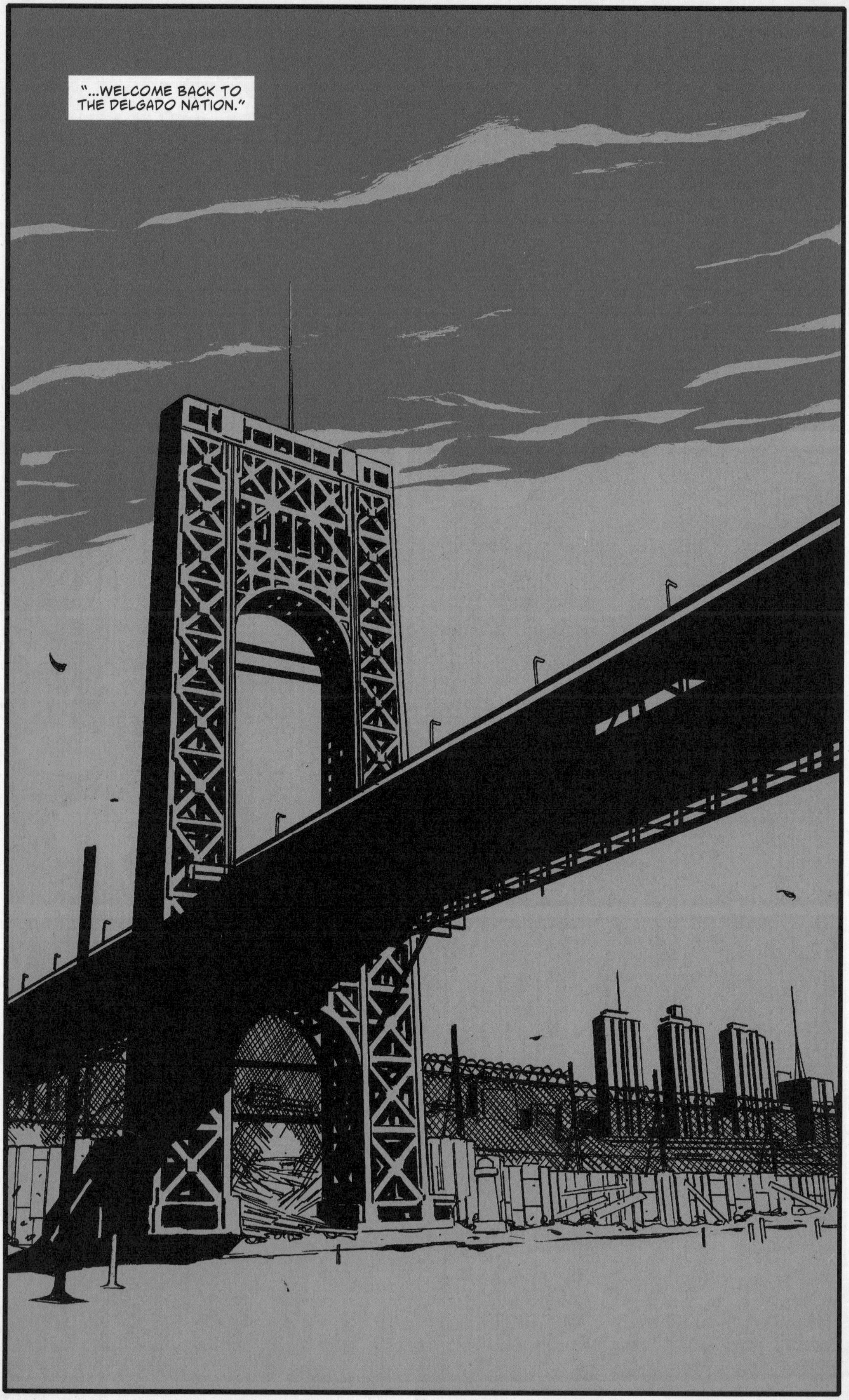
"...WELCOME BACK TO THE DELGADO NATION."

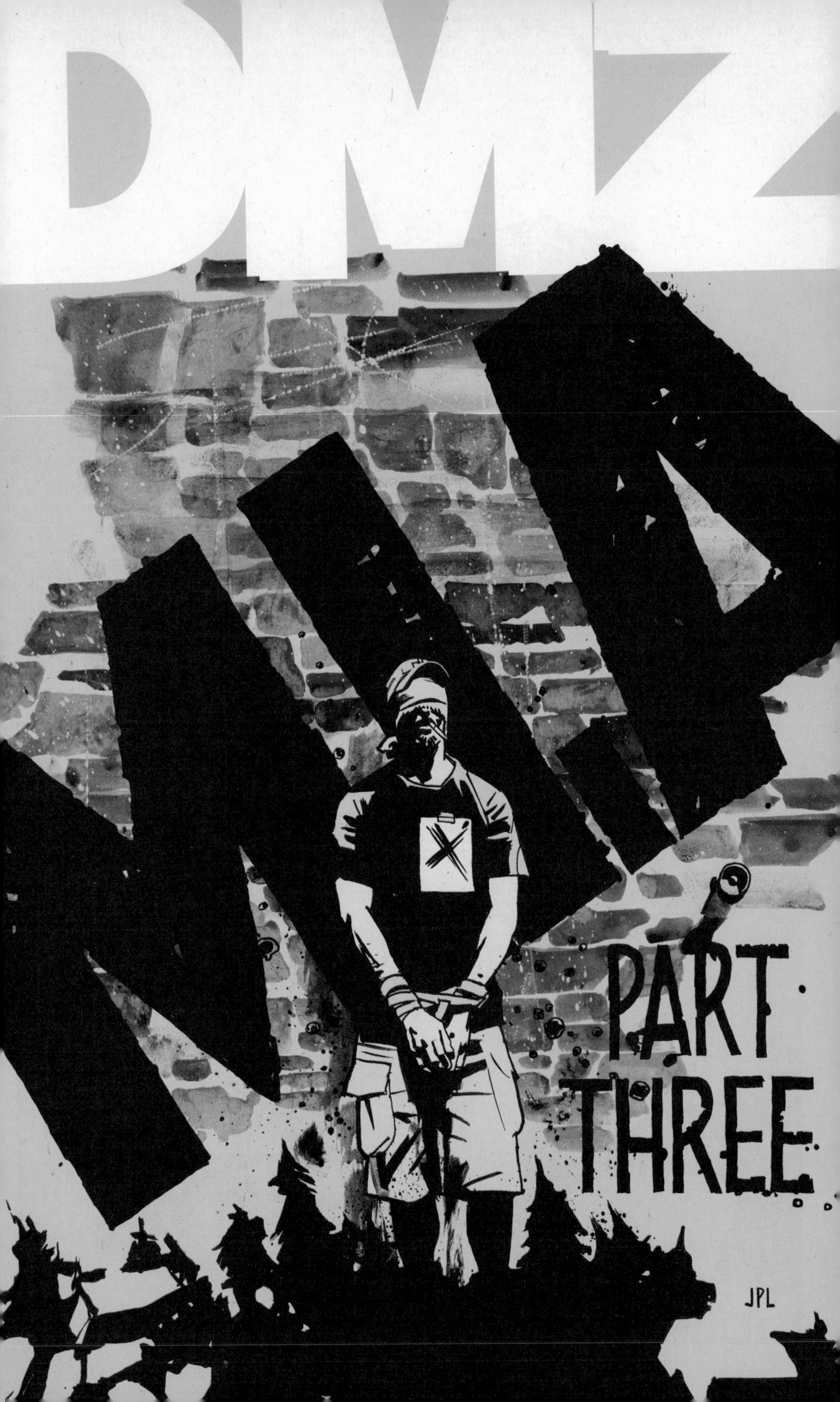
DMZ
PART THREE
JPL

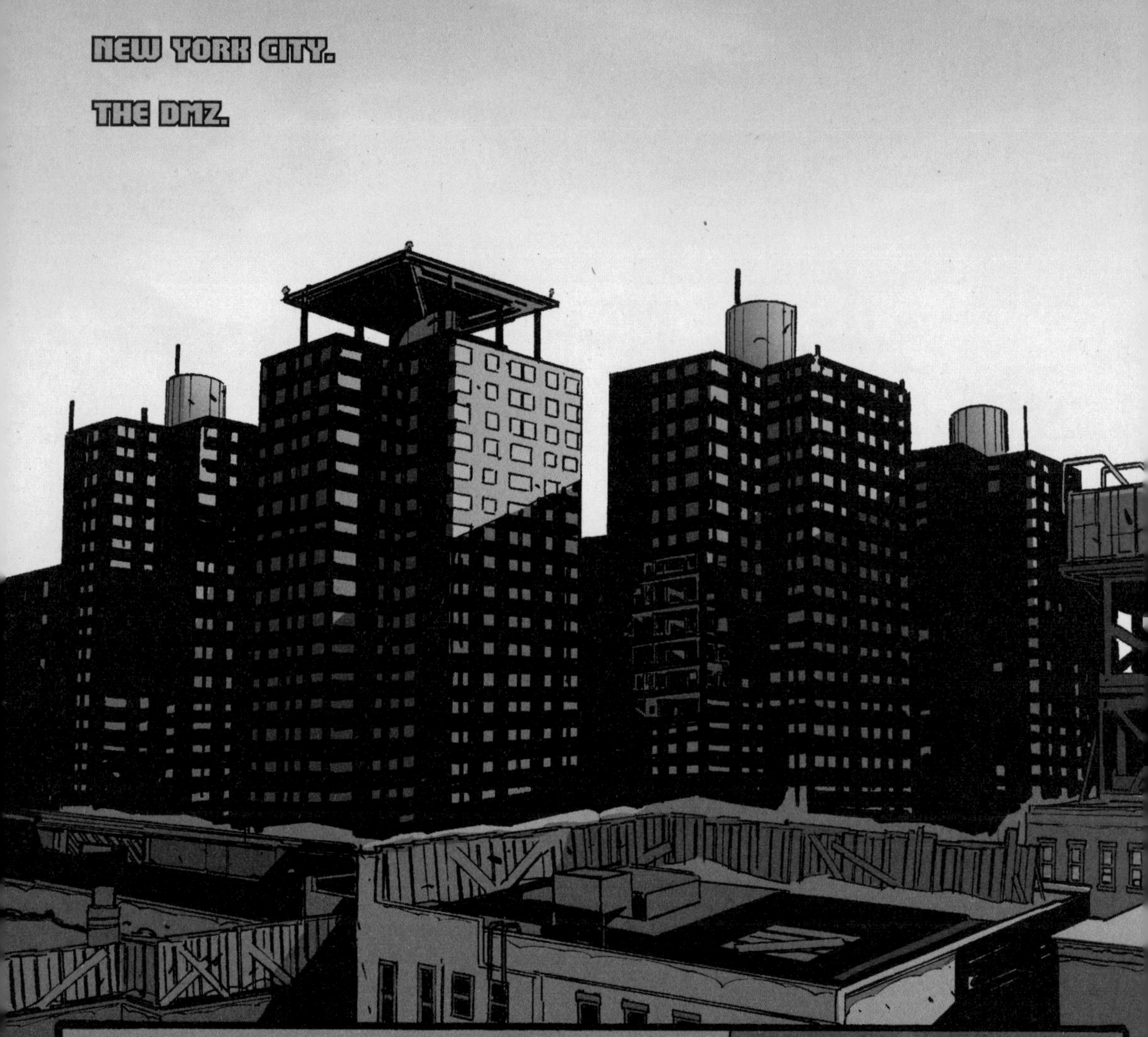
NEW YORK CITY.
THE DMZ.

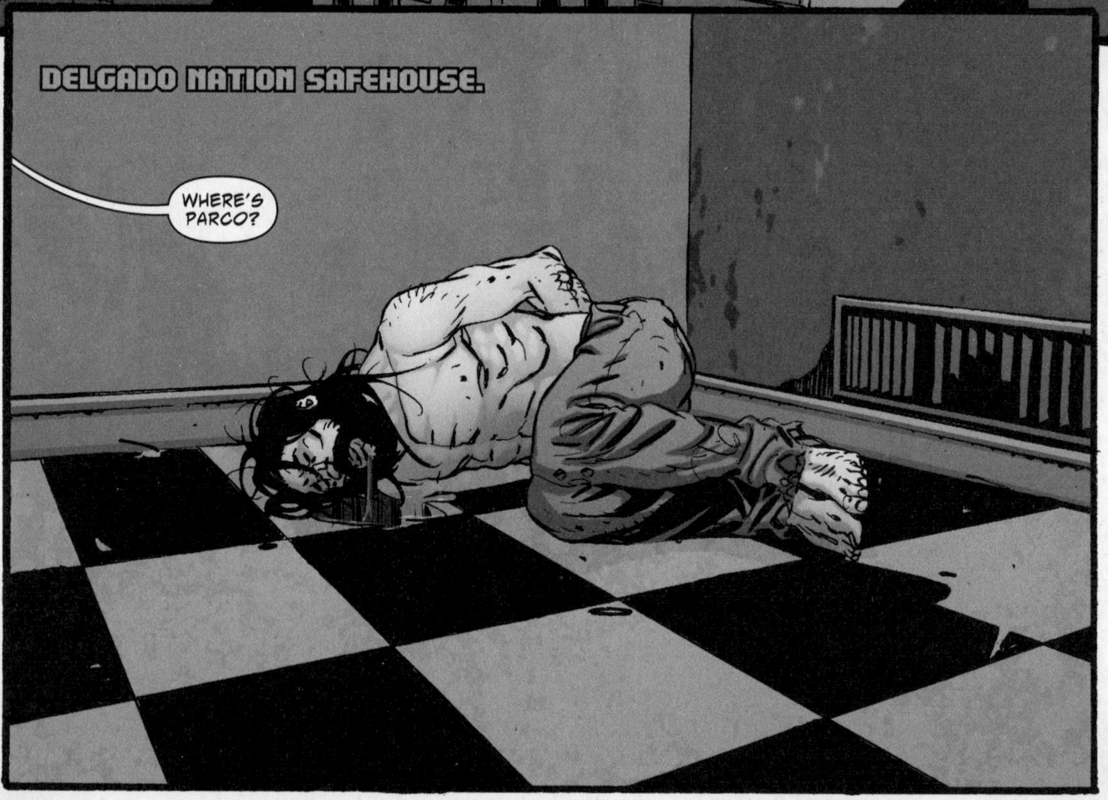
DELGADO NATION SAFEHOUSE.
WHERE'S PARCO?

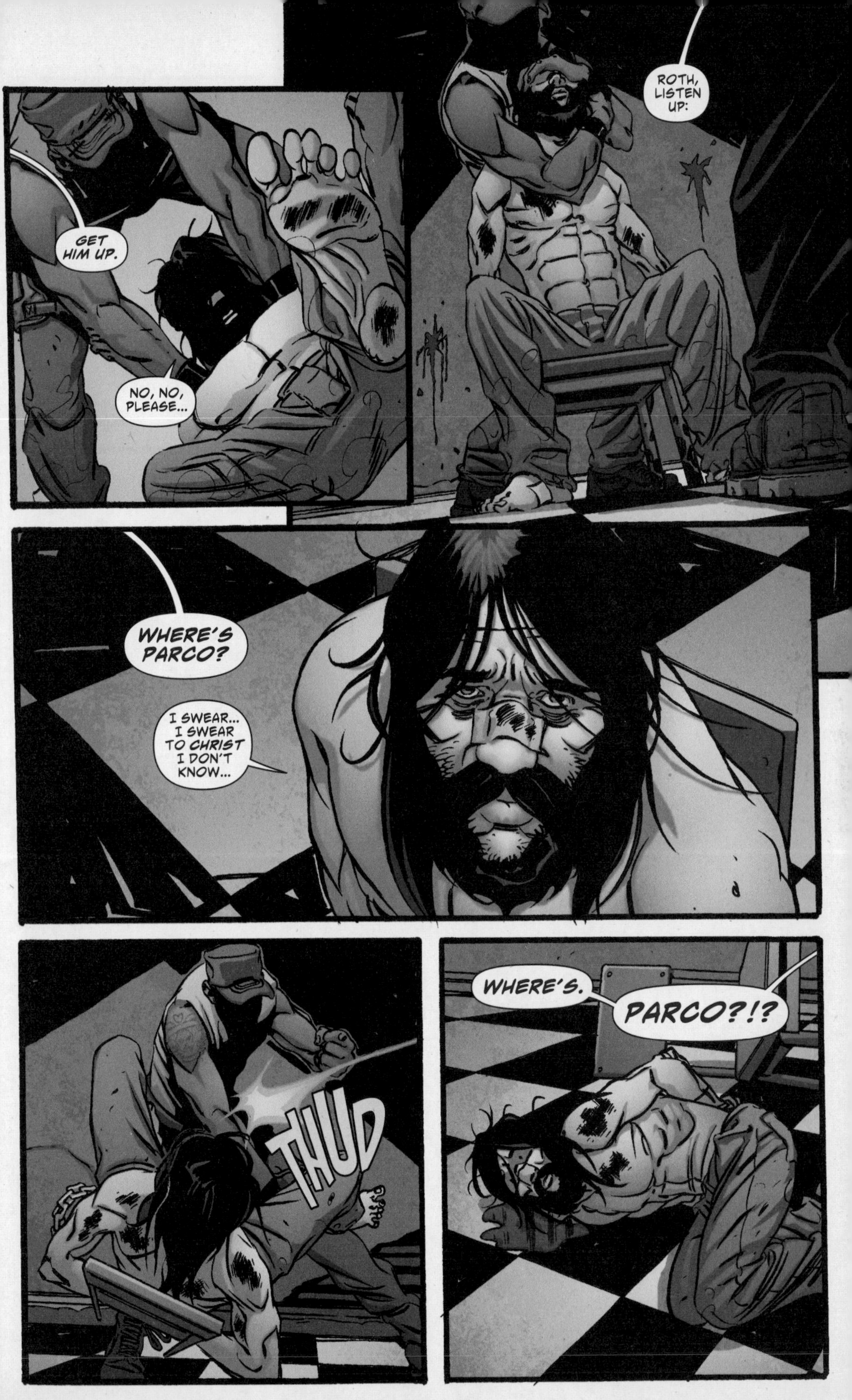
GET HIM UP.
NO, NO, PLEASE...
ROTH, LISTEN UP:
WHERE'S PARCO?
I SWEAR... I SWEAR TO CHRIST I DON'T KNOW...
THUD
WHERE'S.
PARCO?!?

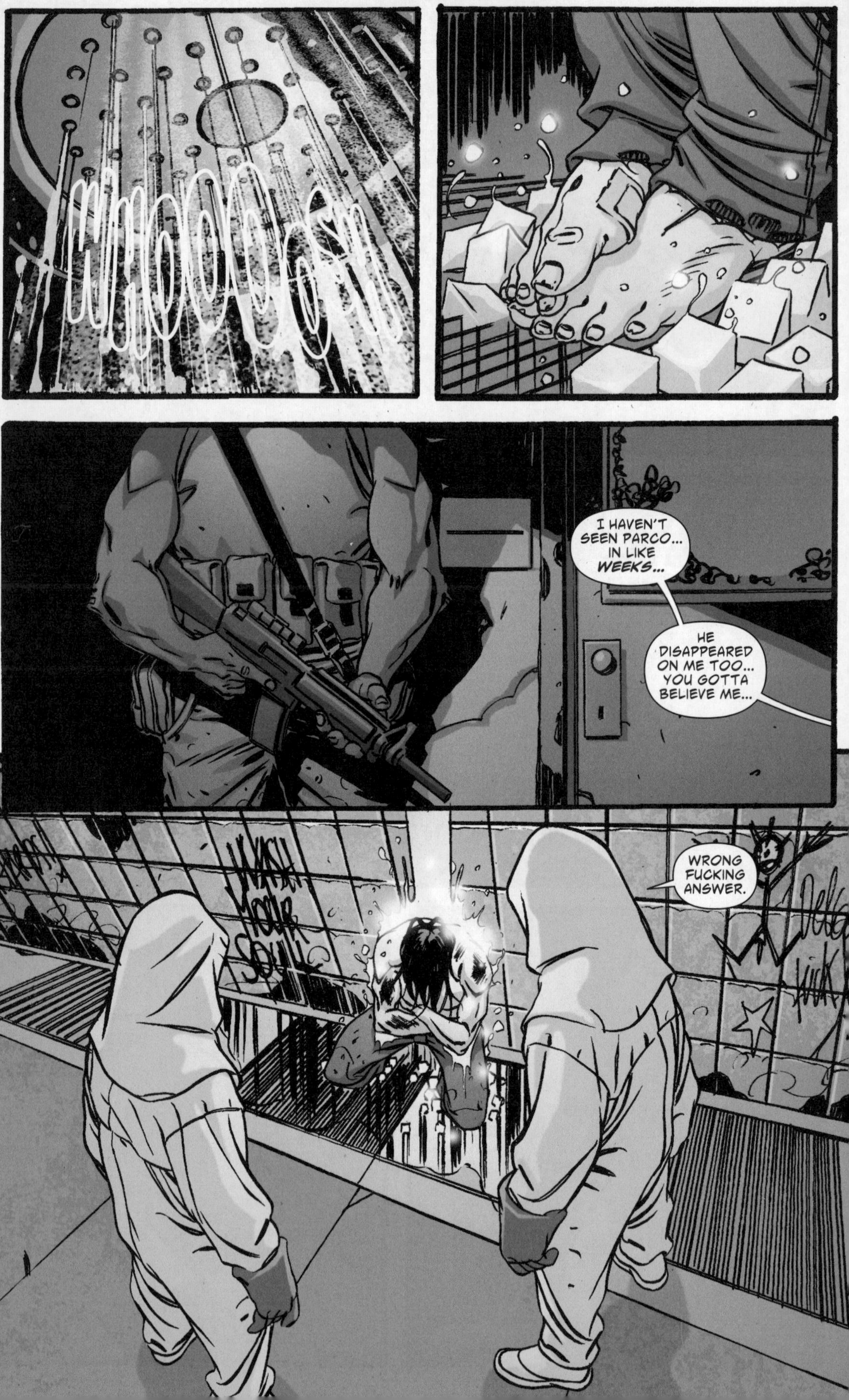
I HAVEN'T SEEN PARCO... IN LIKE WEEKS...
HE DISAPPEARED ON ME TOO... YOU GOTTA BELIEVE ME...
WASH YOUR SOUL
WRONG FUCKING ANSWER.

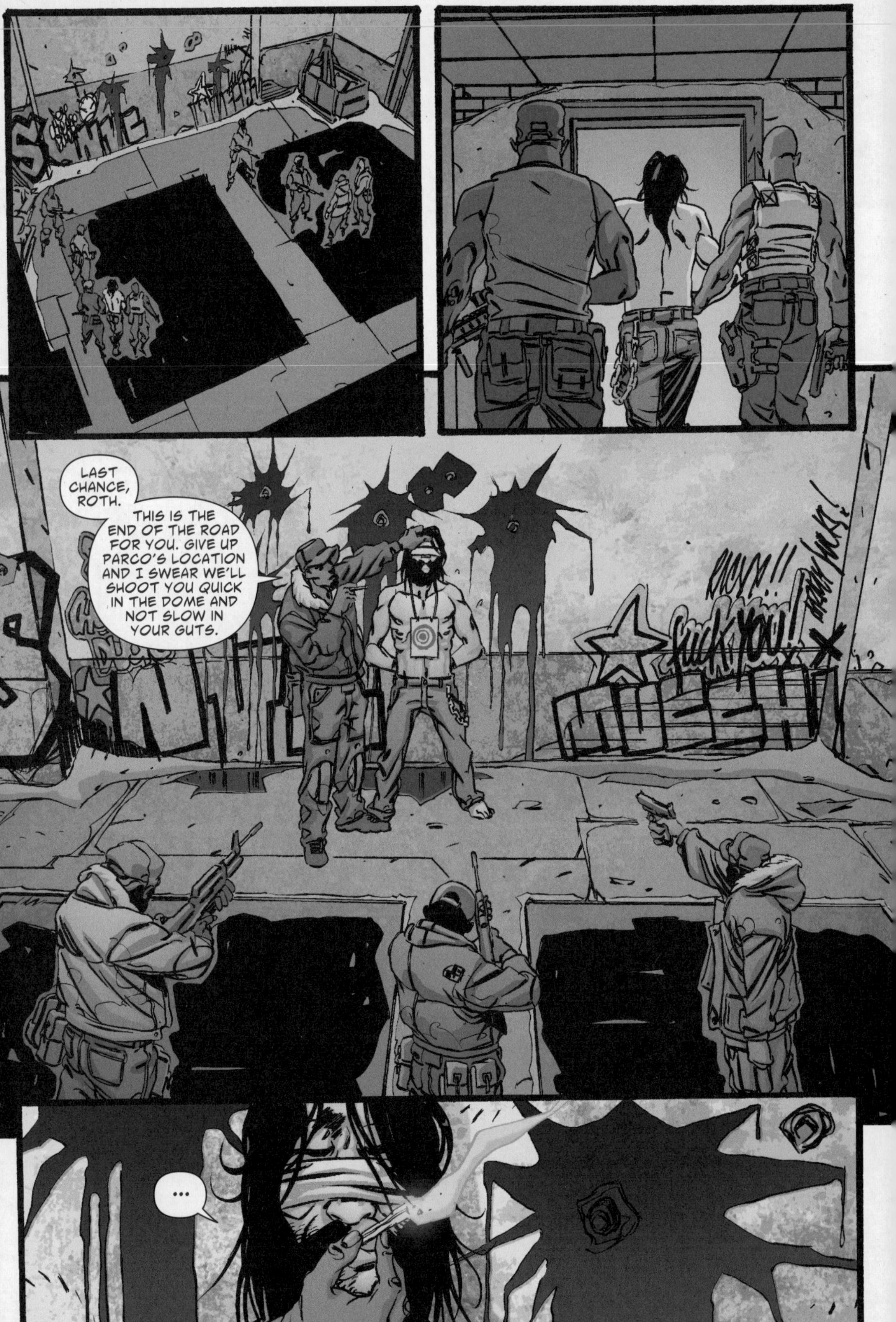
LAST CHANCE, ROTH.
THIS IS THE END OF THE ROAD FOR YOU. GIVE UP PARCO'S LOCATION AND I SWEAR WE'LL SHOOT YOU QUICK IN THE DOME AND NOT SLOW IN YOUR GUTS.
fuck you!
...

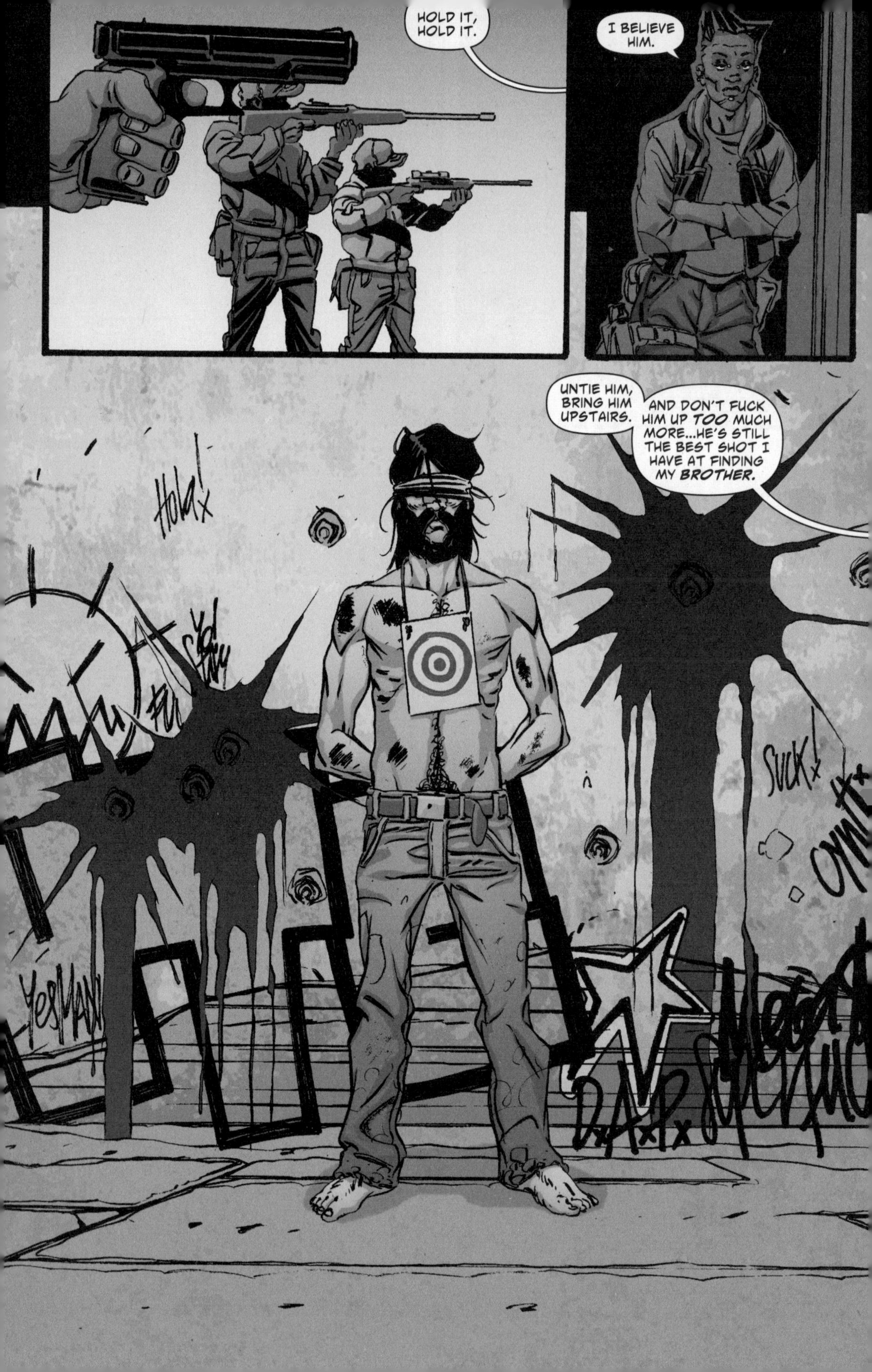
HOLD IT, HOLD IT.
I BELIEVE HIM.
UNTIE HIM, BRING HIM UPSTAIRS.
AND DON'T FUCK HIM UP TOO MUCH MORE...HE'S STILL THE BEST SHOT I HAVE AT FINDING MY BROTHER.
Hola!
SUCK!

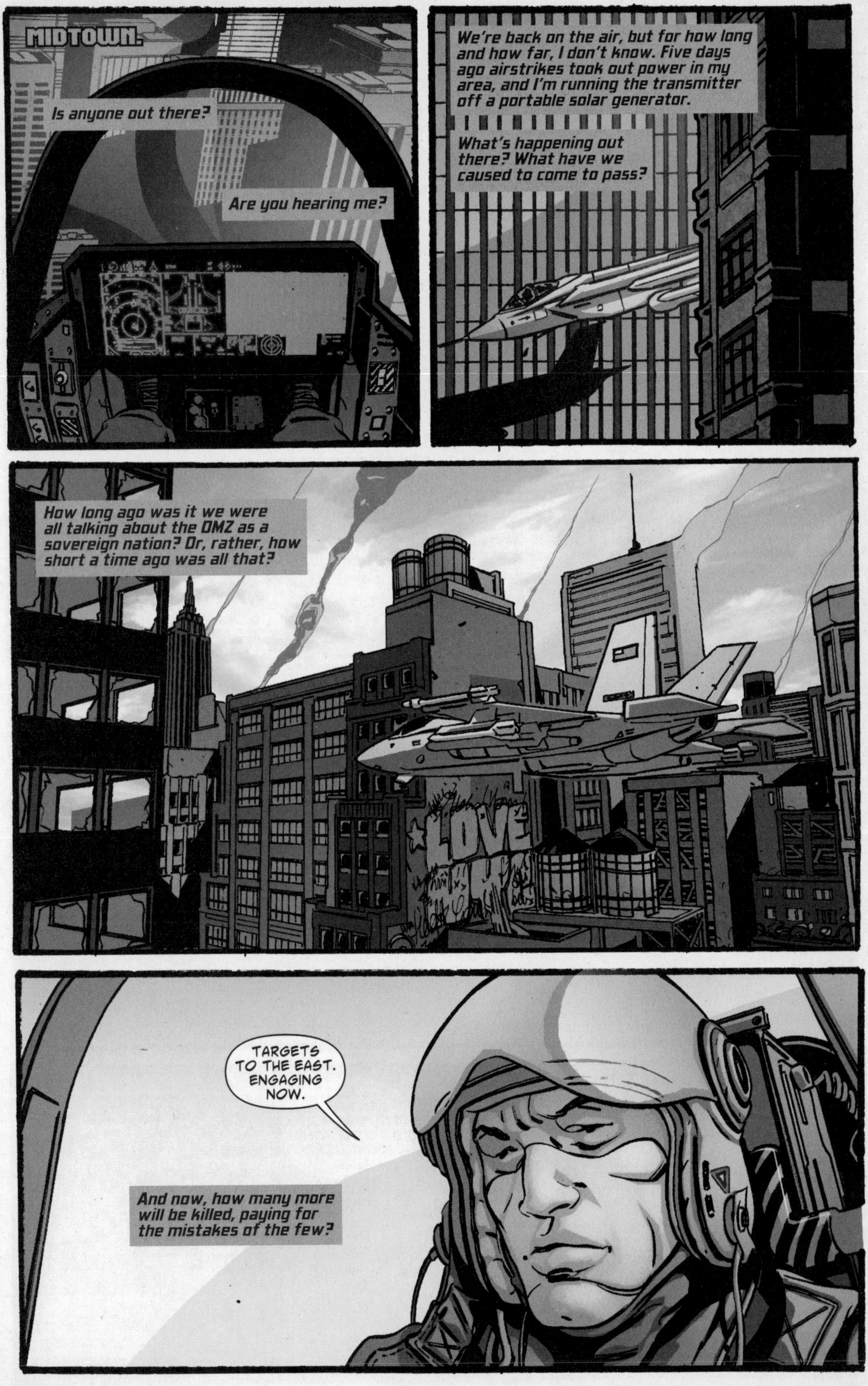
MIDTOWN.
Is anyone out there?
Are you hearing me?
We're back on the air, but for how long and how far, I don't know. Five days ago airstrikes took out power in my area, and I'm running the transmitter off a portable solar generator.
What's happening out there? What have we caused to come to pass?
How long ago was it we were all talking about the DMZ as a sovereign nation? Or, rather, how short a time ago was all that?
LOVE
TARGETS TO THE EAST. ENGAGING NOW.
And now, how many more will be killed, paying for the mistakes of the few?

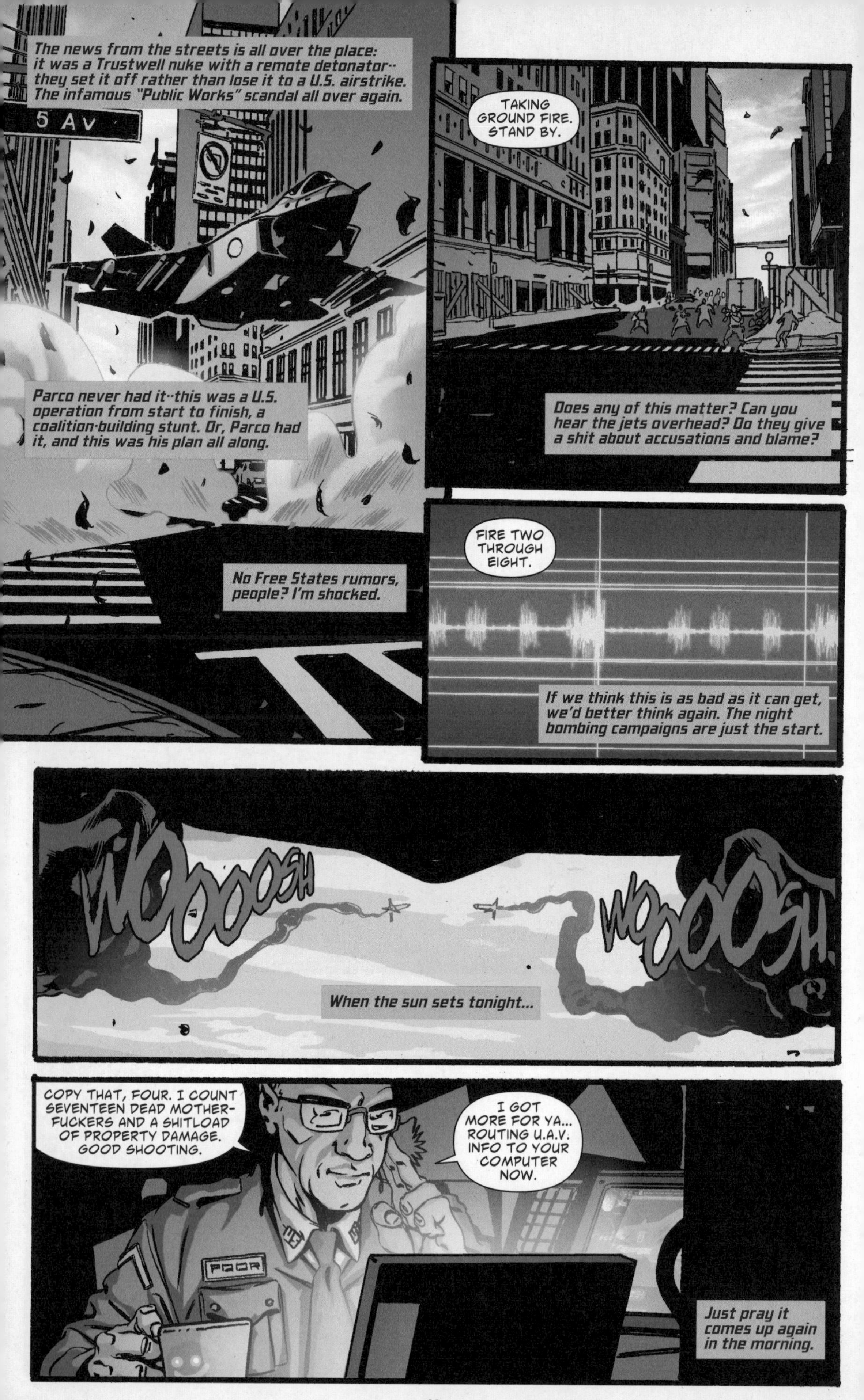
The news from the streets is all over the place: it was a Trustwell nuke with a remote detonator-- they set it off rather than lose it to a U.S. airstrike. The infamous "Public Works" scandal all over again.
5 Av
Parco never had it--this was a U.S. operation from start to finish, a coalition-building stunt. Or, Parco had it, and this was his plan all along.
No Free States rumors, people? I'm shocked.
TAKING GROUND FIRE. STAND BY.
Does any of this matter? Can you hear the jets overhead? Do they give a shit about accusations and blame?
FIRE TWO THROUGH EIGHT.
If we think this is as bad as it can get, we'd better think again. The night bombing campaigns are just the start.
WOOOOSH
WOOOOSH
When the sun sets tonight...
COPY THAT, FOUR. I COUNT SEVENTEEN DEAD MOTHER-FUCKERS AND A SHITLOAD OF PROPERTY DAMAGE. GOOD SHOOTING.
I GOT MORE FOR YA... ROUTING U.A.V. INFO TO YOUR COMPUTER NOW.
Just pray it comes up again in the morning.

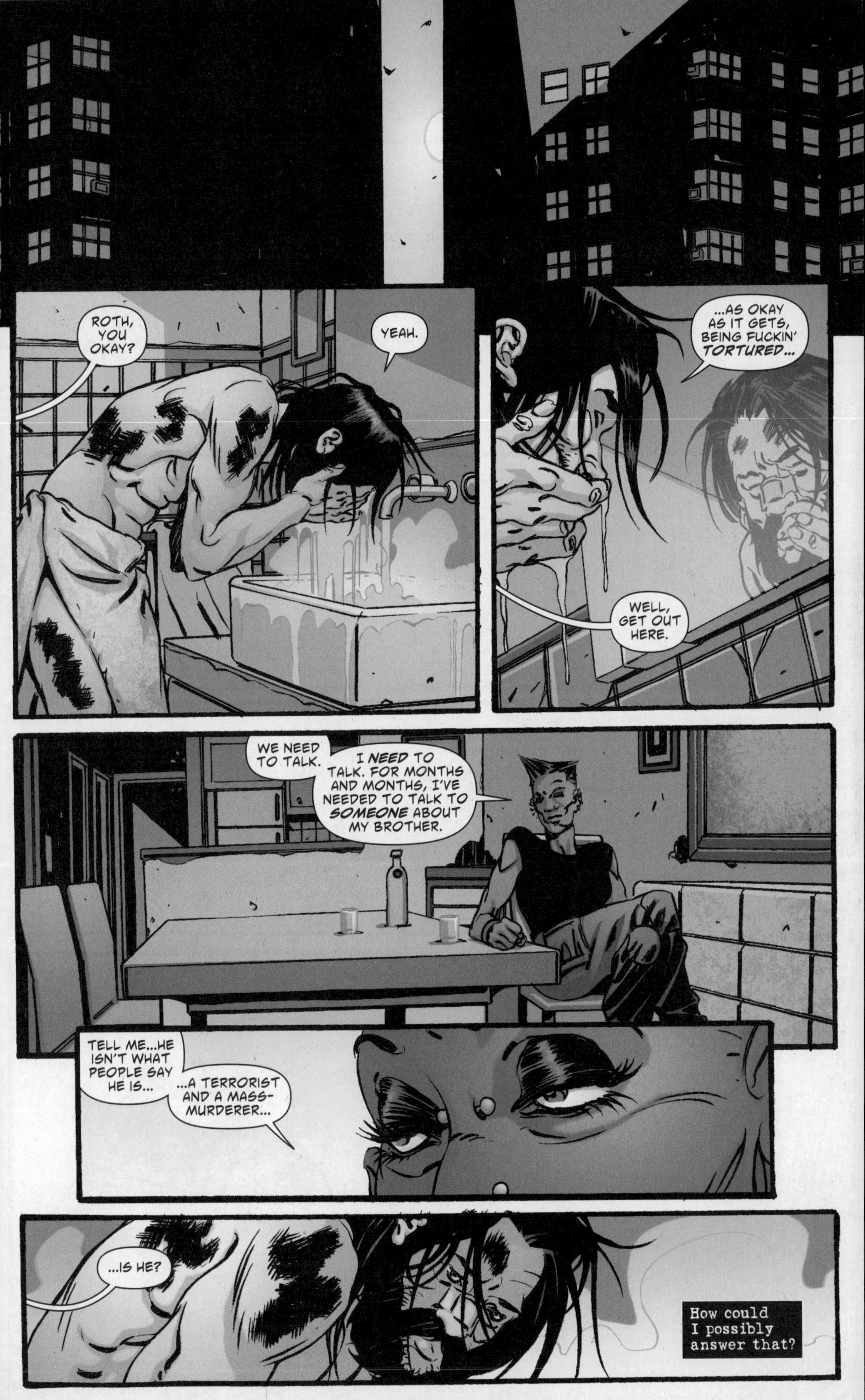
ROTH, YOU OKAY?
YEAH.
...AS OKAY AS IT GETS, BEING FUCKIN' TORTURED...
WELL, GET OUT HERE.
WE NEED TO TALK.
I NEED TO TALK. FOR MONTHS AND MONTHS, I'VE NEEDED TO TALK TO SOMEONE ABOUT MY BROTHER.
TELL ME...HE ISN'T WHAT PEOPLE SAY HE IS...
...A TERRORIST AND A MASS-MURDERER...
...IS HE?
How could I possibly answer that?

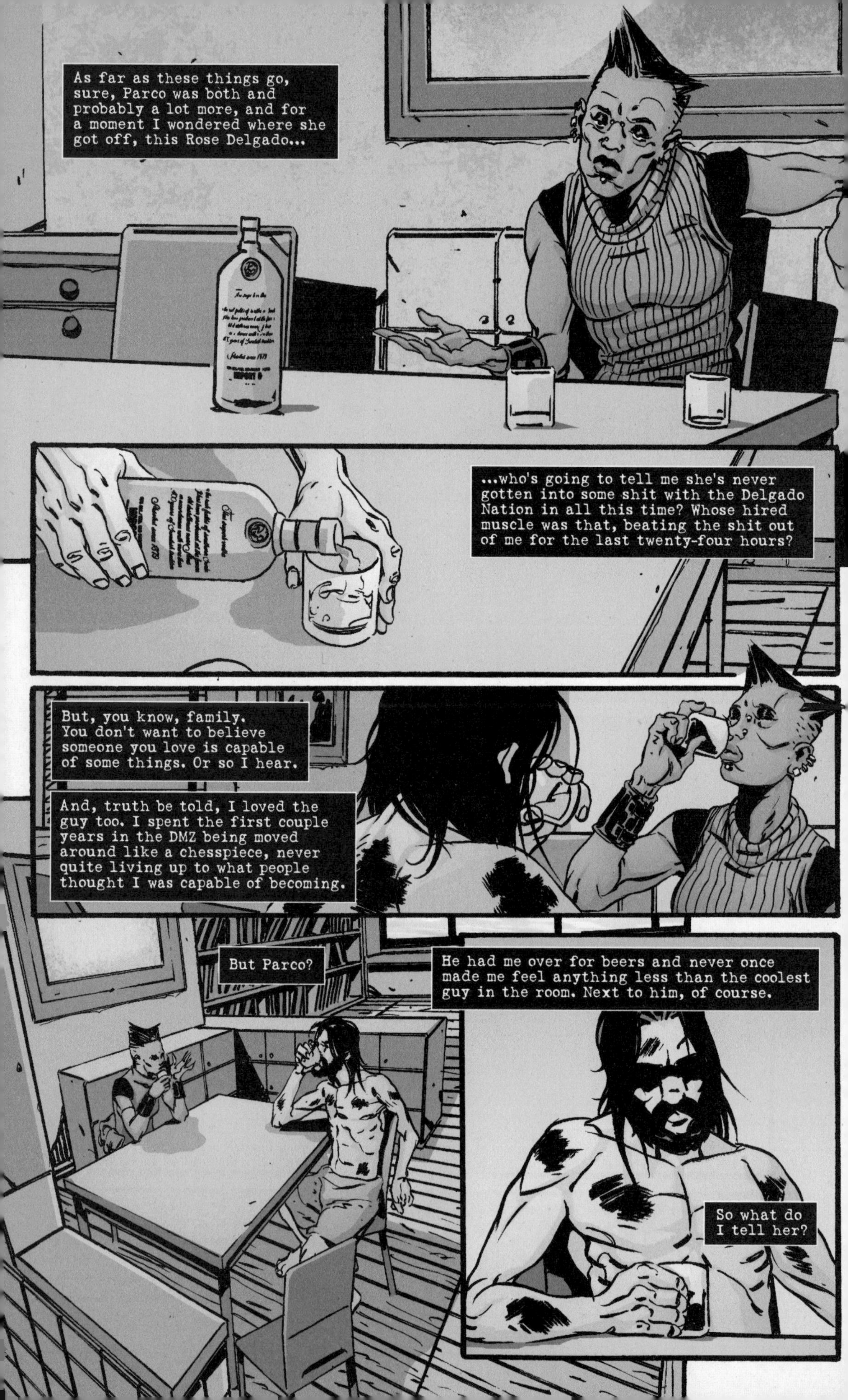
As far as these things go, sure, Parco was both and probably a lot more, and for a moment I wondered where she got off, this Rose Delgado...
...who's going to tell me she's never gotten into some shit with the Delgado Nation in all this time? Whose hired muscle was that, beating the shit out of me for the last twenty-four hours?
But, you know, family. You don't want to believe someone you love is capable of some things. Or so I hear.
And, truth be told, I loved the guy too. I spent the first couple years in the DMZ being moved around like a chesspiece, never quite living up to what people thought I was capable of becoming.
But Parco?
He had me over for beers and never once made me feel anything less than the coolest guy in the room. Next to him, of course.
So what do I tell her?

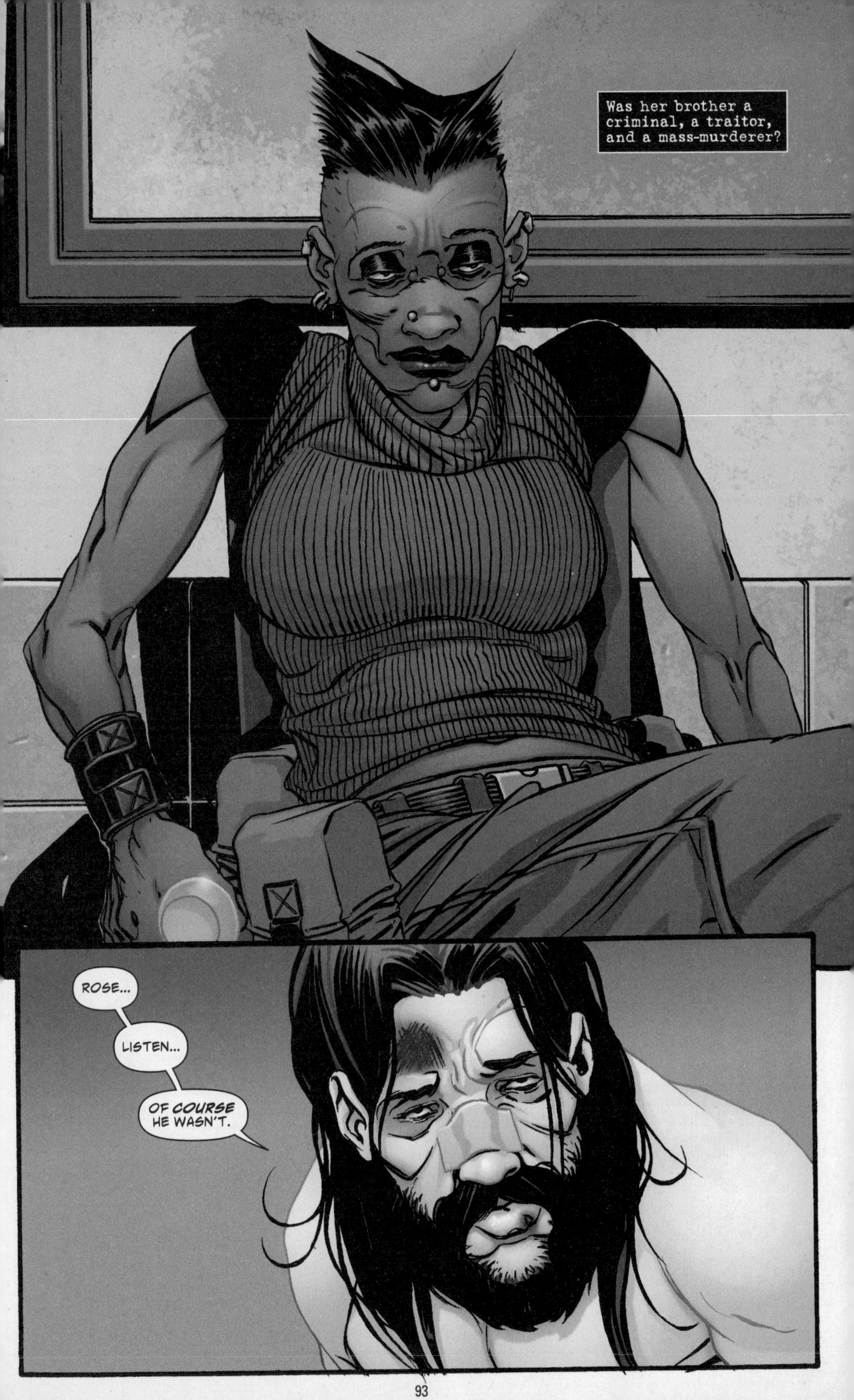
Was her brother a criminal, a traitor, and a mass-murderer?
ROSE...
LISTEN...
OF COURSE HE WASN'T.

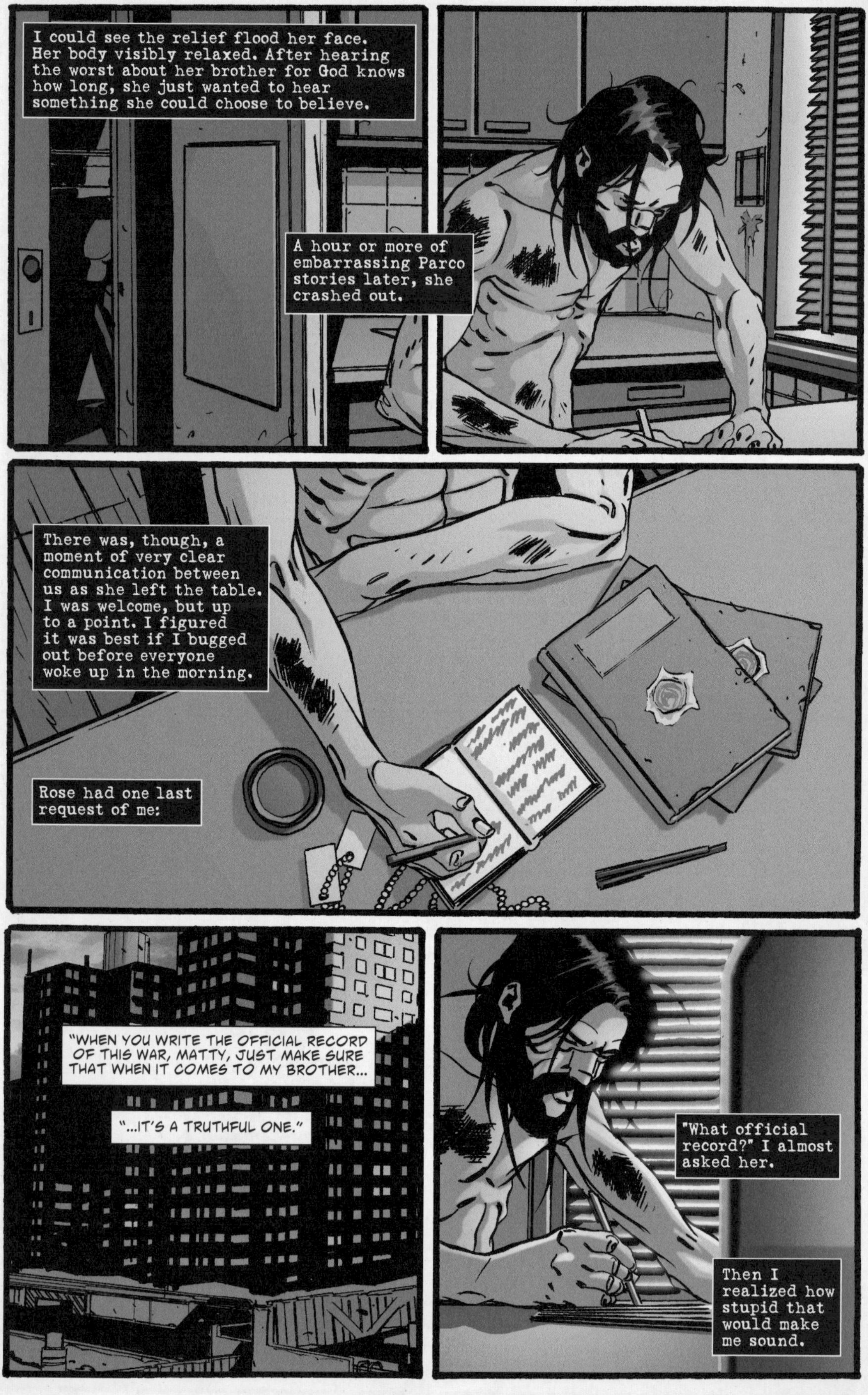
I could see the relief flood her face. Her body visibly relaxed. After hearing the worst about her brother for God knows how long, she just wanted to hear something she could choose to believe.
A hour or more of embarrassing Parco stories later, she crashed out.
There was, though, a moment of very clear communication between us as she left the table. I was welcome, but up to a point. I figured it was best if I bugged out before everyone woke up in the morning.
Rose had one last request of me:
"WHEN YOU WRITE THE OFFICIAL RECORD OF THIS WAR, MATTY, JUST MAKE SURE THAT WHEN IT COMES TO MY BROTHER...
"...IT'S A TRUTHFUL ONE."
"What official record?" I almost asked her.
Then I realized how stupid that would make me sound.

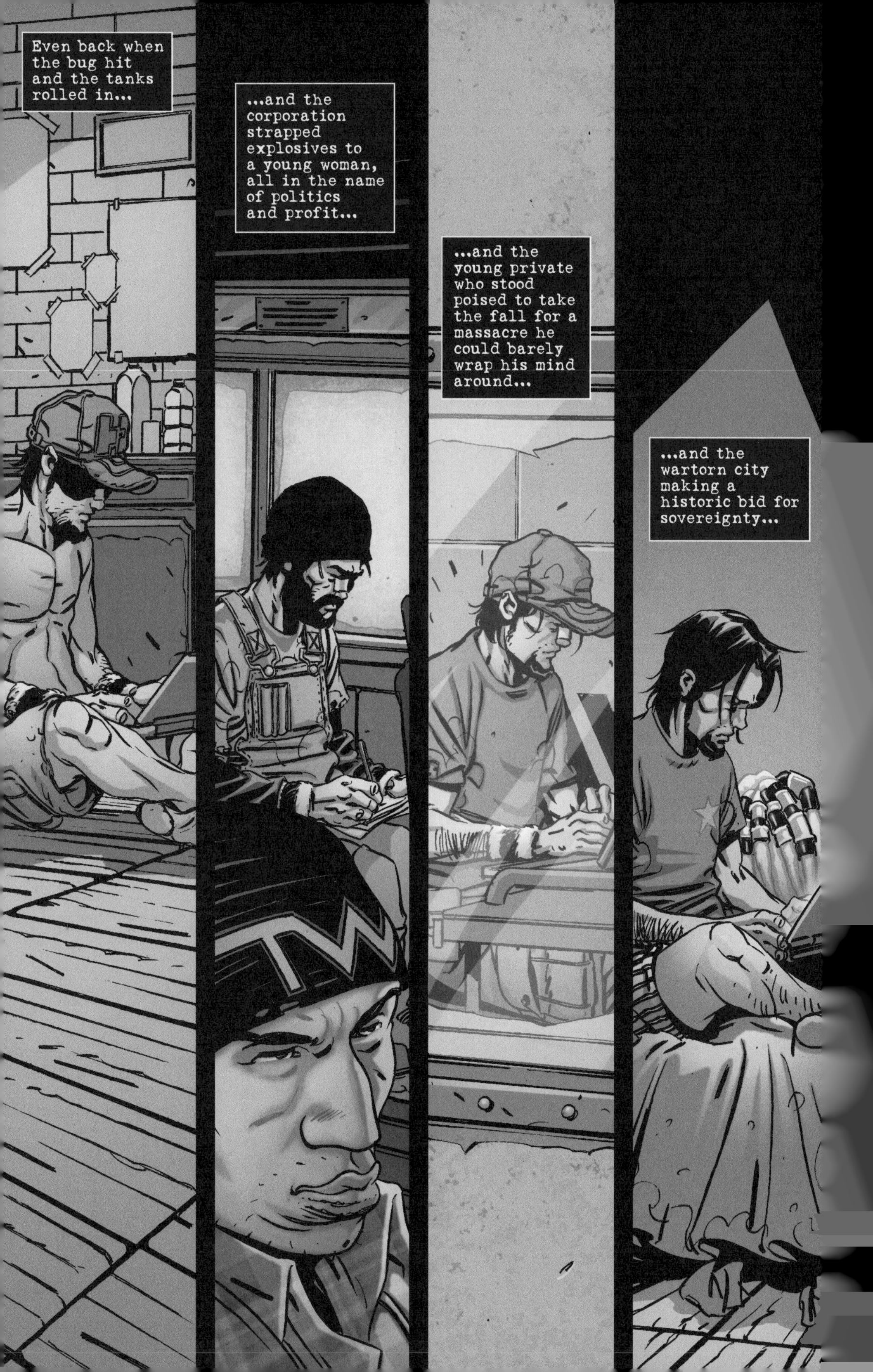
Even back when the bug hit and the tanks rolled in...
...and the corporation strapped explosives to a young woman, all in the name of politics and profit...
...and the young private who stood poised to take the fall for a massacre he could barely wrap his mind around...
...and the wartorn city making a historic bid for sovereignty...

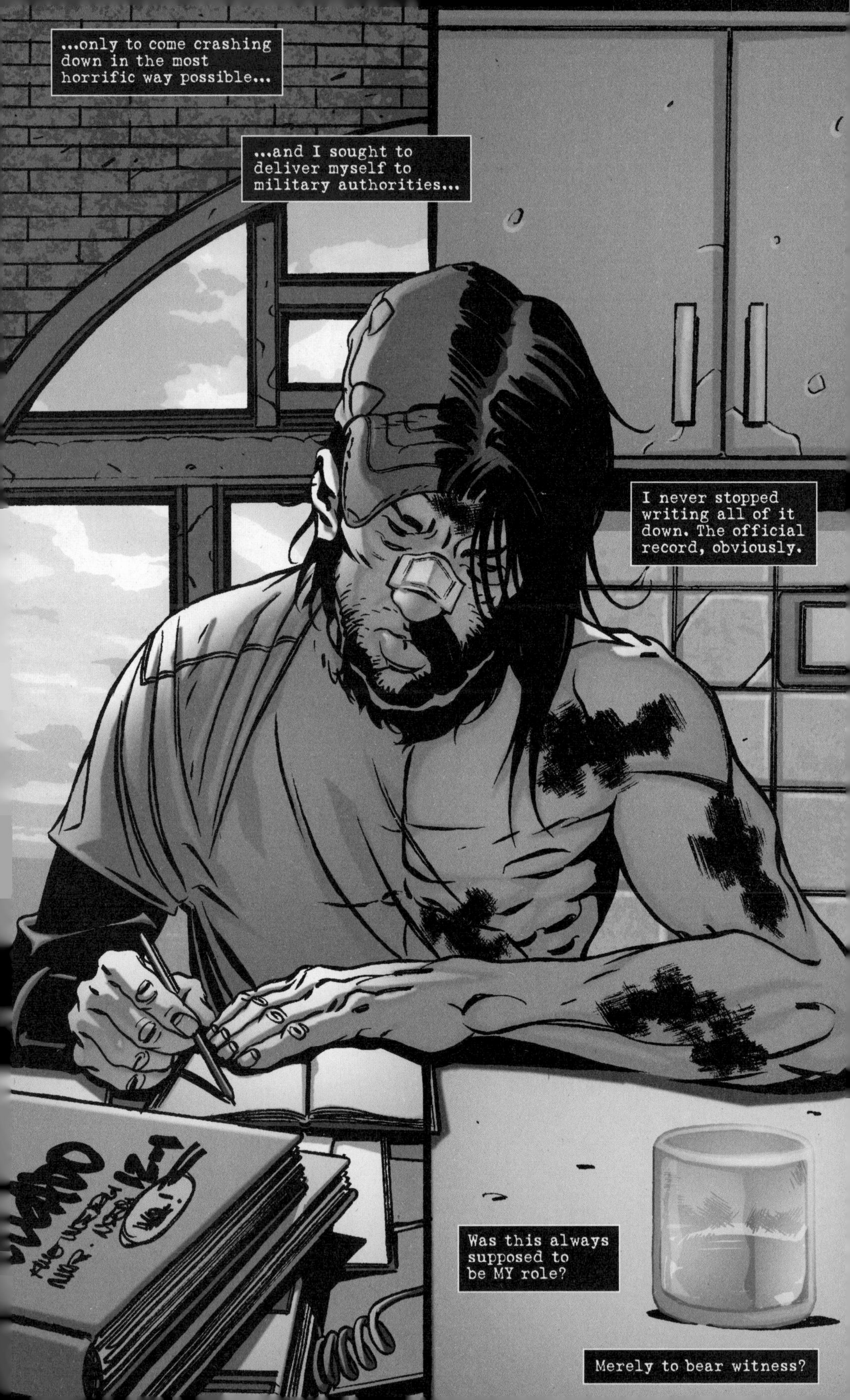

...only to come crashing down in the most horrific way possible...
...and I sought to deliver myself to military authorities...
I never stopped writing all of it down. The official record, obviously.
Was this always supposed to be MY role?
Merely to bear witness?

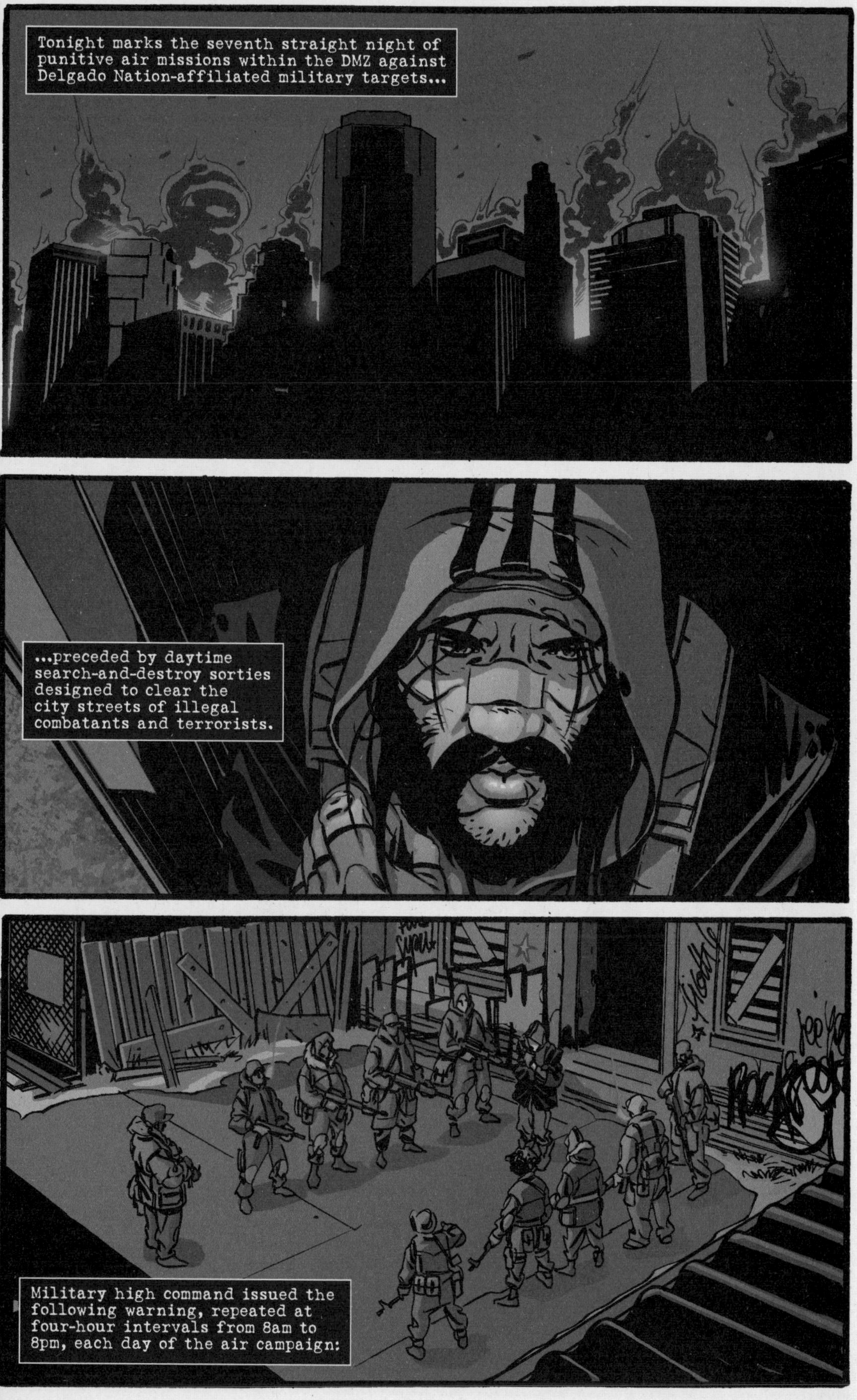
Tonight marks the seventh straight night of punitive air missions within the DMZ against Delgado Nation-affiliated military targets...
...preceded by daytime search-and-destroy sorties designed to clear the city streets of illegal combatants and terrorists.
Military high command issued the following warning, repeated at four-hour intervals from 8am to 8pm, each day of the air campaign:

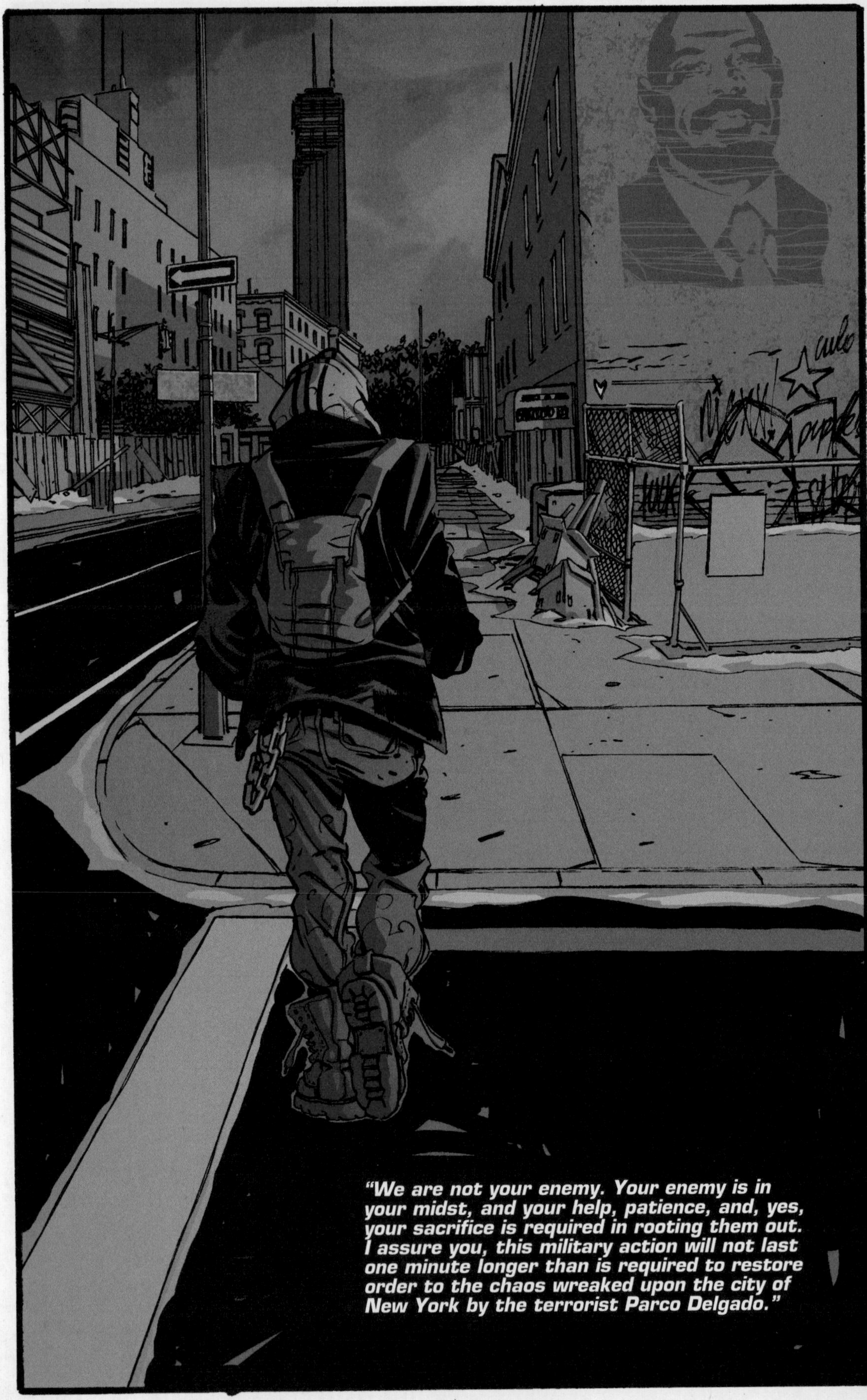
"We are not your enemy. Your enemy is in your midst, and your help, patience, and, yes, your sacrifice is required in rooting them out. I assure you, this military action will not last one minute longer than is required to restore order to the chaos wreaked upon the city of New York by the terrorist Parco Delgado."

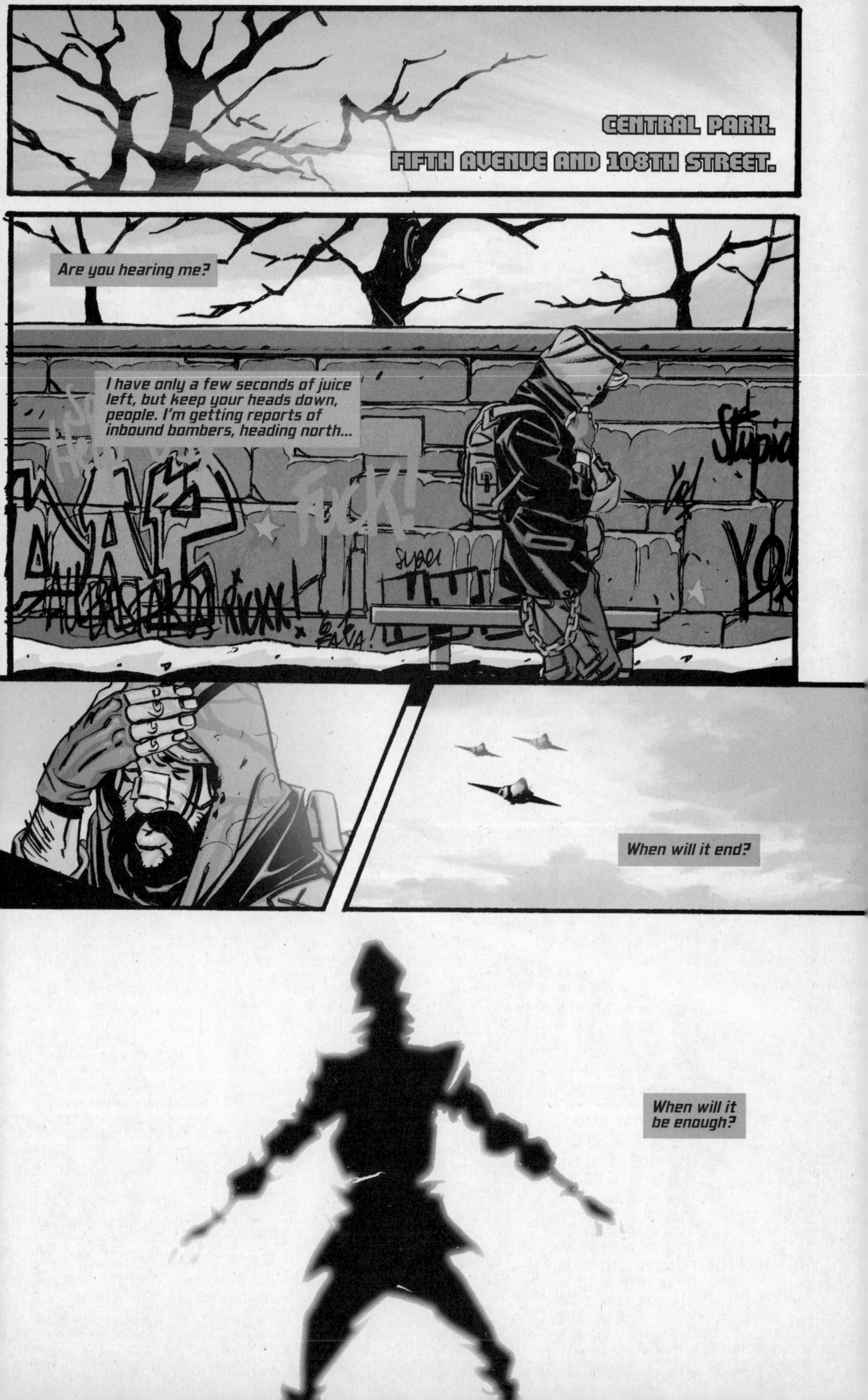
CENTRAL PARK.
FIFTH AVENUE AND 108TH STREET.
Are you hearing me?
I have only a few seconds of juice left, but keep your heads down, people. I'm getting reports of inbound bombers, heading north...
When will it end?
When will it be enough?

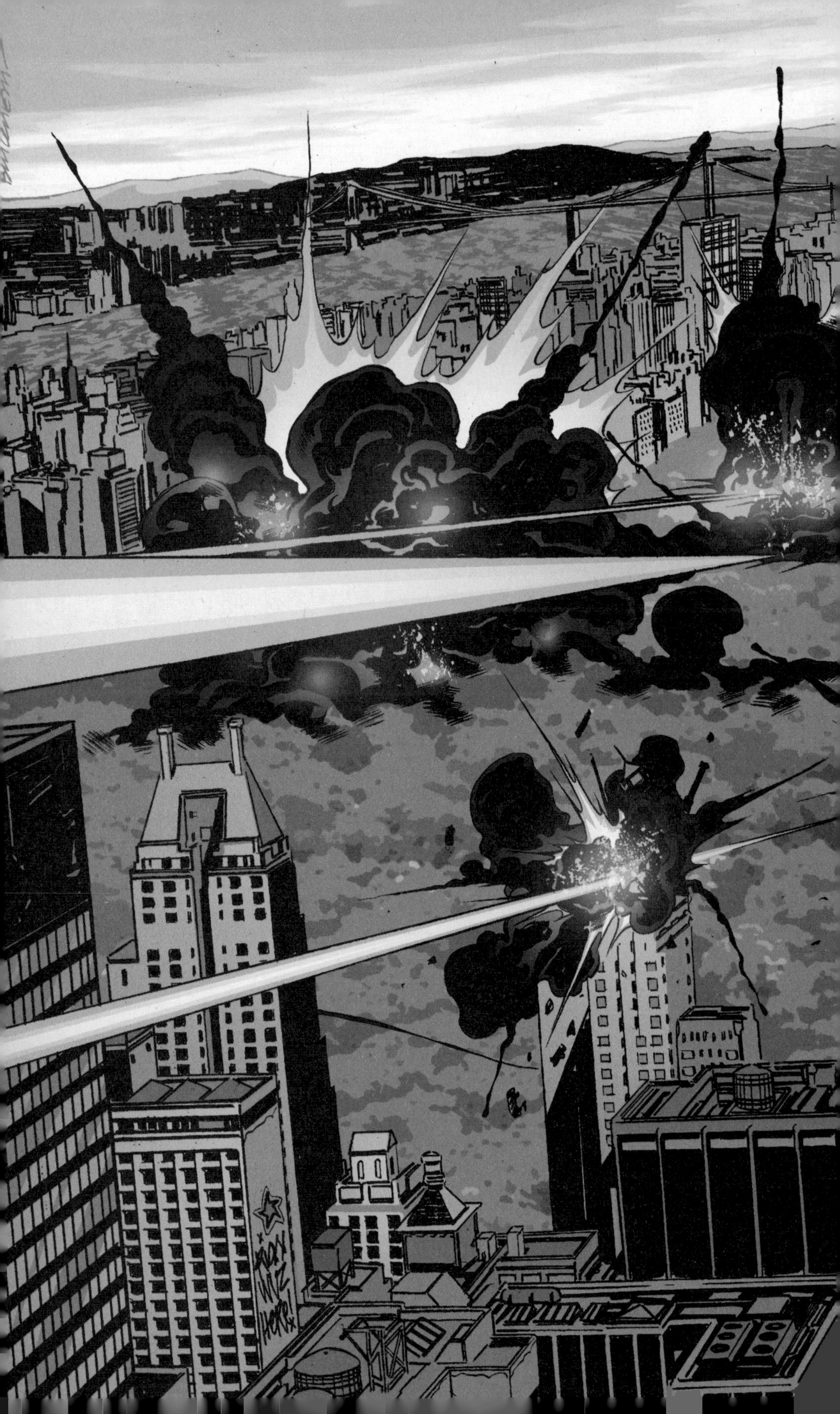
WUZ HERE!

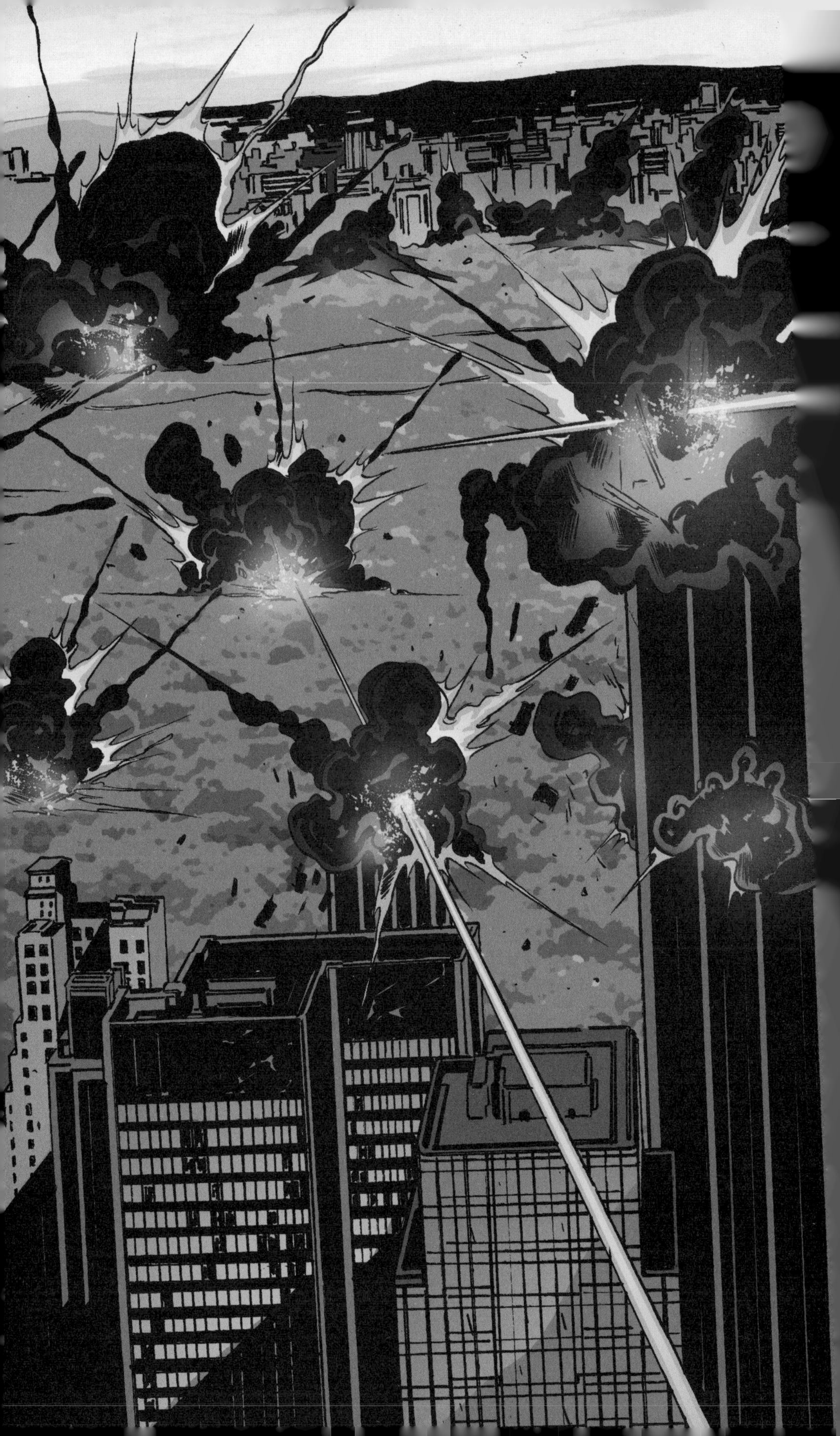

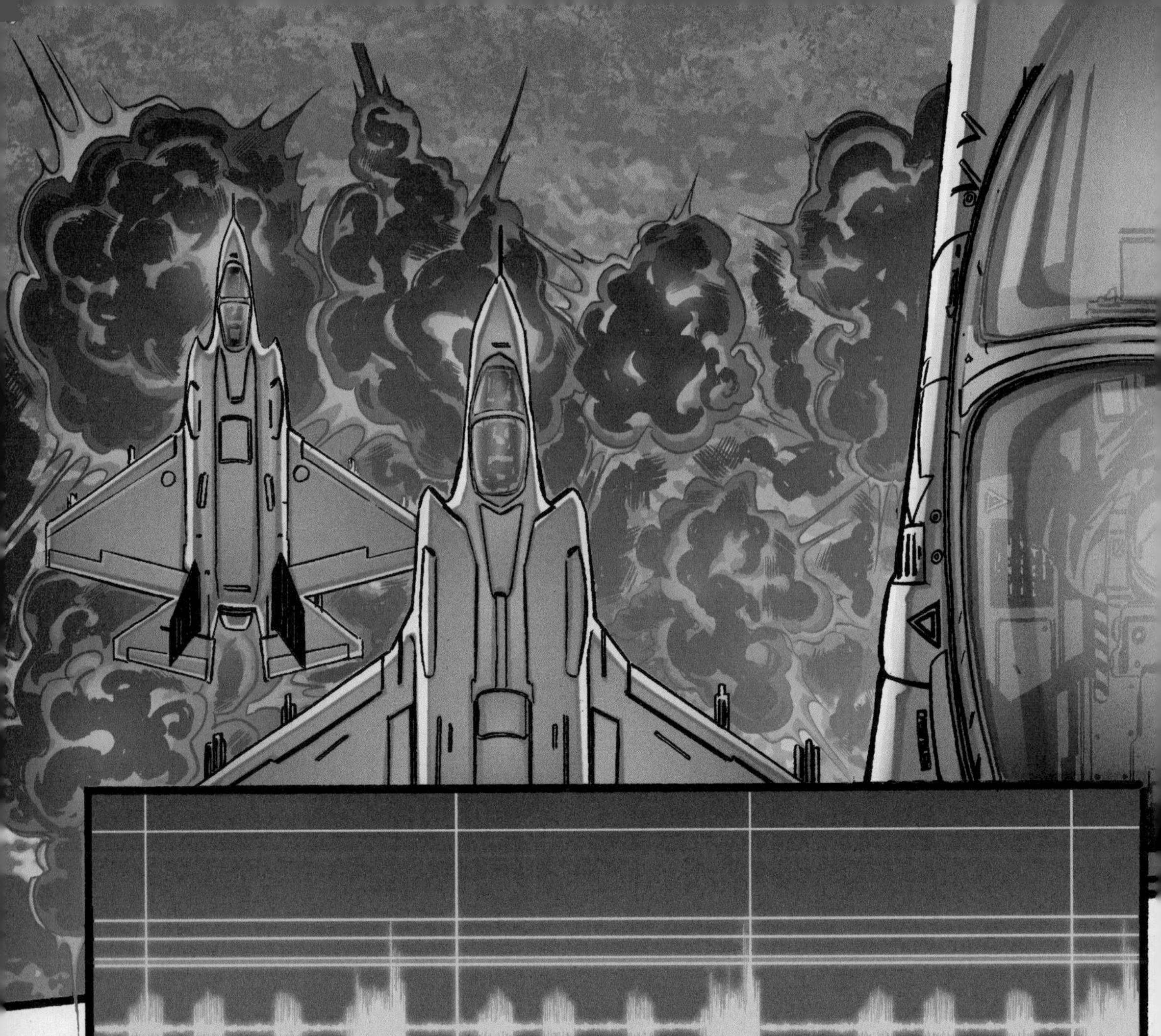

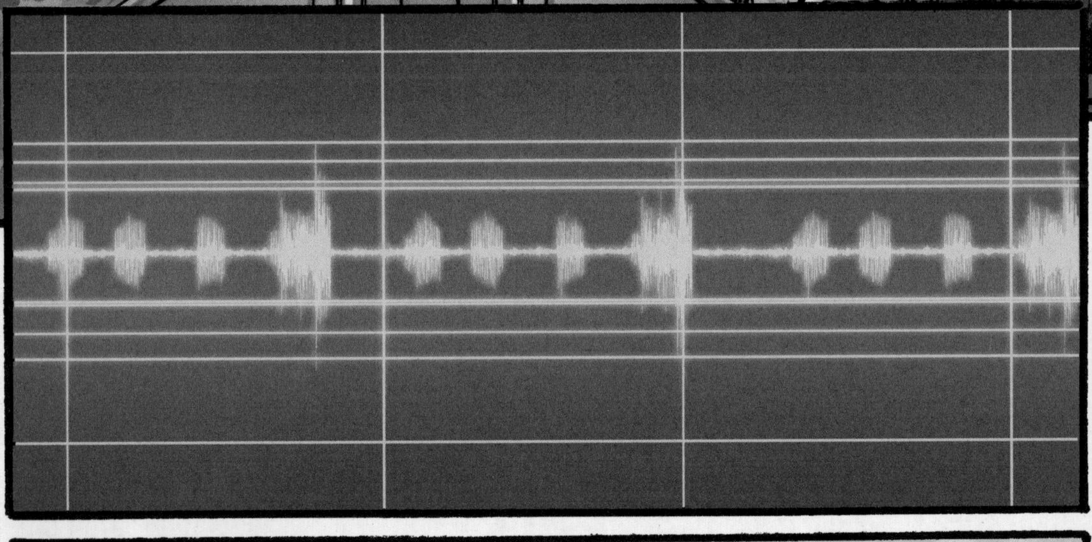

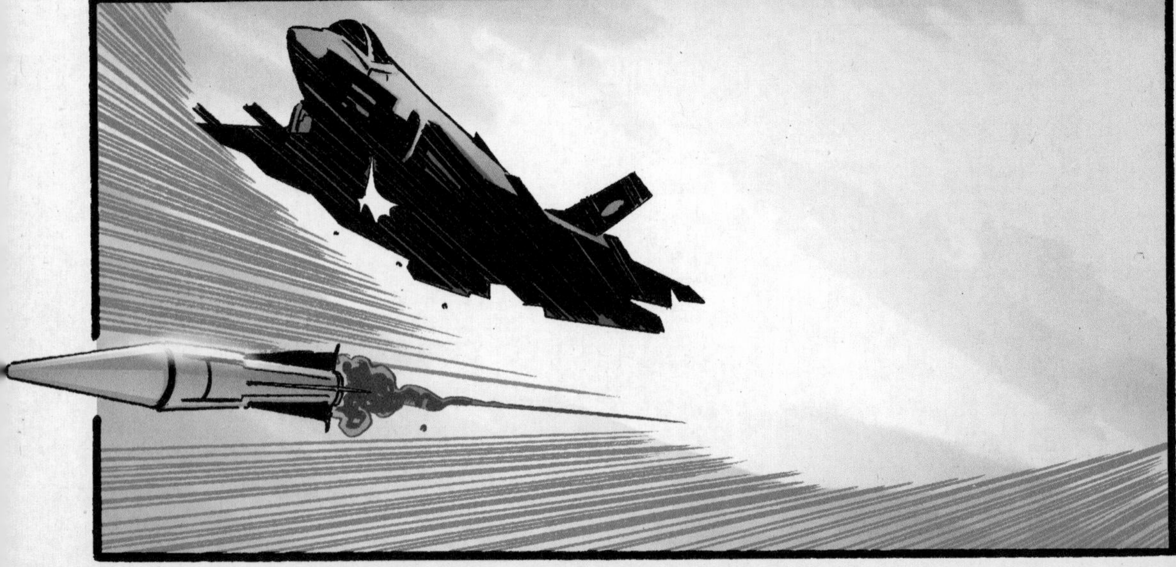

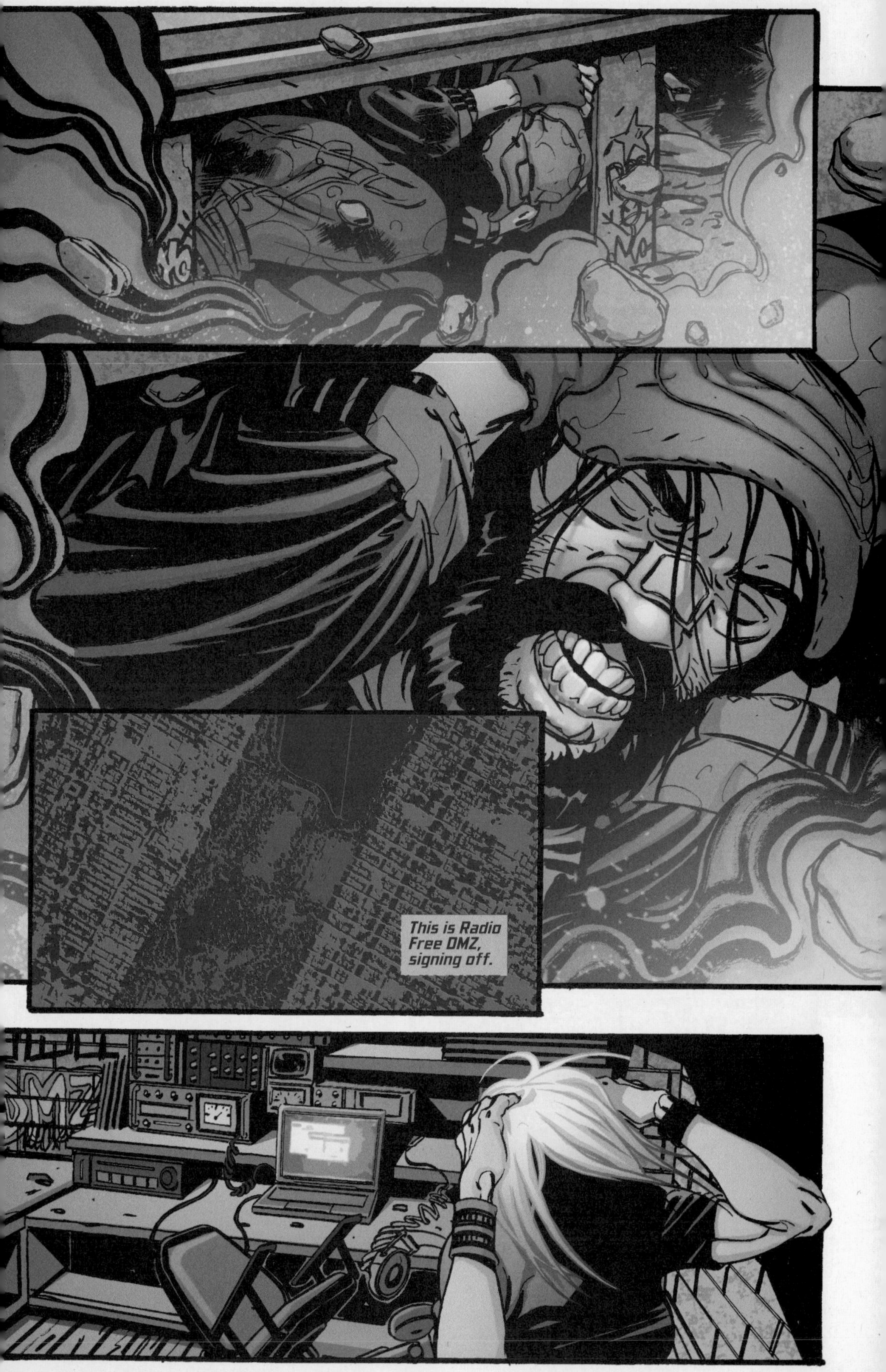
This is Radio Free DMZ, signing off.

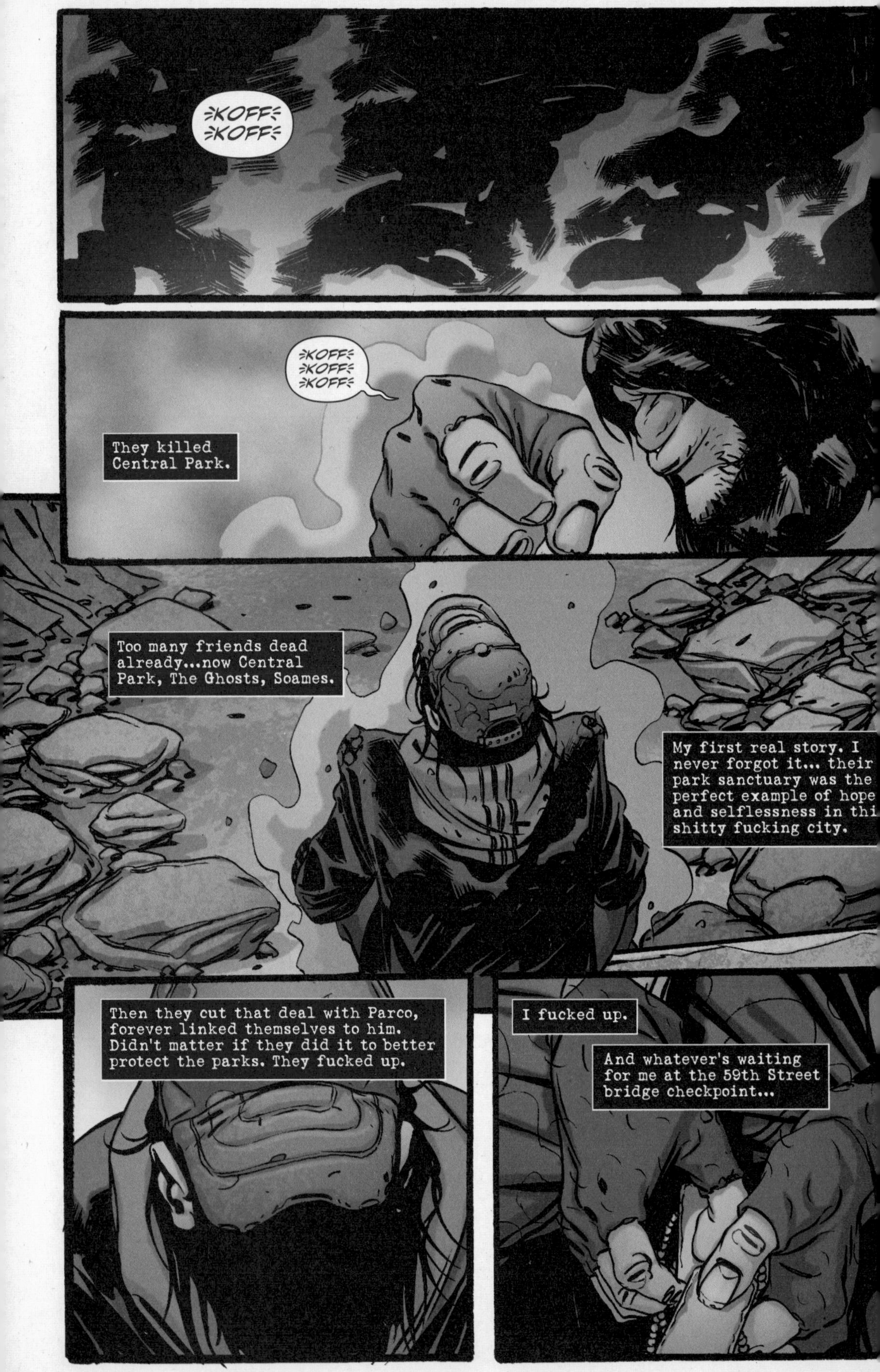

KOFF KOFF
KOFF KOFF KOFF
They killed Central Park.
Too many friends dead already...now Central Park, The Ghosts, Soames.
My first real story. I never forgot it... their park sanctuary was the perfect example of hope and selflessness in thi shitty fucking city.
Then they cut that deal with Parco, forever linked themselves to him. Didn't matter if they did it to better protect the parks. They fucked up.
I fucked up.
And whatever's waiting for me at the 59th Street bridge checkpoint...

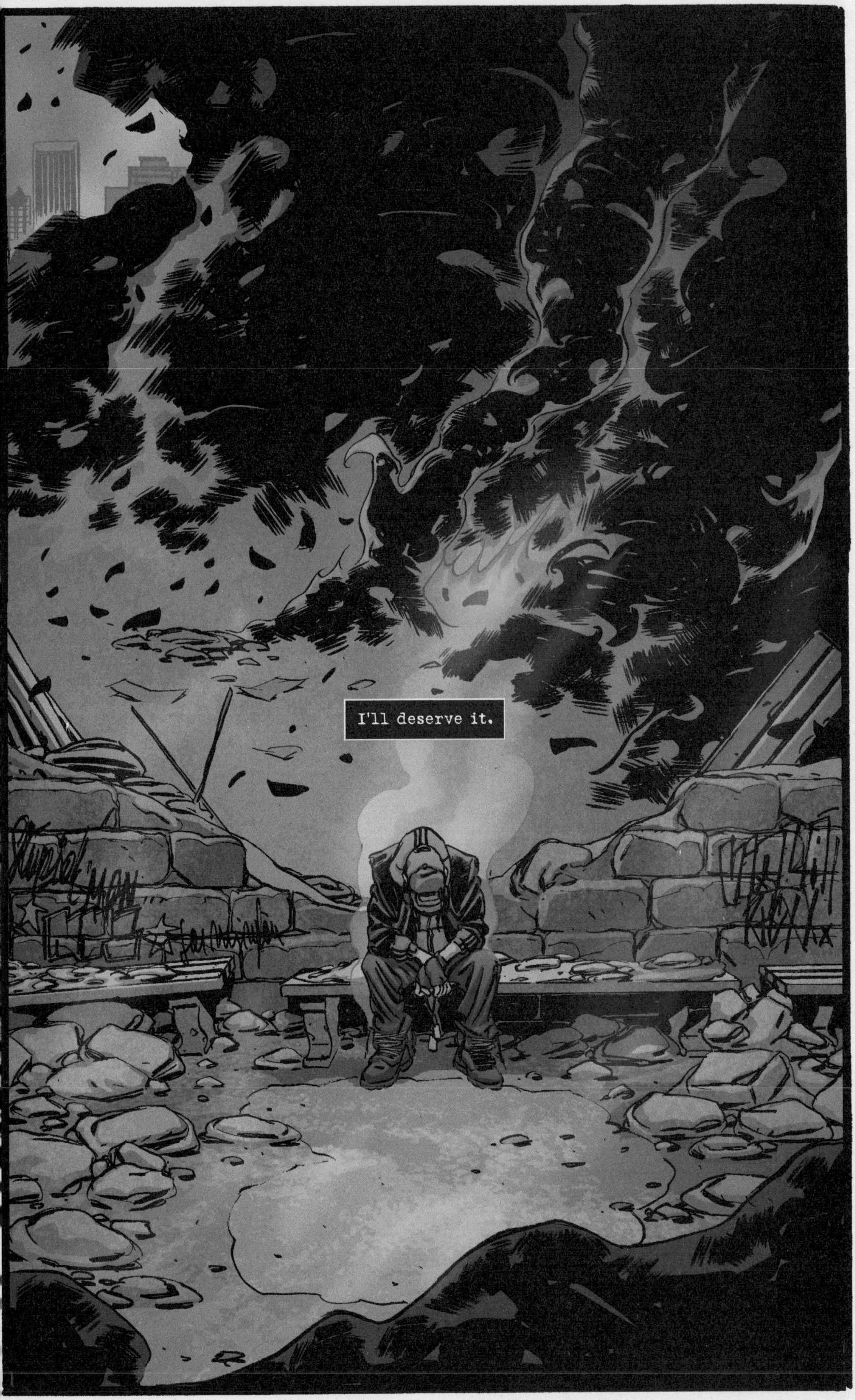
I'll deserve it.

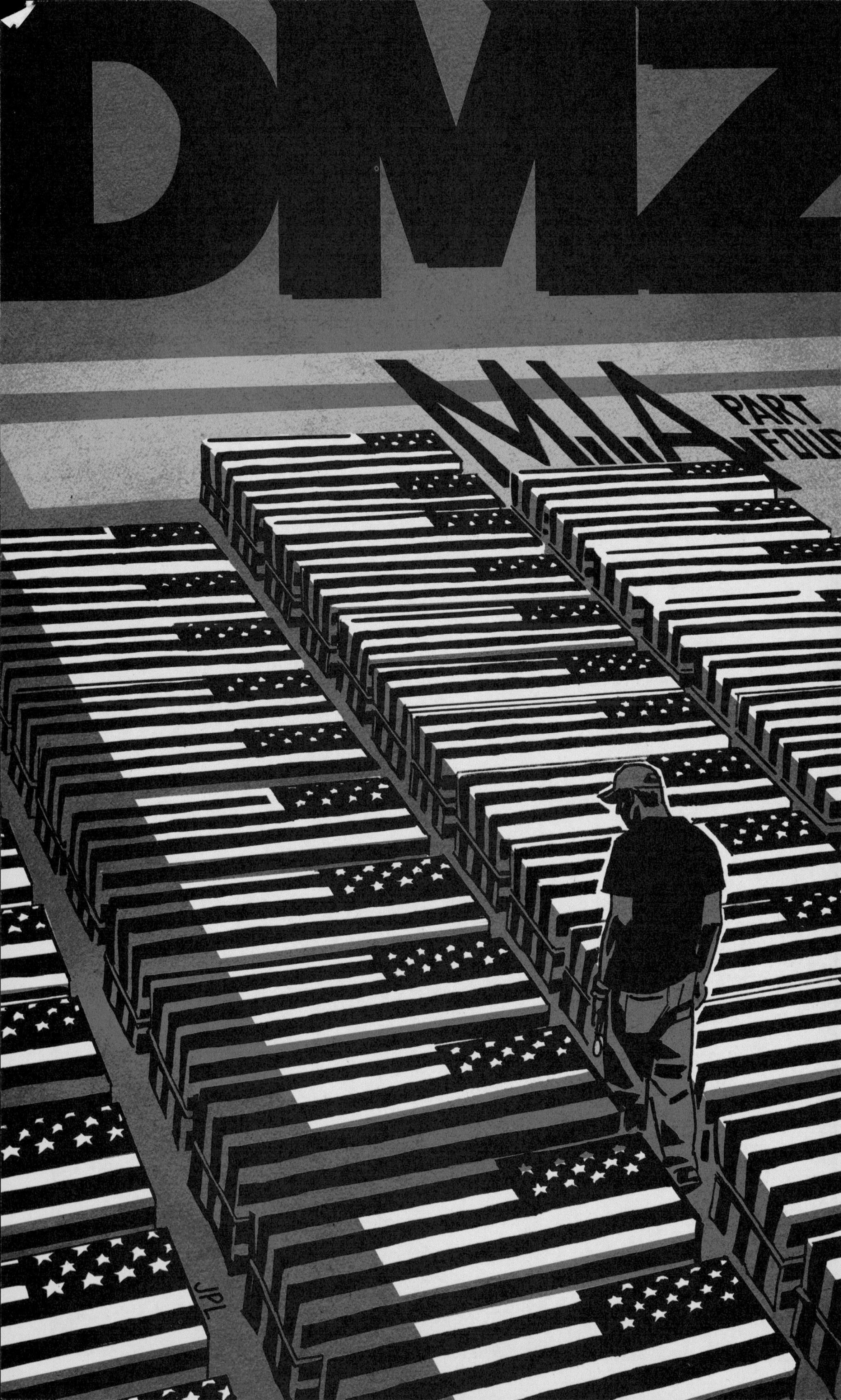
DMZ
M.I.A.
PART FOUR
JPL

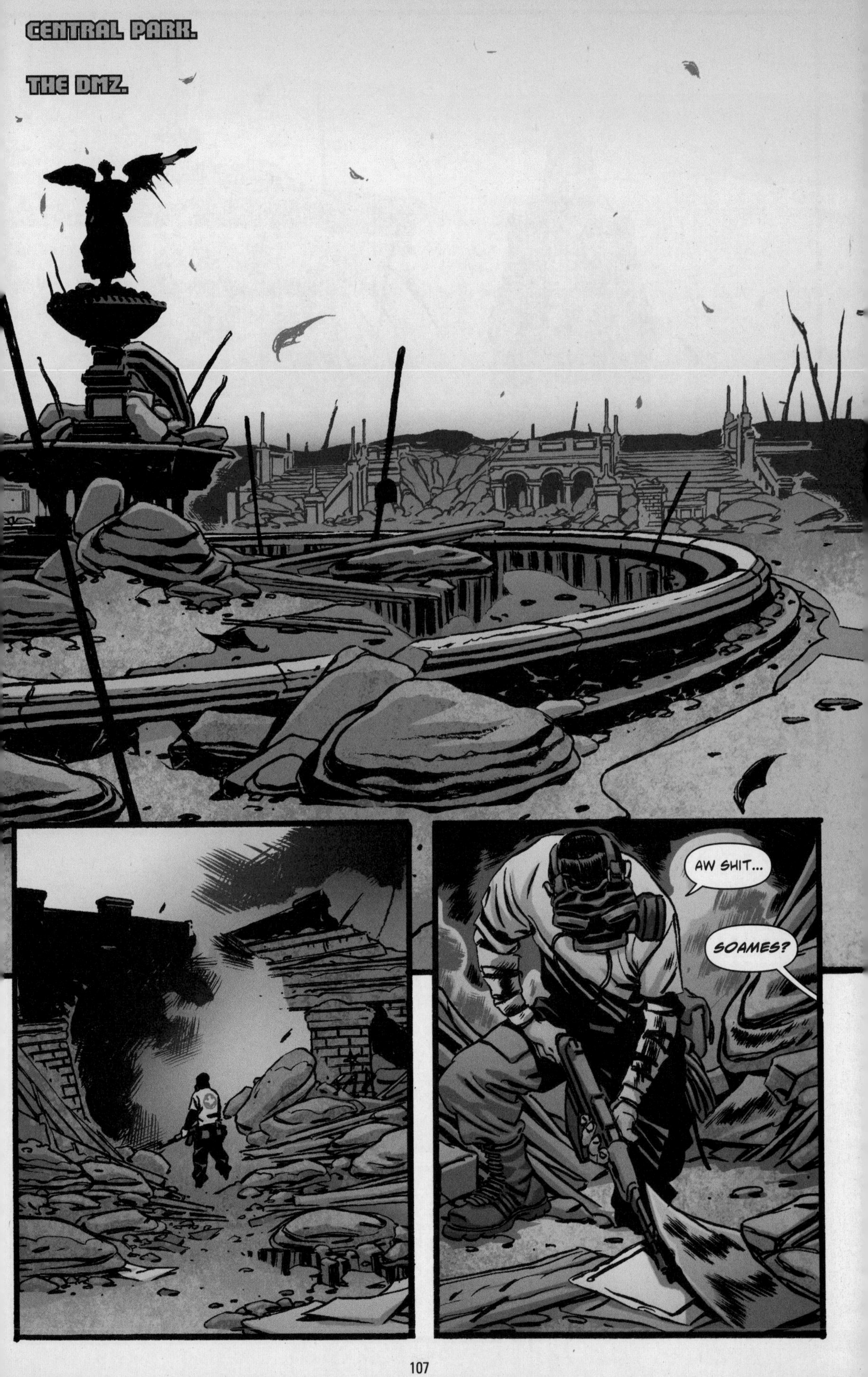
CENTRAL PARK.
THE DMZ.
AW SHIT...
SOAMES?

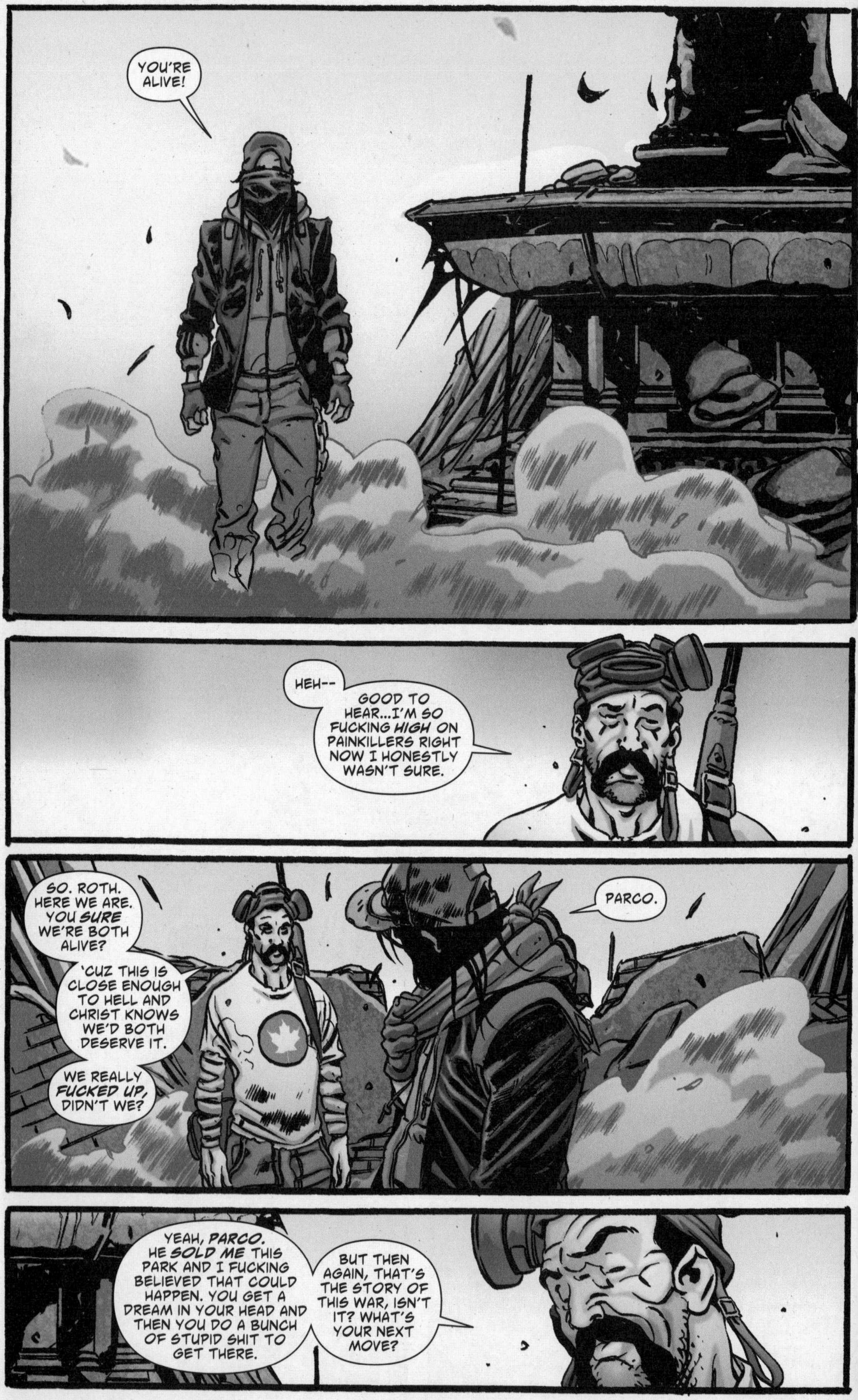

YOU'RE ALIVE!
HEH--
GOOD TO HEAR...I'M SO FUCKING HIGH ON PAINKILLERS RIGHT NOW I HONESTLY WASN'T SURE.
SO. ROTH. HERE WE ARE. YOU SURE WE'RE BOTH ALIVE?
'CUZ THIS IS CLOSE ENOUGH TO HELL AND CHRIST KNOWS WE'D BOTH DESERVE IT.
WE REALLY FUCKED UP, DIDN'T WE?
PARCO.
YEAH, PARCO. HE SOLD ME THIS PARK AND I FUCKING BELIEVED THAT COULD HAPPEN. YOU GET A DREAM IN YOUR HEAD AND THEN YOU DO A BUNCH OF STUPID SHIT TO GET THERE.
BUT THEN AGAIN, THAT'S THE STORY OF THIS WAR, ISN'T IT? WHAT'S YOUR NEXT MOVE?

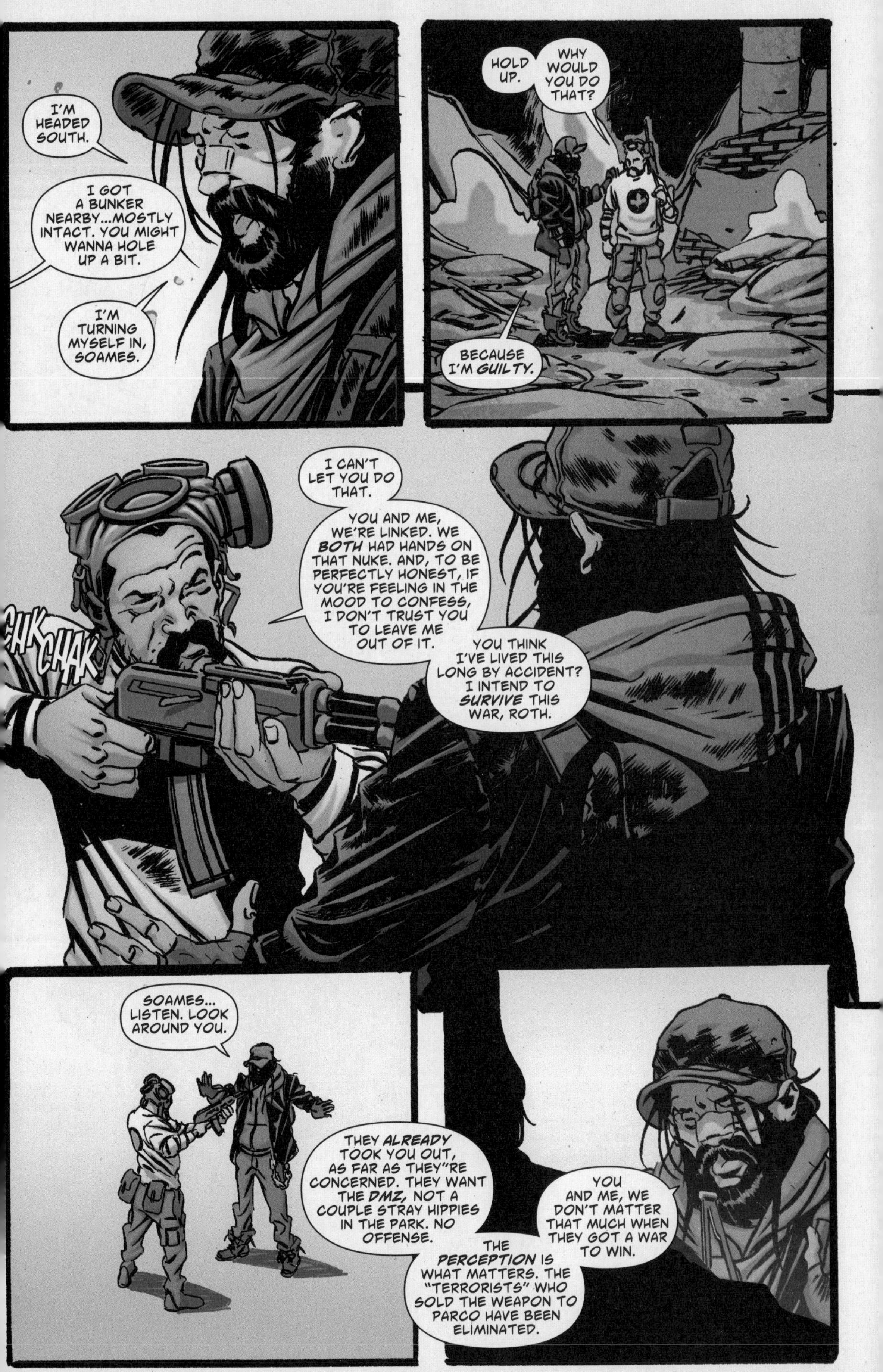
I'M HEADED SOUTH.
I GOT A BUNKER NEARBY...MOSTLY INTACT. YOU MIGHT WANNA HOLE UP A BIT.
I'M TURNING MYSELF IN, SOAMES.
HOLD UP.
WHY WOULD YOU DO THAT?
BECAUSE I'M *GUILTY.*
I CAN'T LET YOU DO THAT.
YOU AND ME, WE'RE LINKED. WE *BOTH* HAD HANDS ON THAT NUKE. AND, TO BE PERFECTLY HONEST, IF YOU'RE FEELING IN THE MOOD TO CONFESS, I DON'T TRUST YOU TO LEAVE ME OUT OF IT.
CHAK
YOU THINK I'VE LIVED THIS LONG BY ACCIDENT? I INTEND TO *SURVIVE* THIS WAR, ROTH.
SOAMES... LISTEN. LOOK AROUND YOU.
THEY *ALREADY* TOOK YOU OUT, AS FAR AS THEY''RE CONCERNED. THEY WANT THE *DMZ,* NOT A COUPLE STRAY HIPPIES IN THE PARK. NO OFFENSE.
YOU AND ME, WE DON'T MATTER THAT MUCH WHEN THEY GOT A WAR TO WIN.
THE *PERCEPTION* IS WHAT MATTERS. THE "TERRORISTS" WHO SOLD THE WEAPON TO PARCO HAVE BEEN ELIMINATED.

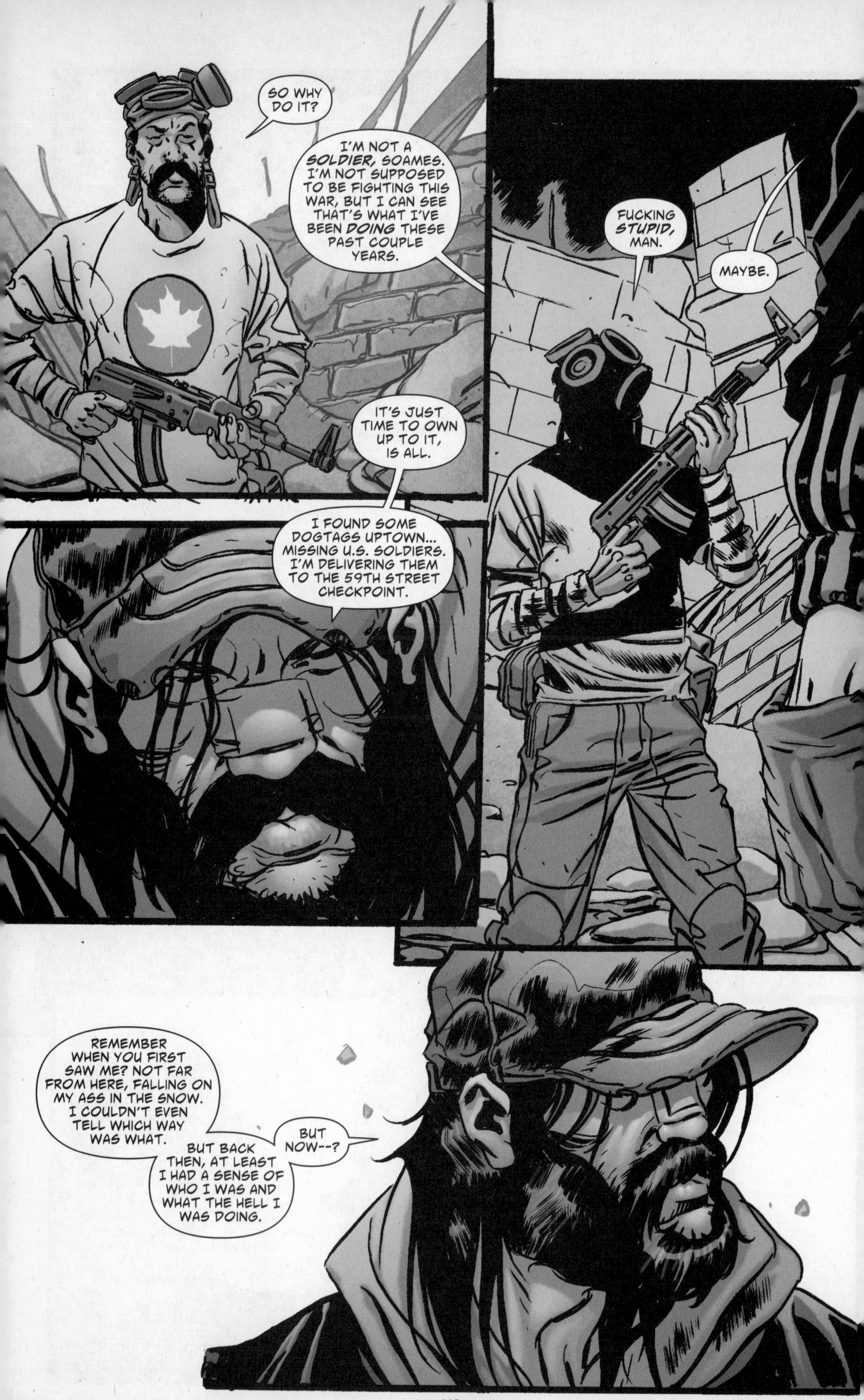
SO WHY DO IT?
I'M NOT A SOLDIER, SOAMES. I'M NOT SUPPOSED TO BE FIGHTING THIS WAR, BUT I CAN SEE THAT'S WHAT I'VE BEEN DOING THESE PAST COUPLE YEARS.
FUCKING STUPID, MAN.
MAYBE.
IT'S JUST TIME TO OWN UP TO IT, IS ALL.
I FOUND SOME DOGTAGS UPTOWN... MISSING U.S. SOLDIERS. I'M DELIVERING THEM TO THE 59TH STREET CHECKPOINT.
REMEMBER WHEN YOU FIRST SAW ME? NOT FAR FROM HERE, FALLING ON MY ASS IN THE SNOW. I COULDN'T EVEN TELL WHICH WAY WAS WHAT.
BUT BACK THEN, AT LEAST I HAD A SENSE OF WHO I WAS AND WHAT THE HELL I WAS DOING.
BUT NOW--?

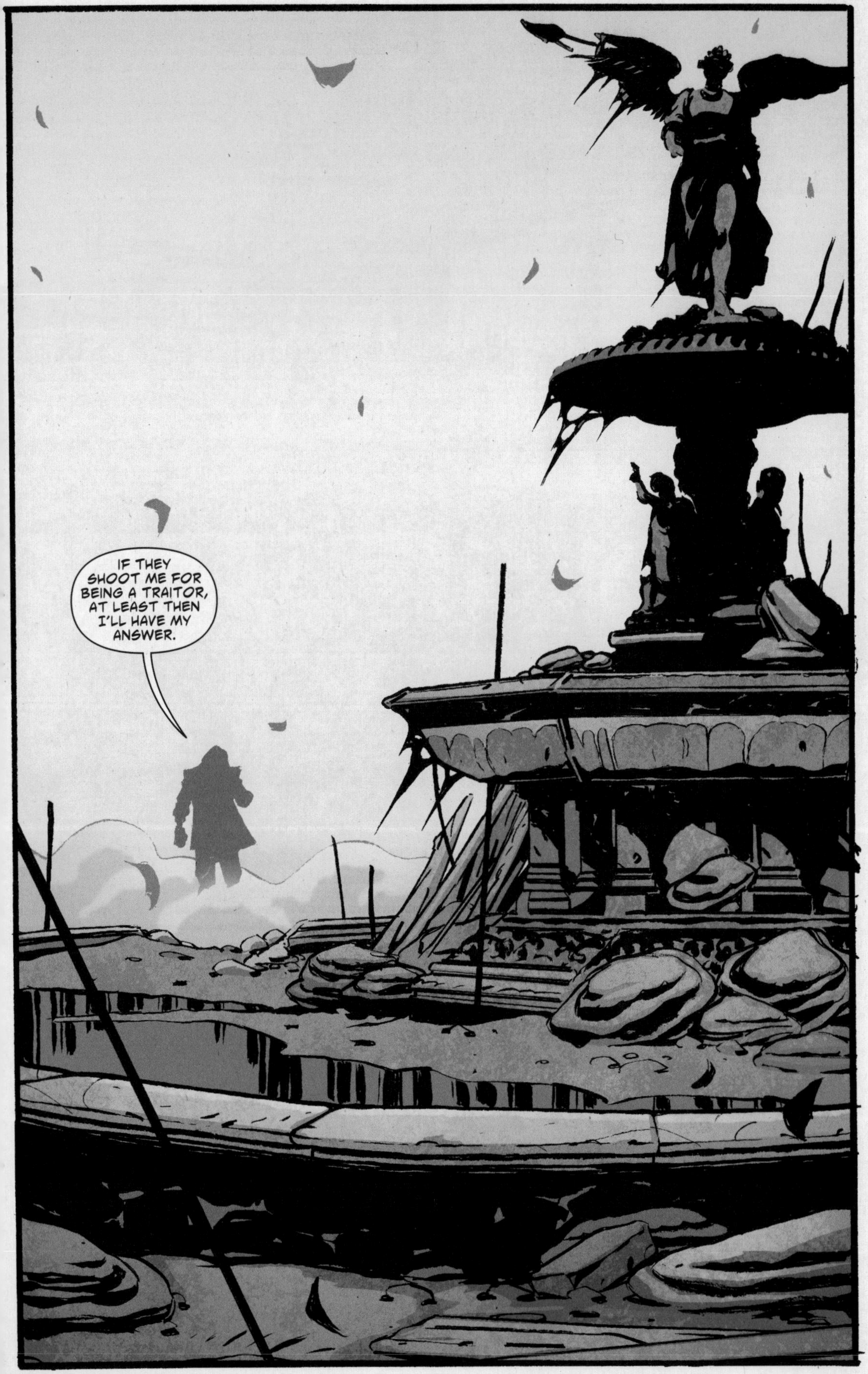
IF THEY SHOOT ME FOR BEING A TRAITOR, AT LEAST THEN I'LL HAVE MY ANSWER.

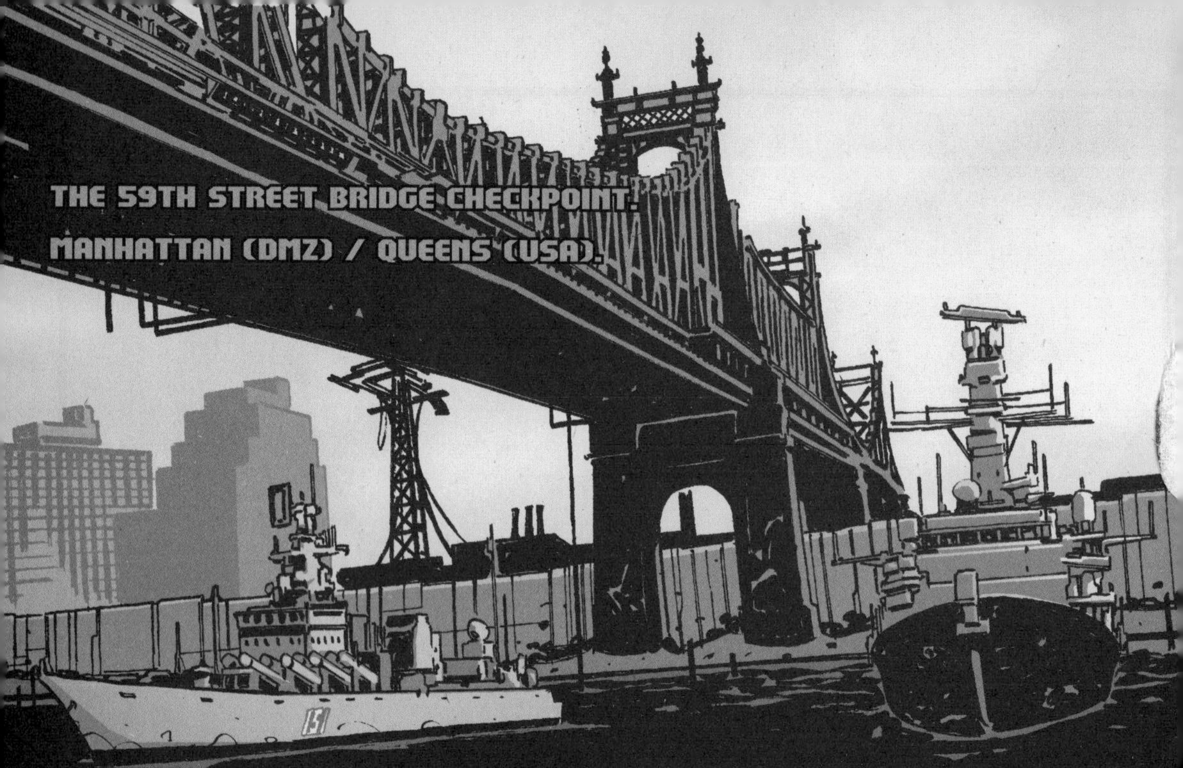
THE 59TH STREET BRIDGE CHECKPOINT.
MANHATTAN (DMZ) / QUEENS (USA).

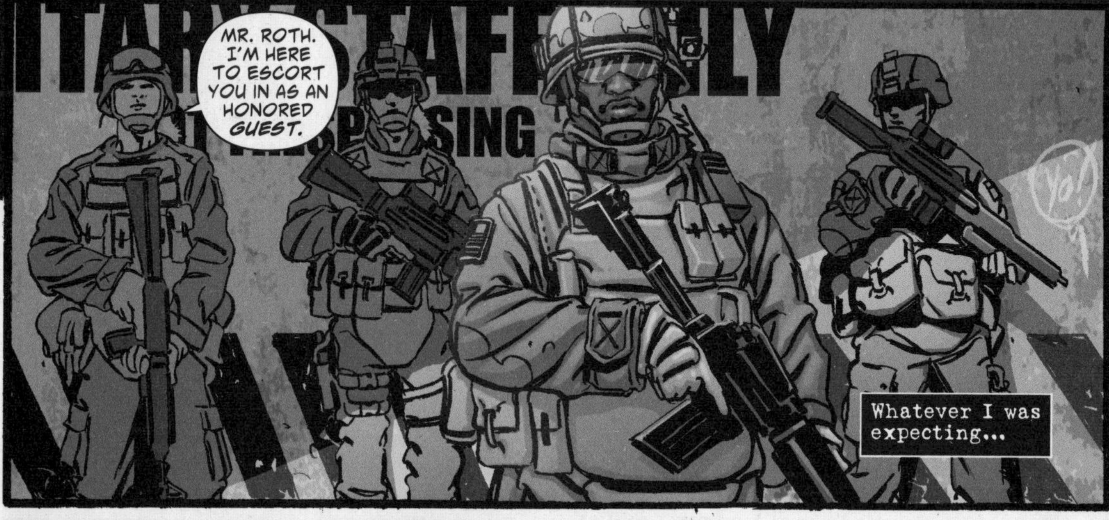
MR. ROTH. I'M HERE TO ESCORT YOU IN AS AN HONORED GUEST.
Whatever I was expecting...

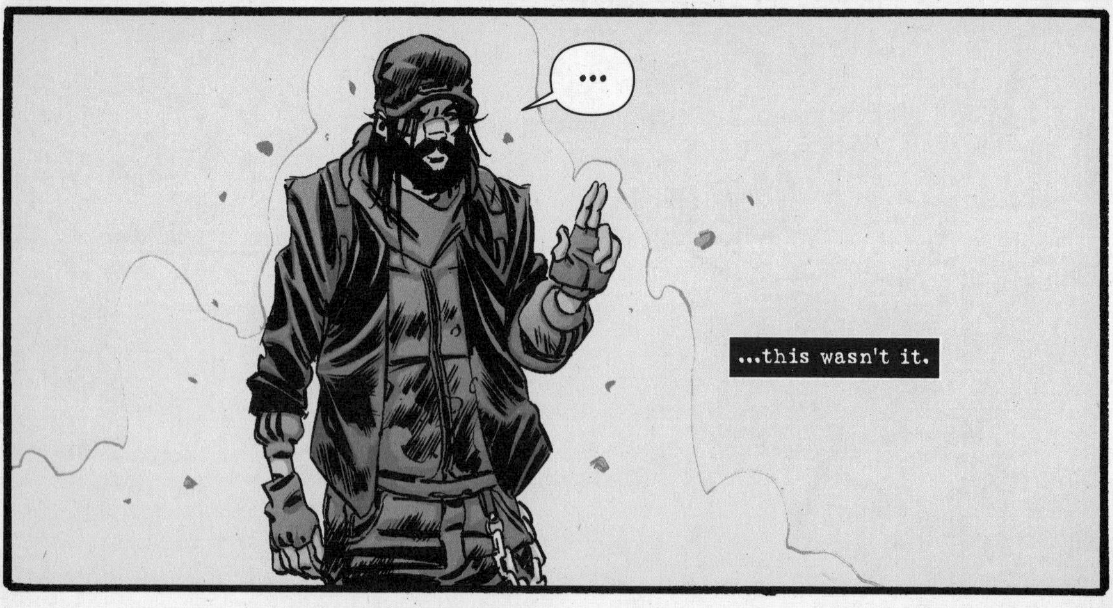
...
...this wasn't it.

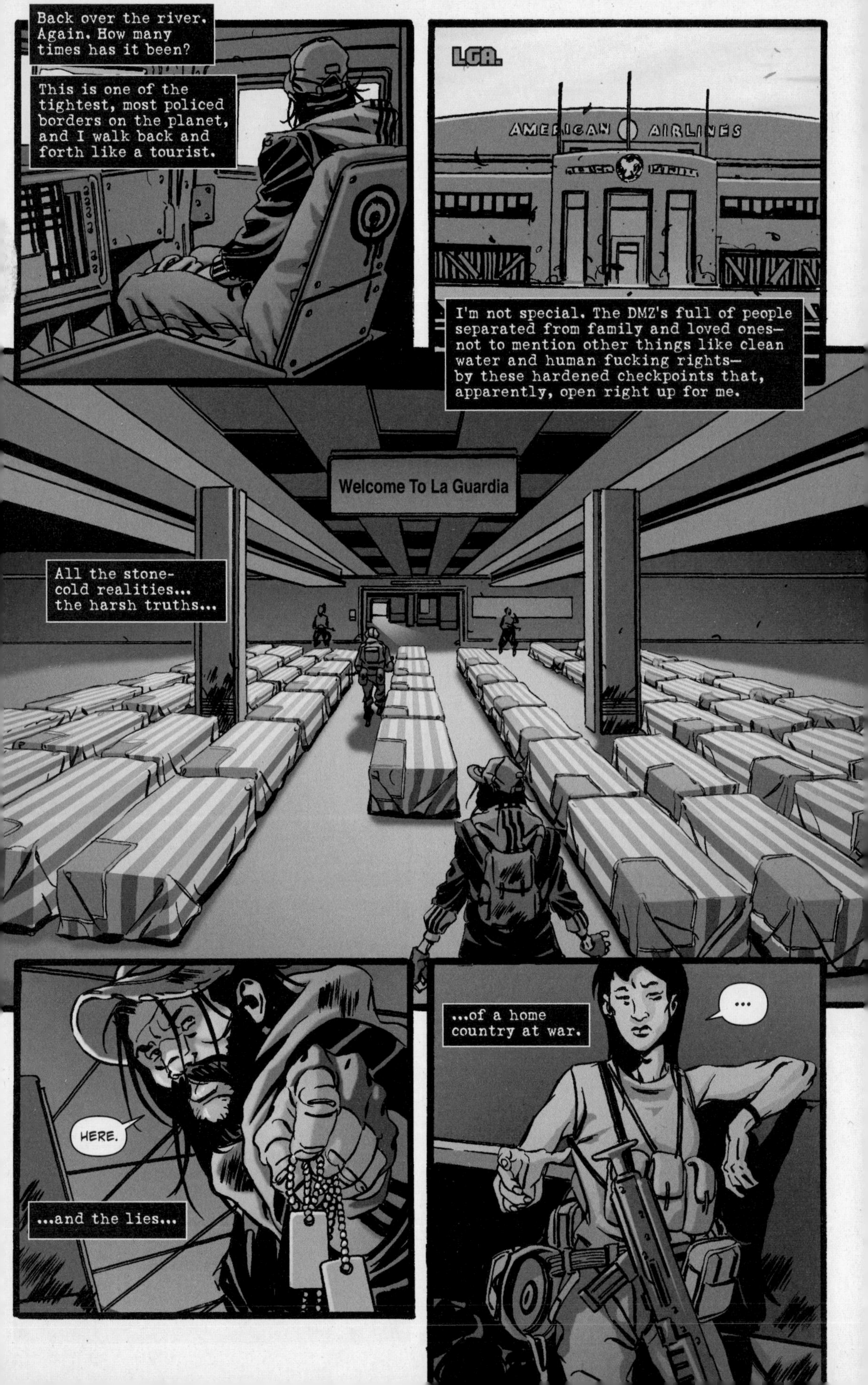
Back over the river. Again. How many times has it been?
This is one of the tightest, most policed borders on the planet, and I walk back and forth like a tourist.
LGA.
AMERICAN AIRLINES
I'm not special. The DMZ's full of people separated from family and loved ones—not to mention other things like clean water and human fucking rights—by these hardened checkpoints that, apparently, open right up for me.
Welcome To La Guardia
All the stone-cold realities... the harsh truths...
HERE.
...and the lies...
...of a home country at war.
...

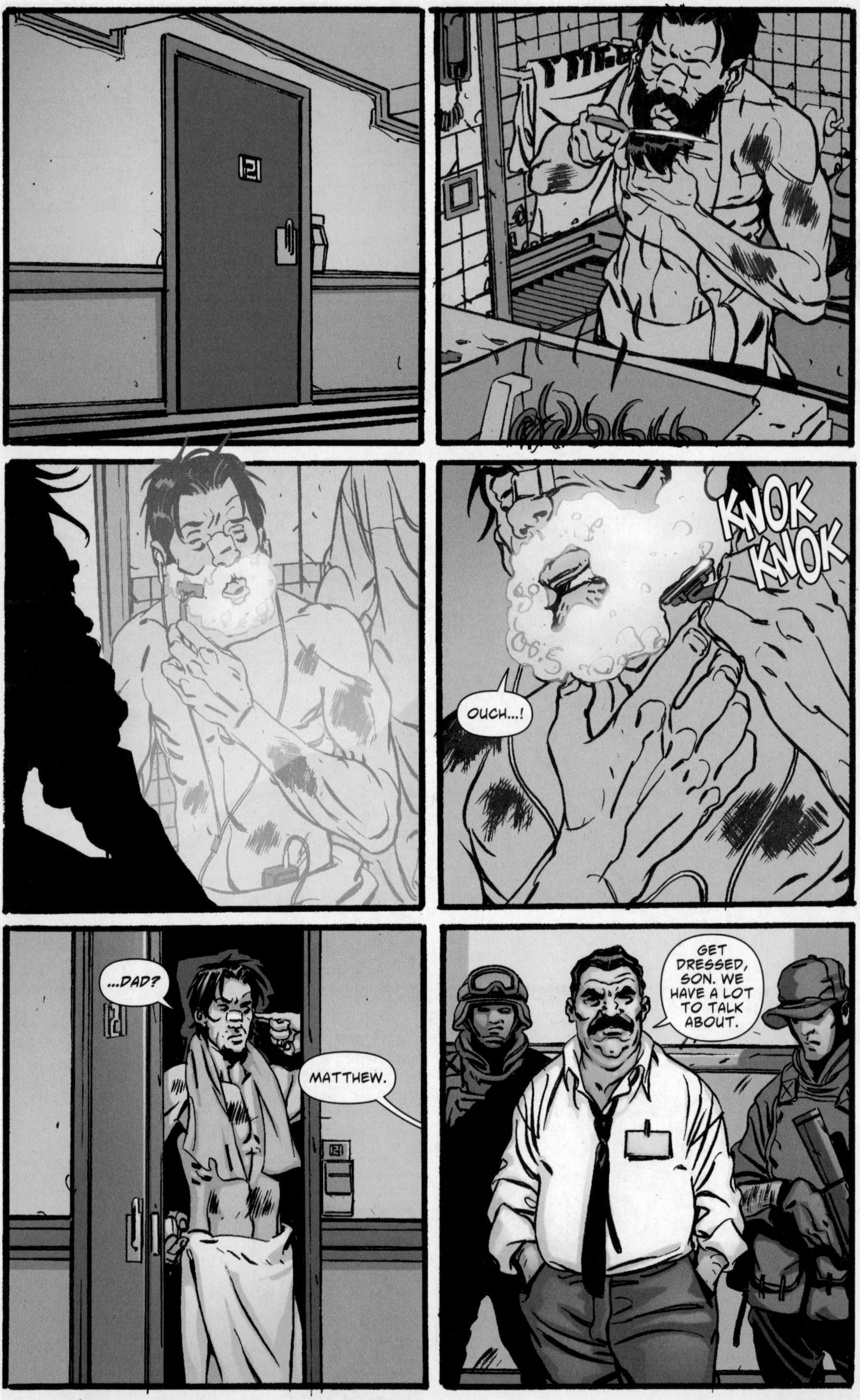
KNOK KNOK
OUCH...!
...DAD?
MATTHEW.
GET DRESSED, SON. WE HAVE A LOT TO TALK ABOUT.

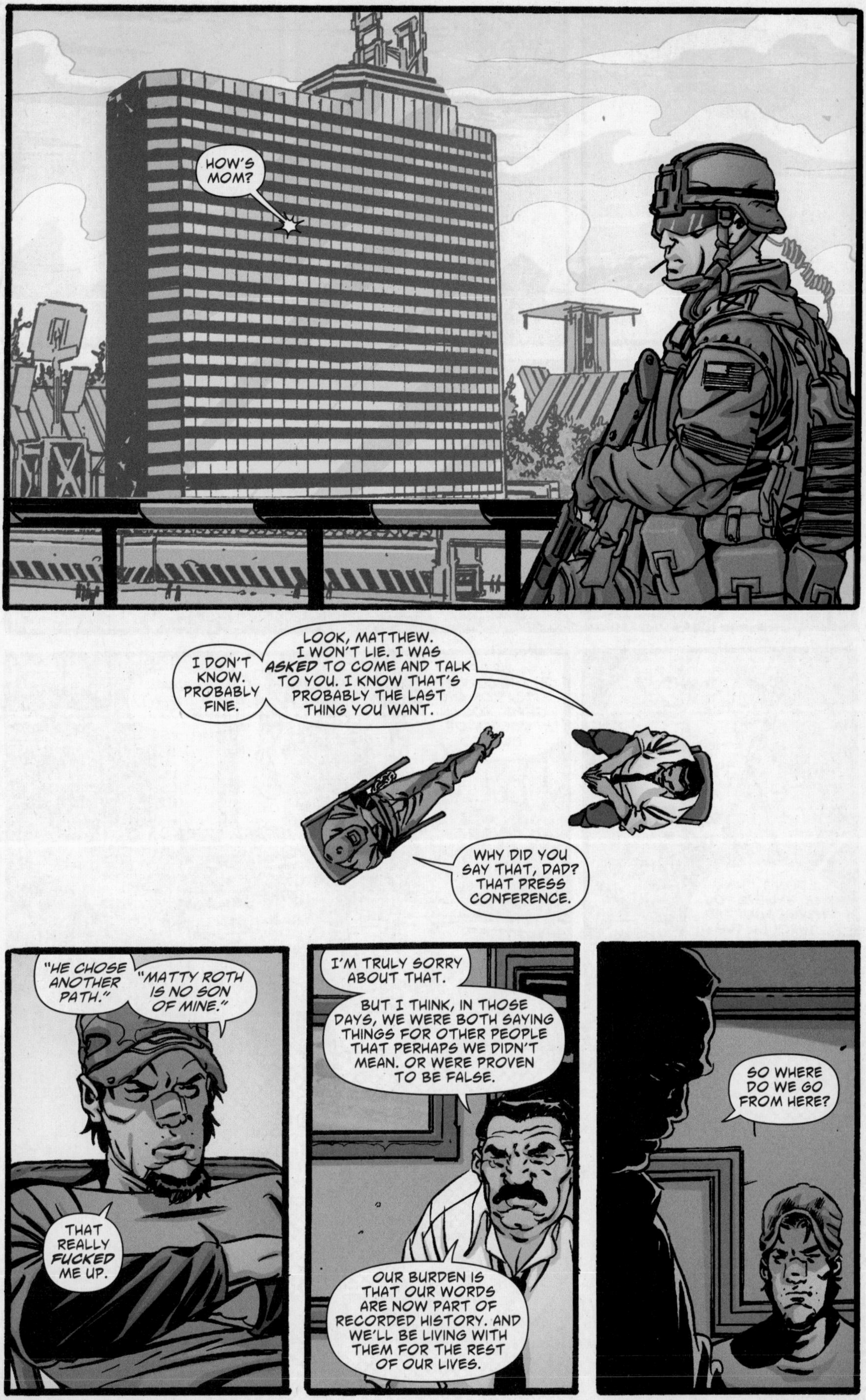
HOW'S MOM?
I DON'T KNOW. PROBABLY FINE.
LOOK, MATTHEW. I WON'T LIE. I WAS ASKED TO COME AND TALK TO YOU. I KNOW THAT'S PROBABLY THE LAST THING YOU WANT.
WHY DID YOU SAY THAT, DAD? THAT PRESS CONFERENCE.
"HE CHOSE ANOTHER PATH."
"MATTY ROTH IS NO SON OF MINE."
THAT REALLY FUCKED ME UP.
I'M TRULY SORRY ABOUT THAT.
BUT I THINK, IN THOSE DAYS, WE WERE BOTH SAYING THINGS FOR OTHER PEOPLE THAT PERHAPS WE DIDN'T MEAN. OR WERE PROVEN TO BE FALSE.
OUR BURDEN IS THAT OUR WORDS ARE NOW PART OF RECORDED HISTORY. AND WE'LL BE LIVING WITH THEM FOR THE REST OF OUR LIVES.
SO WHERE DO WE GO FROM HERE?

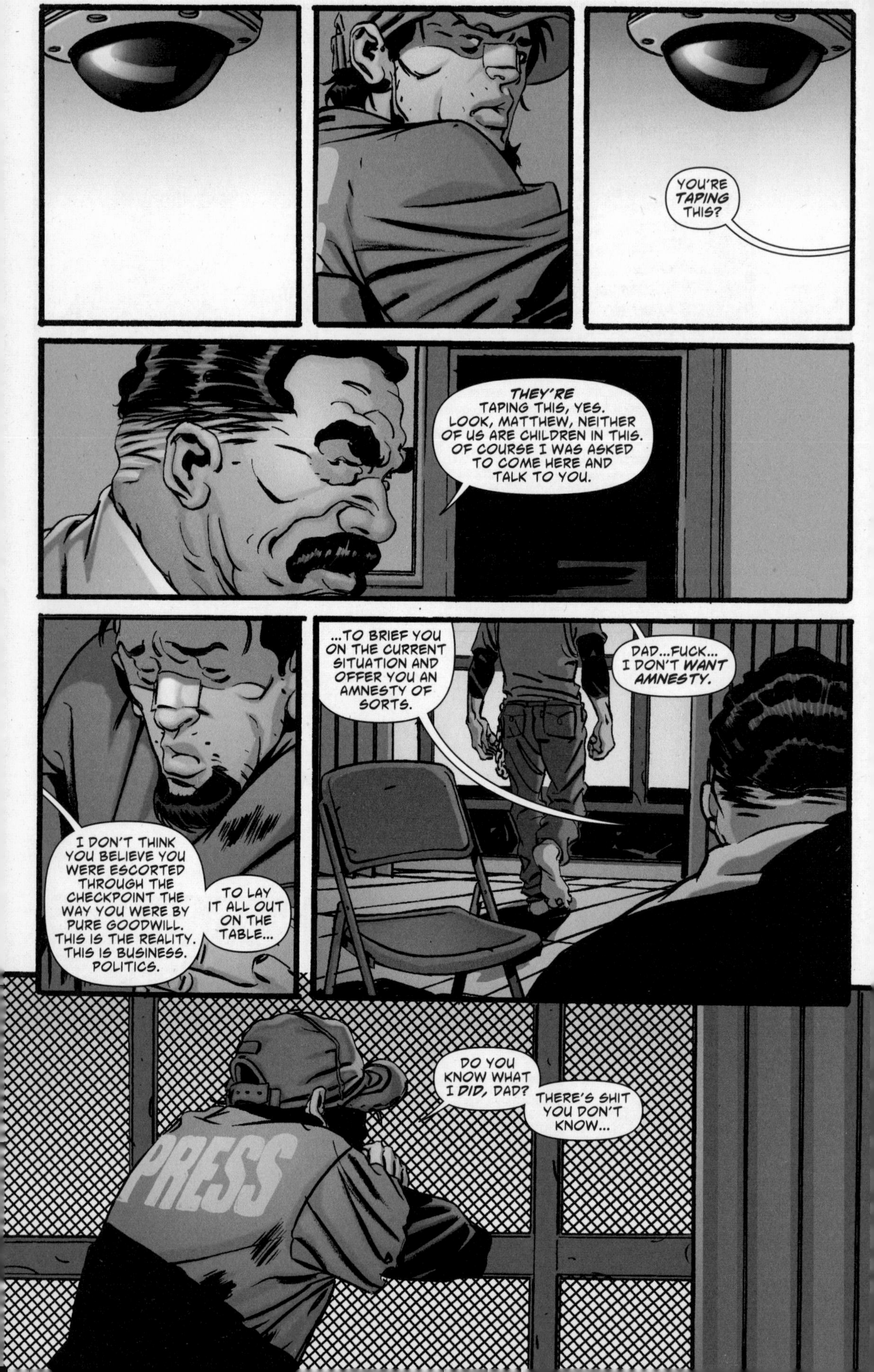
YOU'RE *TAPING* THIS?
*THEY'RE* TAPING THIS, YES. LOOK, MATTHEW, NEITHER OF US ARE CHILDREN IN THIS. OF COURSE I WAS ASKED TO COME HERE AND TALK TO YOU.
I DON'T THINK YOU BELIEVE YOU WERE ESCORTED THROUGH THE CHECKPOINT THE WAY YOU WERE BY PURE GOODWILL. THIS IS THE REALITY. THIS IS BUSINESS. POLITICS.
TO LAY IT ALL OUT ON THE TABLE...
...TO BRIEF YOU ON THE CURRENT SITUATION AND OFFER YOU AN AMNESTY OF SORTS.
DAD...FUCK... I DON'T *WANT* *AMNESTY*.
DO YOU KNOW WHAT I *DID*, DAD?
THERE'S SHIT YOU DON'T KNOW...
PRESS

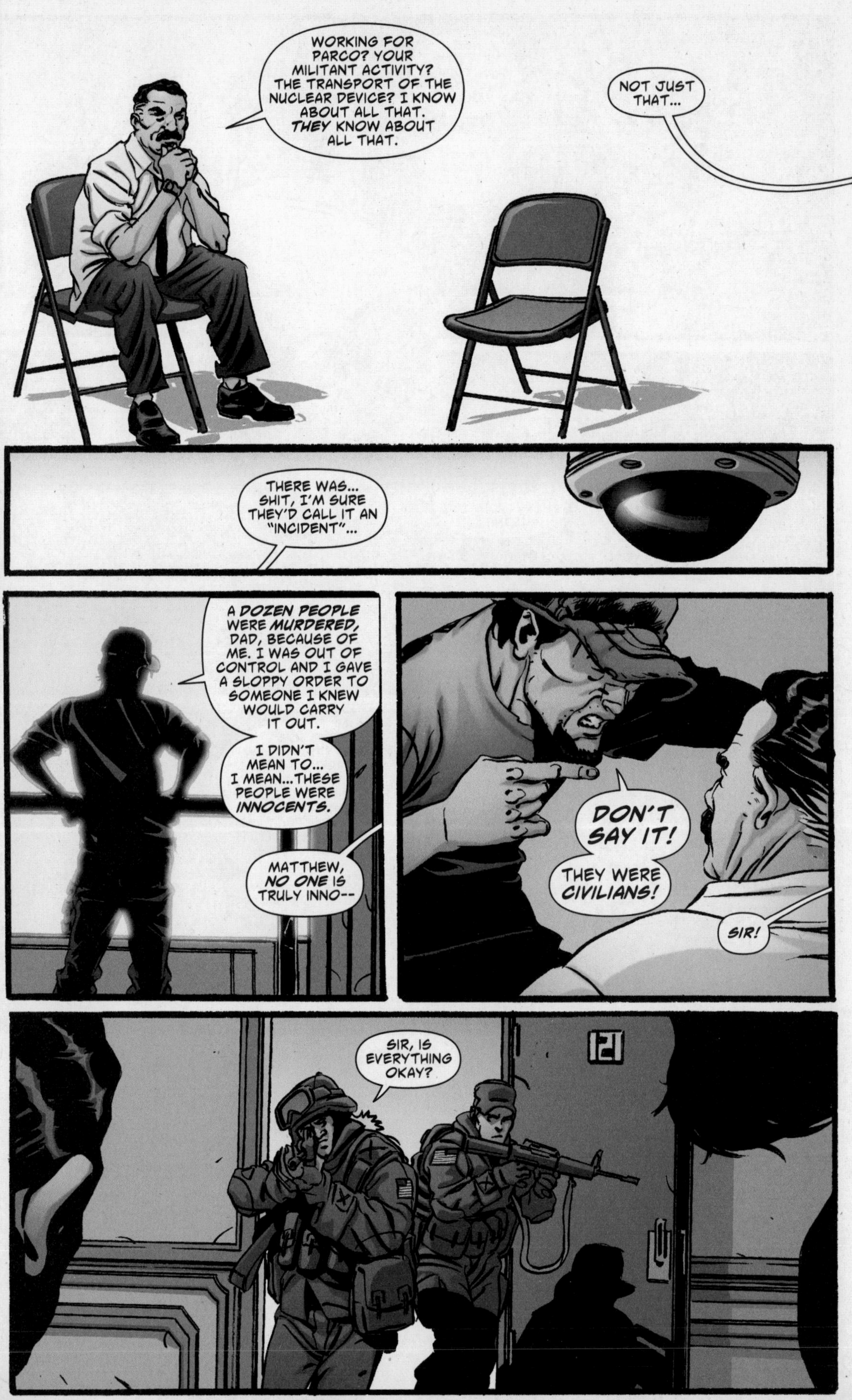
WORKING FOR PARCO? YOUR MILITANT ACTIVITY? THE TRANSPORT OF THE NUCLEAR DEVICE? I KNOW ABOUT ALL THAT. THEY KNOW ABOUT ALL THAT.
NOT JUST THAT...
THERE WAS... SHIT, I'M SURE THEY'D CALL IT AN "INCIDENT"...
A DOZEN PEOPLE WERE MURDERED, DAD, BECAUSE OF ME. I WAS OUT OF CONTROL AND I GAVE A SLOPPY ORDER TO SOMEONE I KNEW WOULD CARRY IT OUT.
I DIDN'T MEAN TO... I MEAN...THESE PEOPLE WERE INNOCENTS.
MATTHEW, NO ONE IS TRULY INNO--
DON'T SAY IT!
THEY WERE CIVILIANS!
SIR!
SIR, IS EVERYTHING OKAY?
121

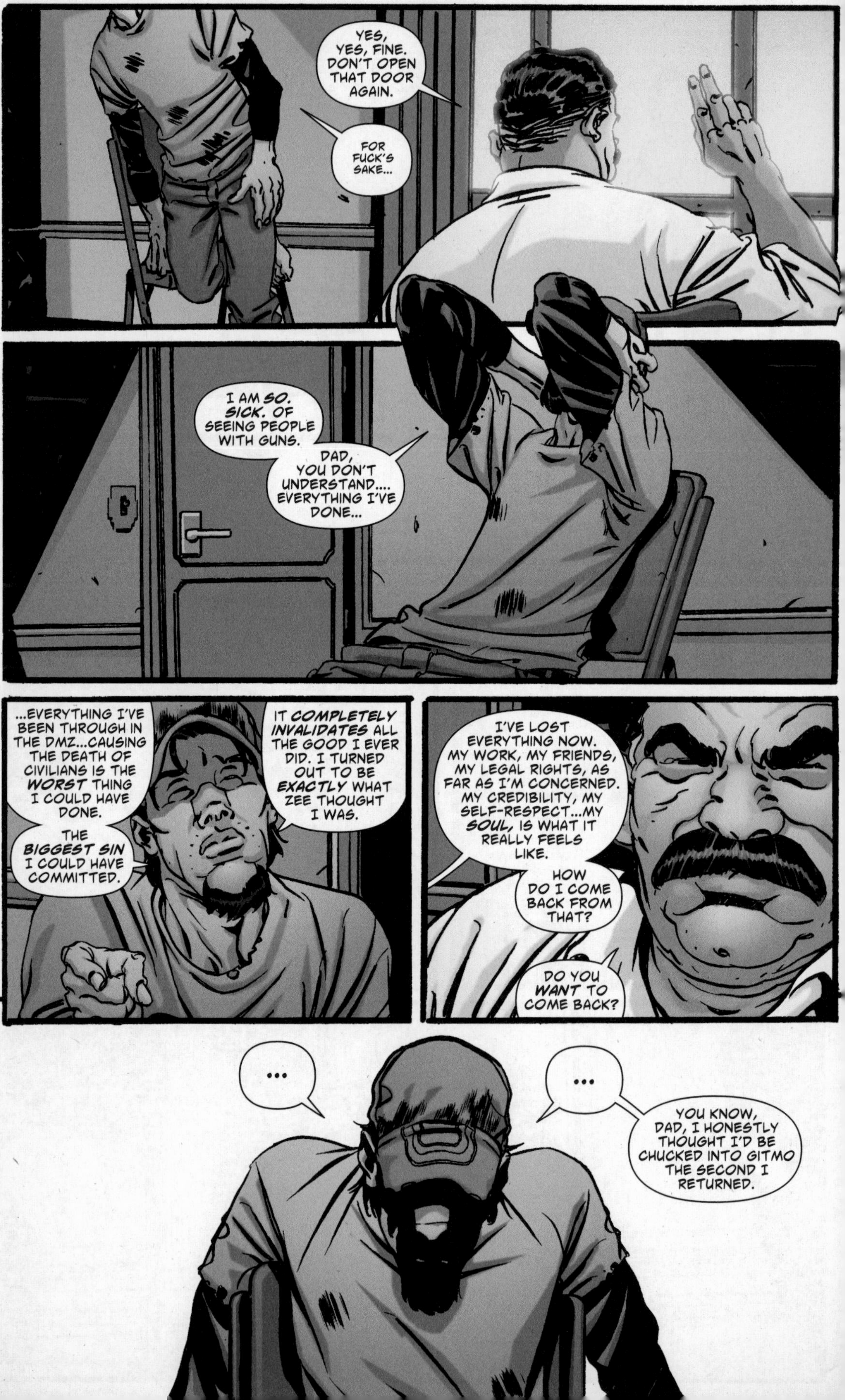
YES, YES, FINE. DON'T OPEN THAT DOOR AGAIN.
FOR FUCK'S SAKE...
I AM SO. SICK. OF SEEING PEOPLE WITH GUNS.
DAD, YOU DON'T UNDERSTAND.... EVERYTHING I'VE DONE...
...EVERYTHING I'VE BEEN THROUGH IN THE DMZ...CAUSING THE DEATH OF CIVILIANS IS THE WORST THING I COULD HAVE DONE.
THE BIGGEST SIN I COULD HAVE COMMITTED.
IT COMPLETELY INVALIDATES ALL THE GOOD I EVER DID. I TURNED OUT TO BE EXACTLY WHAT ZEE THOUGHT I WAS.
I'VE LOST EVERYTHING NOW. MY WORK, MY FRIENDS, MY LEGAL RIGHTS, AS FAR AS I'M CONCERNED. MY CREDIBILITY, MY SELF-RESPECT...MY SOUL, IS WHAT IT REALLY FEELS LIKE.
HOW DO I COME BACK FROM THAT?
DO YOU WANT TO COME BACK?
...
...
YOU KNOW, DAD, I HONESTLY THOUGHT I'D BE CHUCKED INTO GITMO THE SECOND I RETURNED.

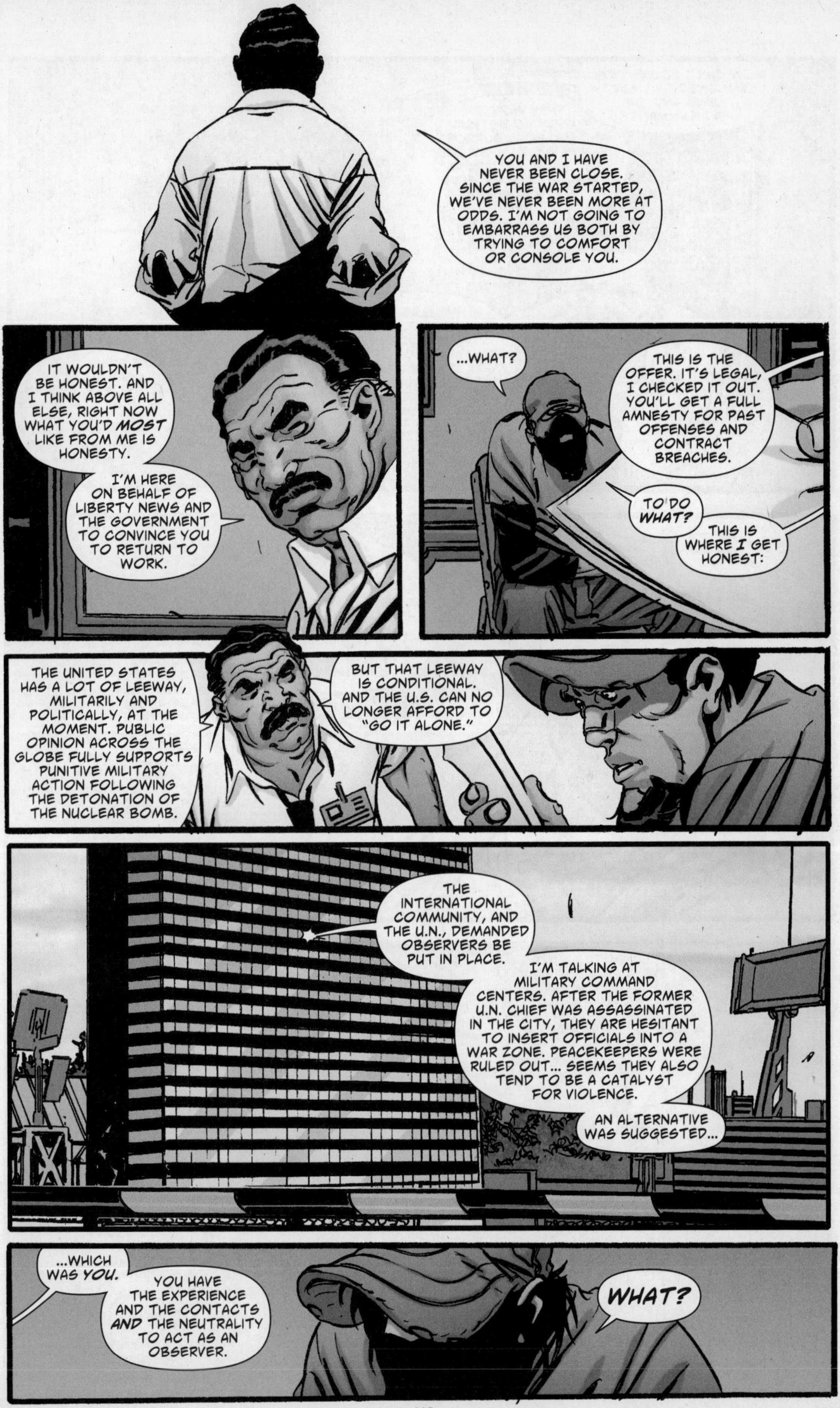
YOU AND I HAVE NEVER BEEN CLOSE. SINCE THE WAR STARTED, WE'VE NEVER BEEN MORE AT ODDS. I'M NOT GOING TO EMBARRASS US BOTH BY TRYING TO COMFORT OR CONSOLE YOU.
IT WOULDN'T BE HONEST. AND I THINK ABOVE ALL ELSE, RIGHT NOW WHAT YOU'D *MOST* LIKE FROM ME IS HONESTY.
I'M HERE ON BEHALF OF LIBERTY NEWS AND THE GOVERNMENT TO CONVINCE YOU TO RETURN TO WORK.
...WHAT?
THIS IS THE OFFER. IT'S LEGAL, I CHECKED IT OUT. YOU'LL GET A FULL AMNESTY FOR PAST OFFENSES AND CONTRACT BREACHES.
TO DO *WHAT?*
THIS IS WHERE *I* GET HONEST:
THE UNITED STATES HAS A LOT OF LEEWAY, MILITARILY AND POLITICALLY, AT THE MOMENT. PUBLIC OPINION ACROSS THE GLOBE FULLY SUPPORTS PUNITIVE MILITARY ACTION FOLLOWING THE DETONATION OF THE NUCLEAR BOMB.
BUT THAT LEEWAY IS CONDITIONAL. AND THE U.S. CAN NO LONGER AFFORD TO "GO IT ALONE."
THE INTERNATIONAL COMMUNITY, AND THE U.N., DEMANDED OBSERVERS BE PUT IN PLACE.
I'M TALKING AT MILITARY COMMAND CENTERS. AFTER THE FORMER U.N. CHIEF WAS ASSASSINATED IN THE CITY, THEY ARE HESITANT TO INSERT OFFICIALS INTO A WAR ZONE. PEACEKEEPERS WERE RULED OUT... SEEMS THEY ALSO TEND TO BE A CATALYST FOR VIOLENCE.
AN ALTERNATIVE WAS SUGGESTED...
...WHICH WAS *YOU.*
YOU HAVE THE EXPERIENCE AND THE CONTACTS *AND* THE NEUTRALITY TO ACT AS AN OBSERVER.
*WHAT?*

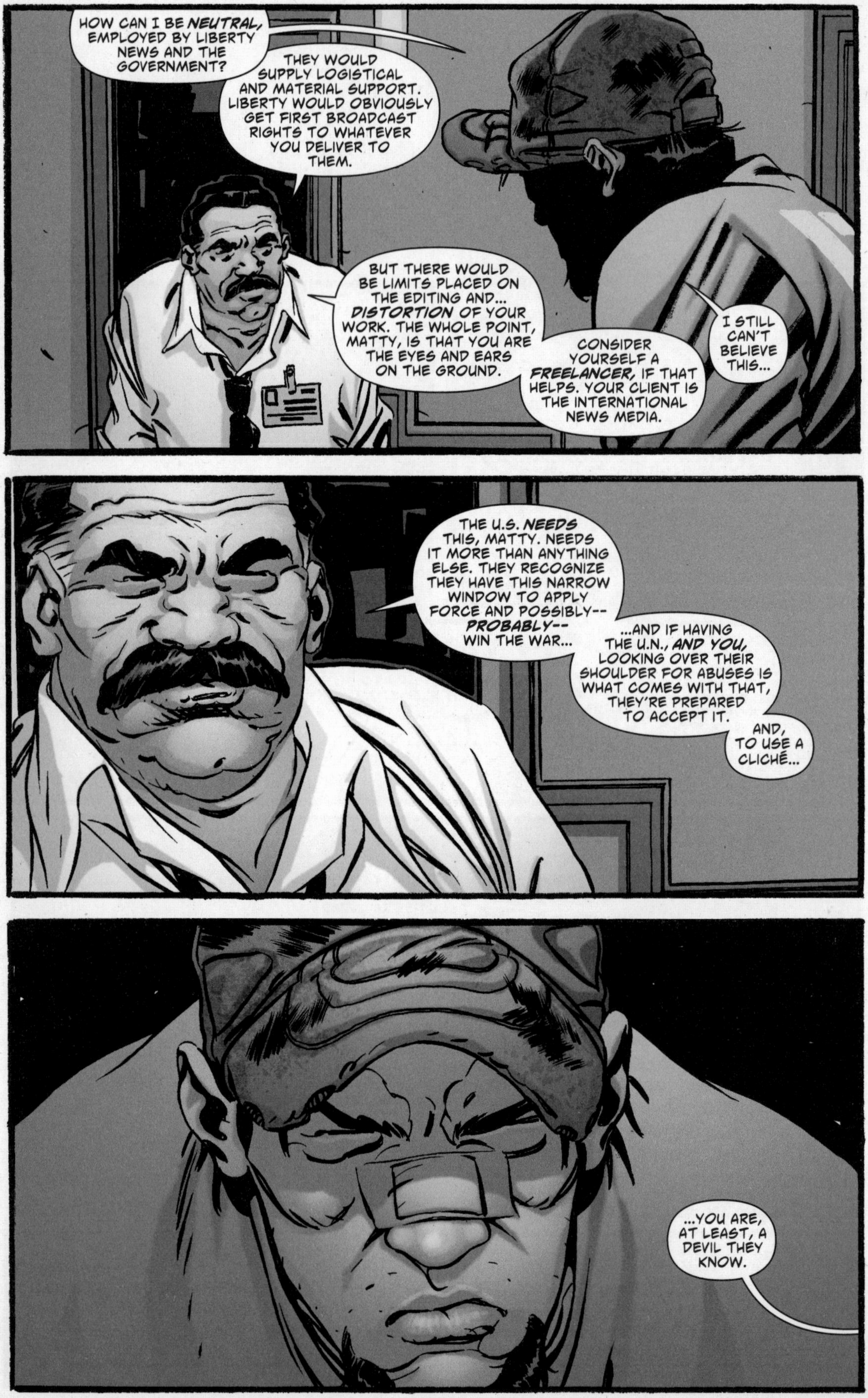
HOW CAN I BE NEUTRAL, EMPLOYED BY LIBERTY NEWS AND THE GOVERNMENT?
THEY WOULD SUPPLY LOGISTICAL AND MATERIAL SUPPORT. LIBERTY WOULD OBVIOUSLY GET FIRST BROADCAST RIGHTS TO WHATEVER YOU DELIVER TO THEM.
BUT THERE WOULD BE LIMITS PLACED ON THE EDITING AND... DISTORTION OF YOUR WORK. THE WHOLE POINT, MATTY, IS THAT YOU ARE THE EYES AND EARS ON THE GROUND.
I STILL CAN'T BELIEVE THIS...
CONSIDER YOURSELF A FREELANCER, IF THAT HELPS. YOUR CLIENT IS THE INTERNATIONAL NEWS MEDIA.
THE U.S. NEEDS THIS, MATTY. NEEDS IT MORE THAN ANYTHING ELSE. THEY RECOGNIZE THEY HAVE THIS NARROW WINDOW TO APPLY FORCE AND POSSIBLY-- PROBABLY-- WIN THE WAR...
...AND IF HAVING THE U.N., AND YOU, LOOKING OVER THEIR SHOULDER FOR ABUSES IS WHAT COMES WITH THAT, THEY'RE PREPARED TO ACCEPT IT.
AND, TO USE A CLICHÉ...
...YOU ARE, AT LEAST, A DEVIL THEY KNOW.

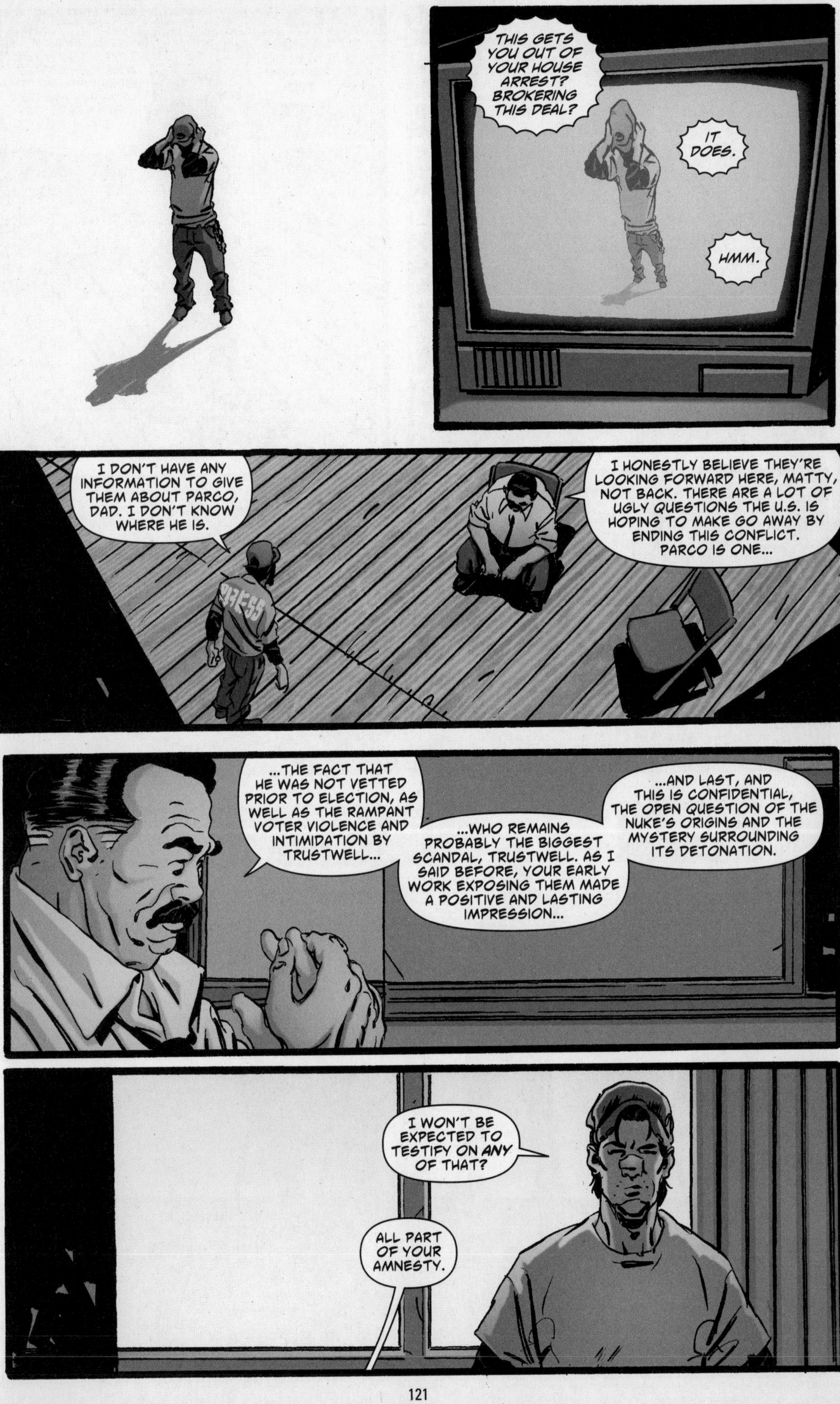
THIS GETS YOU OUT OF YOUR HOUSE ARREST? BROKERING THIS DEAL?
IT DOES.
HMM.
I DON'T HAVE ANY INFORMATION TO GIVE THEM ABOUT PARCO, DAD. I DON'T KNOW WHERE HE IS.
I HONESTLY BELIEVE THEY'RE LOOKING FORWARD HERE, MATTY, NOT BACK. THERE ARE A LOT OF UGLY QUESTIONS THE U.S. IS HOPING TO MAKE GO AWAY BY ENDING THIS CONFLICT. PARCO IS ONE...
...THE FACT THAT HE WAS NOT VETTED PRIOR TO ELECTION, AS WELL AS THE RAMPANT VOTER VIOLENCE AND INTIMIDATION BY TRUSTWELL...
...WHO REMAINS PROBABLY THE BIGGEST SCANDAL, TRUSTWELL. AS I SAID BEFORE, YOUR EARLY WORK EXPOSING THEM MADE A POSITIVE AND LASTING IMPRESSION...
...AND LAST, AND THIS IS CONFIDENTIAL, THE OPEN QUESTION OF THE NUKE'S ORIGINS AND THE MYSTERY SURROUNDING ITS DETONATION.
I WON'T BE EXPECTED TO TESTIFY ON ANY OF THAT?
ALL PART OF YOUR AMNESTY.

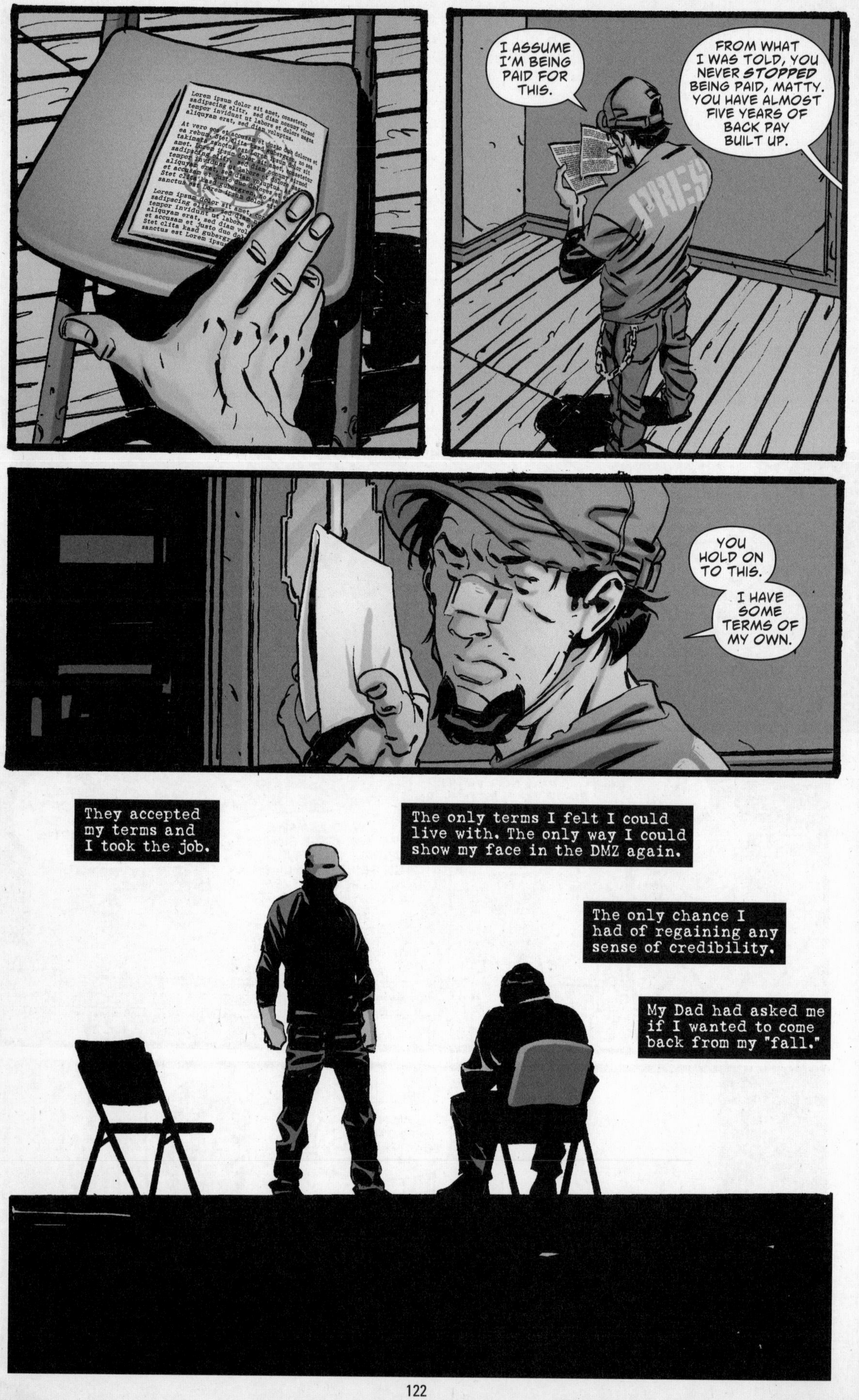
I ASSUME I'M BEING PAID FOR THIS.
FROM WHAT I WAS TOLD, YOU NEVER STOPPED BEING PAID, MATTY. YOU HAVE ALMOST FIVE YEARS OF BACK PAY BUILT UP.
YOU HOLD ON TO THIS.
I HAVE SOME TERMS OF MY OWN.
They accepted my terms and I took the job.
The only terms I felt I could live with. The only way I could show my face in the DMZ again.
The only chance I had of regaining any sense of credibility.
My Dad had asked me if I wanted to come back from my "fall."

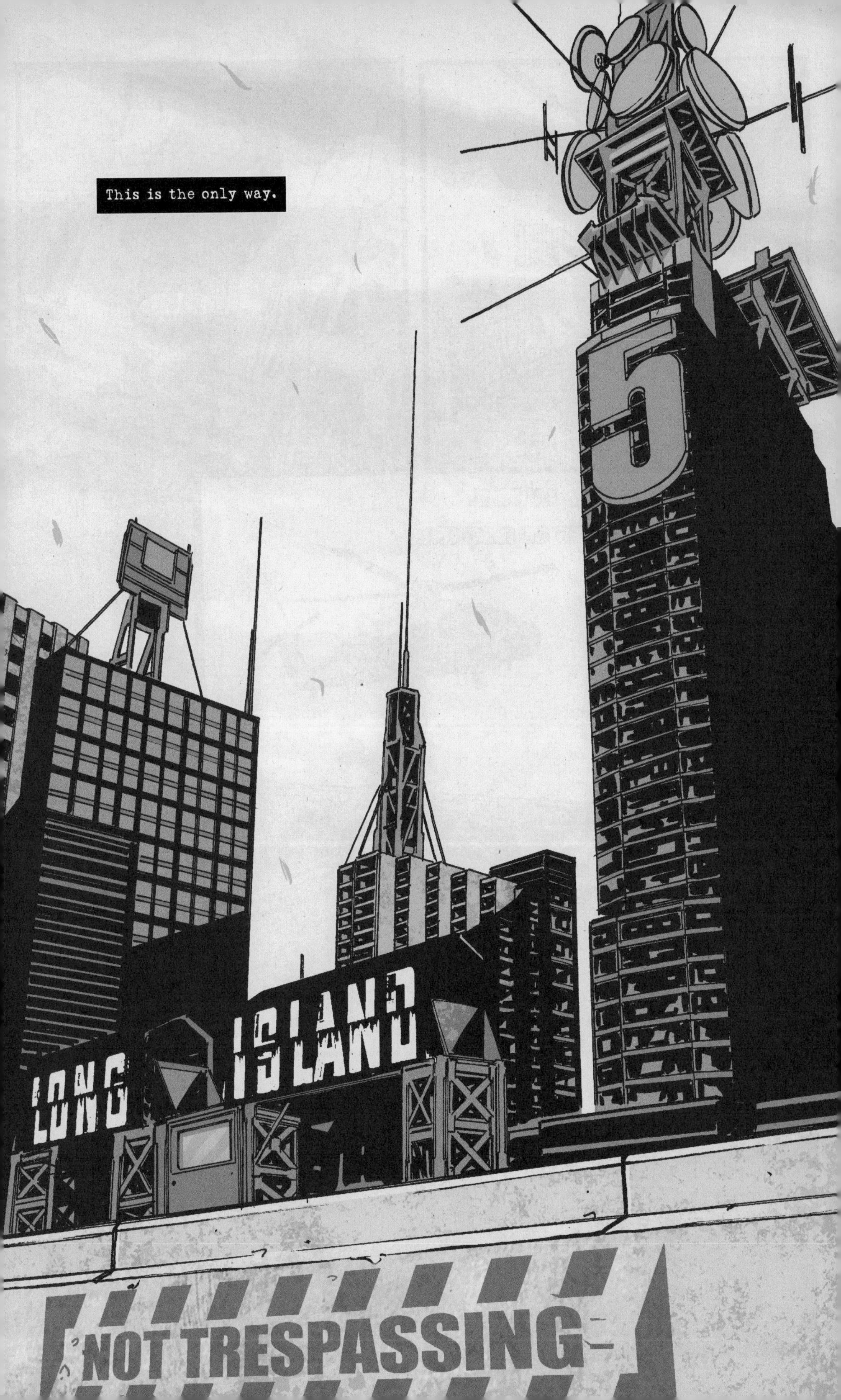
This is the only way.
5
LONG ISLAND
NOT TRESPASSING

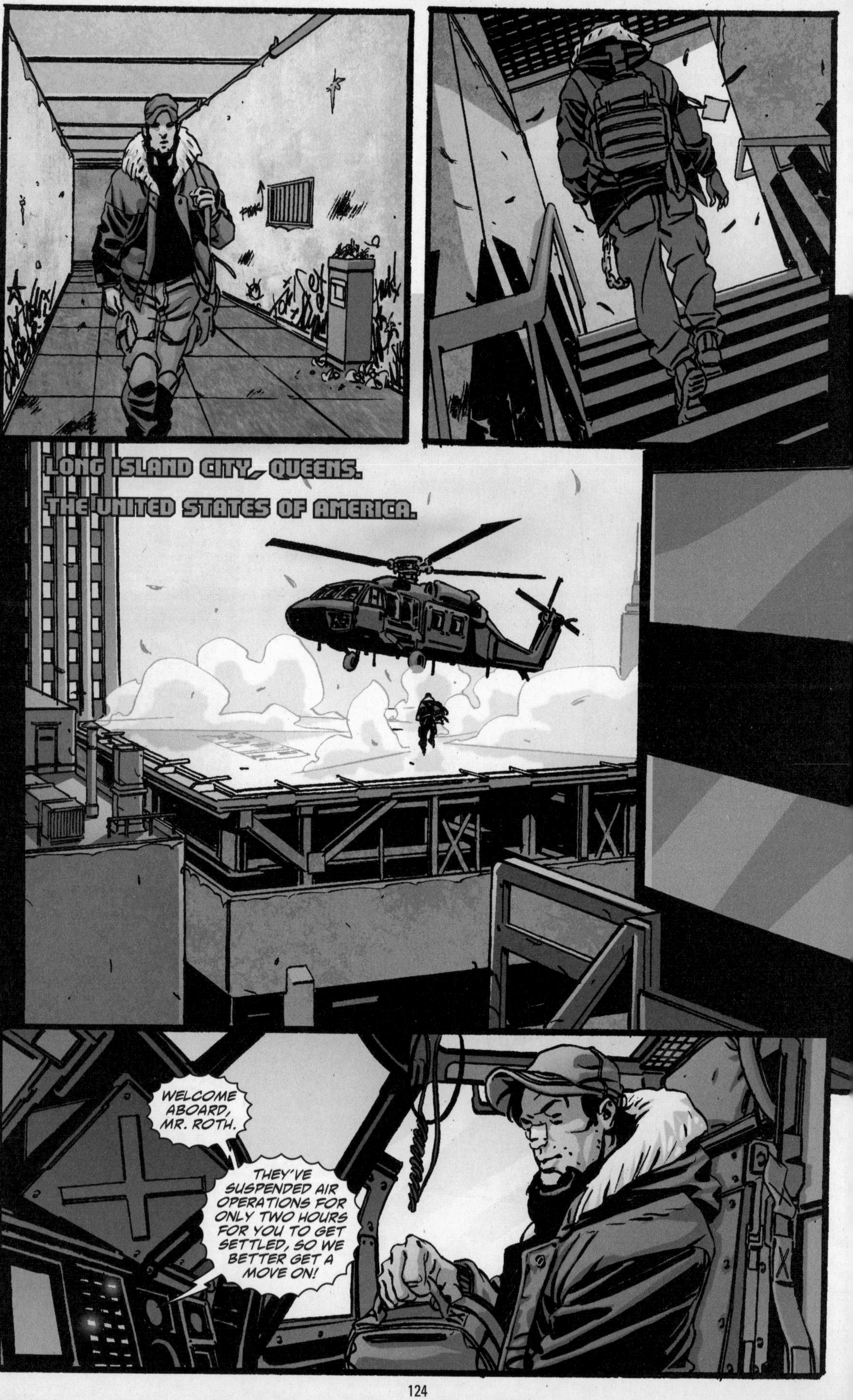

LONG ISLAND CITY, QUEENS.
THE UNITED STATES OF AMERICA.
WELCOME ABOARD, MR. ROTH.
THEY'VE SUSPENDED AIR OPERATIONS FOR ONLY TWO HOURS FOR YOU TO GET SETTLED, SO WE BETTER GET A MOVE ON!

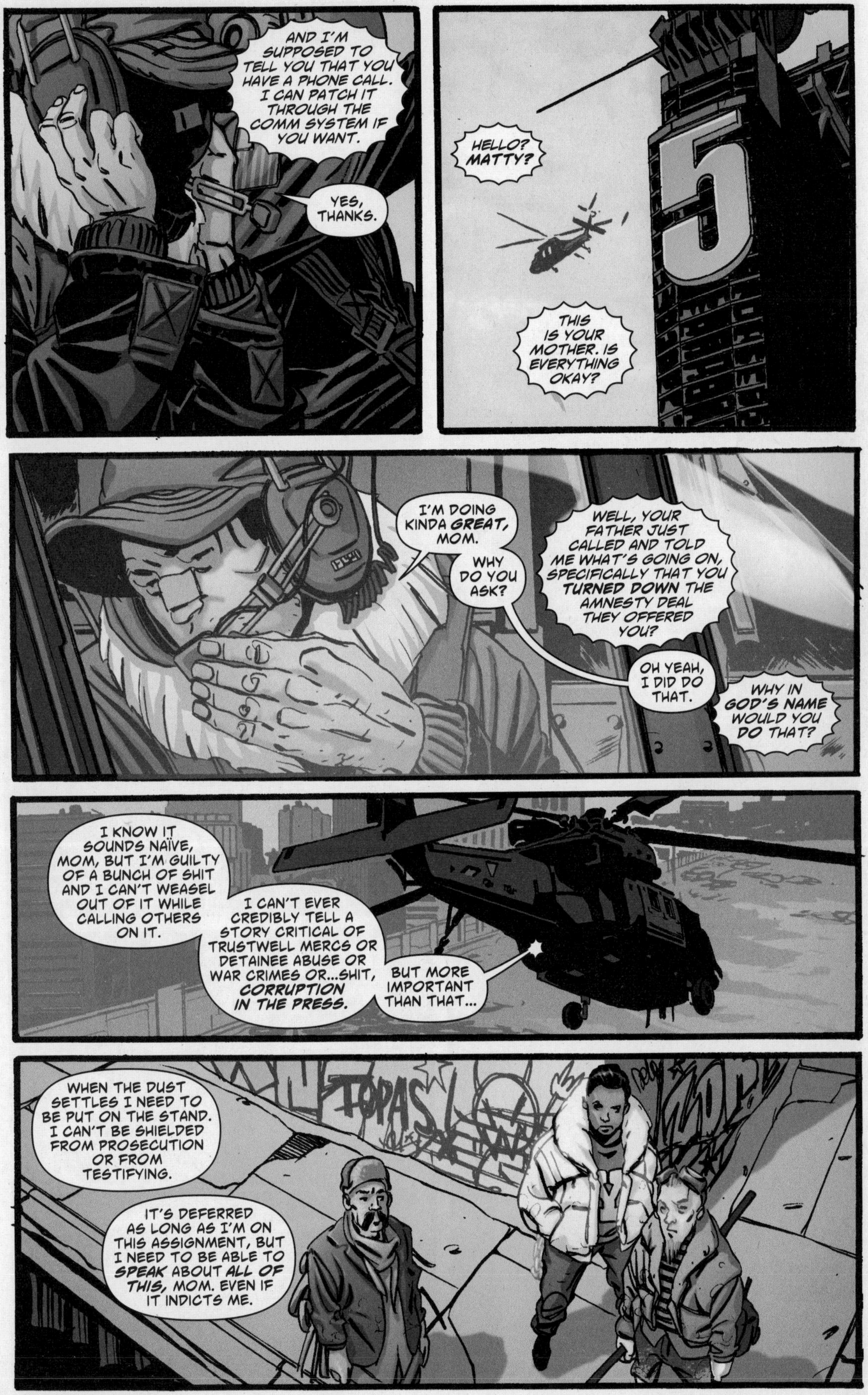
AND I'M SUPPOSED TO TELL YOU THAT YOU HAVE A PHONE CALL. I CAN PATCH IT THROUGH THE COMM SYSTEM IF YOU WANT.
YES, THANKS.
HELLO? MATTY?
THIS IS YOUR MOTHER. IS EVERYTHING OKAY?
I'M DOING KINDA GREAT, MOM.
WHY DO YOU ASK?
WELL, YOUR FATHER JUST CALLED AND TOLD ME WHAT'S GOING ON, SPECIFICALLY THAT YOU TURNED DOWN THE AMNESTY DEAL THEY OFFERED YOU?
OH YEAH, I DID DO THAT.
WHY IN GOD'S NAME WOULD YOU DO THAT?
I KNOW IT SOUNDS NAÏVE, MOM, BUT I'M GUILTY OF A BUNCH OF SHIT AND I CAN'T WEASEL OUT OF IT WHILE CALLING OTHERS ON IT.
I CAN'T EVER CREDIBLY TELL A STORY CRITICAL OF TRUSTWELL MERCS OR DETAINEE ABUSE OR WAR CRIMES OR...SHIT, CORRUPTION IN THE PRESS.
BUT MORE IMPORTANT THAN THAT...
WHEN THE DUST SETTLES I NEED TO BE PUT ON THE STAND. I CAN'T BE SHIELDED FROM PROSECUTION OR FROM TESTIFYING.
IT'S DEFERRED AS LONG AS I'M ON THIS ASSIGNMENT, BUT I NEED TO BE ABLE TO SPEAK ABOUT ALL OF THIS, MOM. EVEN IF IT INDICTS ME.

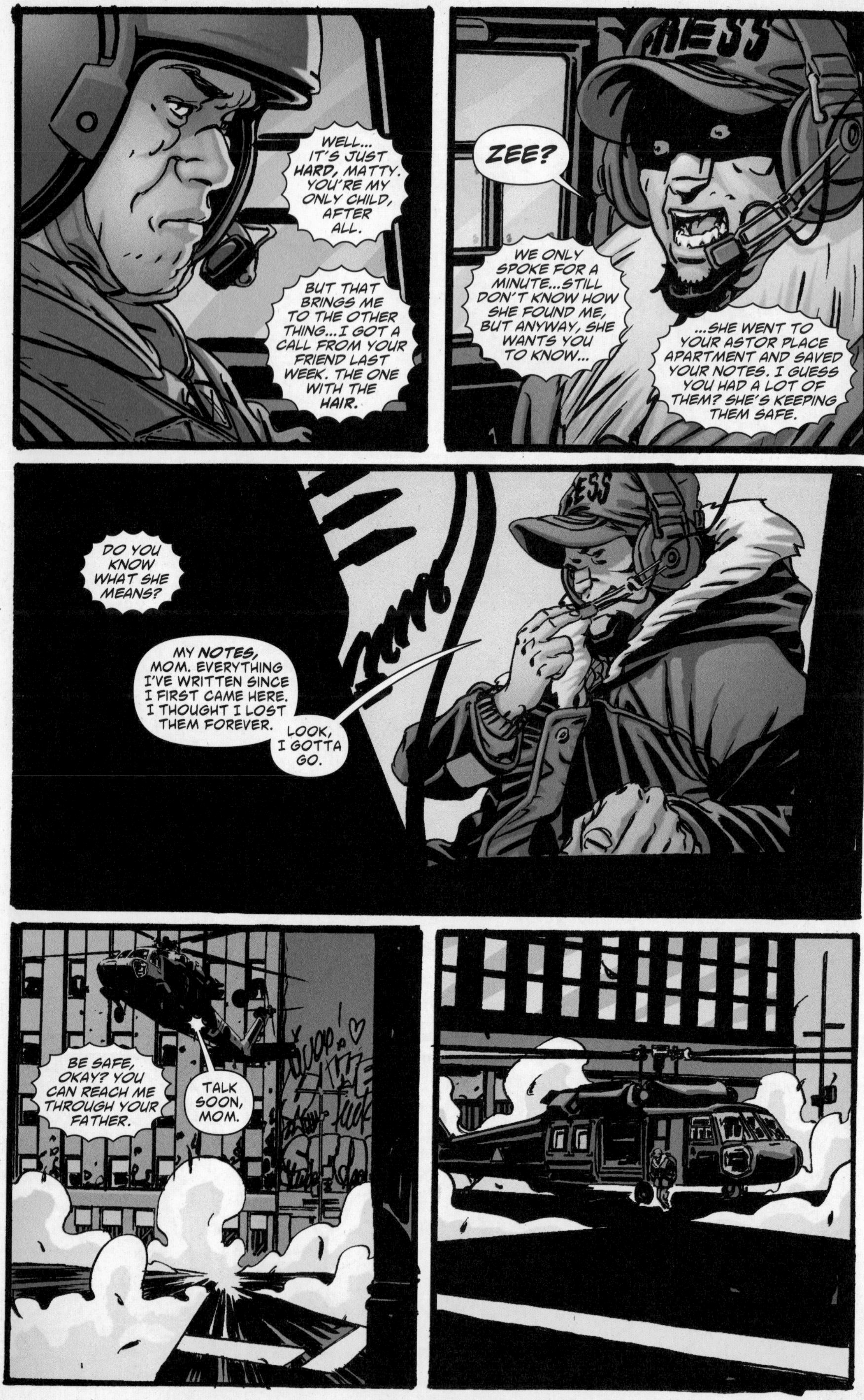
WELL... IT'S JUST HARD, MATTY. YOU'RE MY ONLY CHILD, AFTER ALL.
BUT THAT BRINGS ME TO THE OTHER THING... I GOT A CALL FROM YOUR FRIEND LAST WEEK. THE ONE WITH THE HAIR.
ZEE?
WE ONLY SPOKE FOR A MINUTE... STILL DON'T KNOW HOW SHE FOUND ME, BUT ANYWAY, SHE WANTS YOU TO KNOW...
...SHE WENT TO YOUR ASTOR PLACE APARTMENT AND SAVED YOUR NOTES. I GUESS YOU HAD A LOT OF THEM? SHE'S KEEPING THEM SAFE.
DO YOU KNOW WHAT SHE MEANS?
MY NOTES, MOM. EVERYTHING I'VE WRITTEN SINCE I FIRST CAME HERE. I THOUGHT I LOST THEM FOREVER.
LOOK, I GOTTA GO.
BE SAFE, OKAY? YOU CAN REACH ME THROUGH YOUR FATHER.
TALK SOON, MOM.